100 Bollywood Films

100 BOLLYWOOD FILMS

BFI Screen Guides

Rachel Dwyer

To the menagerie:
SEMPER FIDELIS

First published in 2005 by the
British Film Institute
21 Stephen Street, London W1T 1LN

The British Film Institute's purpose is to champion moving image culture in all its
richness and diversity across the UK, for the benefit of as wide an audience as
possible, and to create and encourage debate.

Cover design: Paul Wright
Cover image: *Sholay* (Ramesh Sippy, 1975, Sippy Films)
Series design: Ketchup/couch
Set by: Fakenham Photosetting Ltd, Fakenham, Norfolk
Printed in the UK by The Cromwell Press, Trowbridge, Wiltshire

British Library Cataloguing-in-Publication Data
A catalogue record for this book is available from the British Library

ISBN 1–84457–099–1 (pbk)
ISBN 1–84457–098–3 (hbk)

Contents

Acknowledgments

I should like to thank all my friends for their patience and for taking my random phone calls, persistent emails and frantic SMSes about this book. The encyclopaedic knowledge of Kaushik Bhaumik, Jerry Pinto and Maithili Rao meant they suffered more than others, but they endlessly gave me prompt and helpful advice, which they may think I wilfully ignored. I also discussed my selection with Sikander Berry, Anurag Kashyap, Gautam Pemmaraju, Shaad Ali Sahgal, Sameer Sharma, Shanoo Sharma and Kush Varia.

The indefatigable Jerry Pinto deserves special thanks for making many visits to Video Plaza at Leamington Road and Rhythm House at Kala Ghoda, whether with me, or on his own, working from emailed lists or having three-way conversations with the staff and me on the phone, getting copies sent to London and arranging rental copies when I was in Bombay.

I should like to thank Rajni Bhatia for her great generosity in helping to compile the filmographic details at the end of each film. I am not sure she had any idea of how much work this would involve, but she spent several days on this task with good humour.

Special thanks are due also to Ramdas Bhatkal, who gave me sound advice on Marathi items relating to Shantaram's films; Anna Morcom for helping me collect materials from Kamat Foto Flash; thanks to Randhir Kapoor for his suggestion we do this; and to Fifi Haroon, who supplied me with DVDs and VCDs.

I should like to thank everyone at the National Film Archive of India (Pune), who often act more like a team of research assistants than archive staff, for their help in supplying me with photographs, films and printed materials; in particular, Mr Shashidharan, Mrs Joshi, Aarti Karkhanis and Laxmi Iyer, Dilip Rajput and others involved in the screening.

Several producers supplied me with photographs and permissions at no cost. These include Farhan Akhtar, Rajkumar Barjatya, Puja Bedi, Shyam Benegal, B. R. Chopra, Yash Chopra, Subhash Ghai and Meghna Ghai-Puri, Vidhu Vinod Chopra, Shaukat Khan, the late Gulshan Rai, Ram Gopal Varma, Vinci Wadia and the National Film Development Corporation.

Once again, thanks to my friends in Bombay and Pune for their endless kindness and hospitality during my research for this book. It is hard to list you all, but special thanks to Pam Chopra for her extraordinary hospitality; and to Mohan Agashe, Ashim Ahluwalia, Titu Ahluwalia, Apurva Asrani, Aarti Bajaj, Shyam Benegal, Harsha and Smita Bhatkal, Christophe Carvalho, Priya and Suresh Chabria, Gayatri Chatterjee, Angad Chowdhry, Harish Dayani, Shobhaa Dé, Richard Delacy, Abhay Deol, Faisal Devji, Ayesha Dharker, Imtiaz Dharker, Naresh Fernandes, Sanjay Gadhvi, Shumona Goel, Rumana Hameid, Udita Jhunjhunwala, Meera Mehta, A. G. Noorani, Gautam Pemmaraju, Satya Pemmaraju, Swamy Rao, Vyjayanthi Rao, Shaad Ali Sahgal, Asim Shah, Sonal Shah, Navdeep and Madhuri Singh, Paul Smith, Rahul Srivastava, Paromita Vora, the late Riyad Wadia and Vinci Wadia.

Thanks as ever to Michael.

Introduction

The films in this volume have been chosen for different reasons. The only common ground is that they should be recognisable as a 'Bollywood' or a Hindi film. I suggest the following parameters: the films are produced in India, their language is Hindi (or Urdu) and they had a theatrical release across the usual distribution circuits of (north) India.

Although this is not a selection of the '100 best' films, some of the movies here are widely held to be 'better' than others, in terms of structure, style, acting and other features that would be recognisable to those who know other cinemas. Perhaps one could suggest that the films of Bimal Roy, Guru Dutt, Mani Ratnam and some outstanding films (such as *Sholay* [1975], *Deewaar* [1975], *Pakeezah* [1971]) could be assessed under the umbrella term 'world cinema', where despite their noticeable differences from other cinemas, they can be appraised on some of the same critical and aesthetic terms.

Yet to those unfamiliar with Hindi cinema, some of the films in this volume do not look like 'good' movies, yet most of them would be regarded as such by their audiences. There is no defined aesthetics of Hindi cinema, but these films share noticeable features, such as the use of melodrama and heightened emotion, especially around the family, an engaging narrative, stars, a certain *mise en scène*, usually one of glamour, grandiloquent dialogues and the all-important songs. These are therefore the topics upon which I have focused in my discussion, as indicators of why these films are significant.

The pleasures of cinema, as of other art forms, are complex, and it is never easy to analyse people's responses to films. Box-office success should ne noted as it suggests that the audiences found these films to be 'good', although we do not usually know for what reasons. Statistics for Bollywood films are notoriously unreliable as figures are said to be 'adjusted', in the face of rampant piracy, but I have taken into account films that were clearly major hits.

Another criterion for selection is the film's importance in the history of Hindi cinema. For example, *Bobby* (1973), a film that would deserve inclusion by any of my criteria, also brought in the 'love as friendship' theme which flourished in the 1990s; *Lagaan* (2001) for its 'Oscar' success; *Hum aapke hain koun...!* (1994) for its marketing; *Dilwale dulhaniya le jayenge* (1995) for Hindi film and the diaspora (and for its 500-week run in India); *Dil chahta hai* (2001) for changing style within the Hindi movie format, and so on.

I have omitted silent films, although they are foundational to Indian cinema history, on several grounds. Few silents were made in Bombay and to call them 'Hindi' films is wildly inaccurate. Were I to choose any examples, Phalke's work would have been the obvious choice, but we do not have complete versions of his films. Other films might have been *Shiraz* (1928) or *Light of Asia* (1926) but these are English films, as a very basic grasp of lip-reading shows. All India's remaining silent films are available in the Film and Television Archives of India in Pune and can be watched over a few days. They may be of historical interest but I am not sure how many would count as good cinema.

The important talkie cinema of pre-independent India is under-represented here, as it is only gradually becoming available beyond the Archives. While many films are lost, including *Alam ara* (1931), India's first talkie, some studios' outputs are fairly well preserved, notably those of Calcutta's New Theatres, Bombay Talkies and Pune's Prabhat Studios. Prabhat Studios have issued many of their films with subtitles on VHS and VCD. However, some of the work of New Theatres and Prabhat is excluded on the grounds of language (Bengali and Marathi respectively), and only their Hindi films (mostly made in parallel to the Bengali or Marathi versions) may be considered. The hugely influential Bombay Talkies which spawned Filmistan has only two films here, while Prabhat has only one, as some of their best features were in Marathi only (*Sant Tukaram* [1936], *Ramshastri* [1944], *Sant Dnyaneshwar*); New Theatres made some of the key early films (*Vidyapati* [1937], *Chandidas* [1927], *Devdas*) and nurtured major talent such as K. L. Saigal, Prithviraj Kapoor and Bimal Roy, but I have included the work of these figures only once they had moved to Bombay.

It is hard not to allow the 1950s to dominate, as this was the era in which so many classic films were made and the great directors Mehboob Khan, Bimal Roy, Raj Kapoor and Guru Dutt were at their peak. The 1970s was also an extraordinarily fertile period when, alongside the great Salim–Javed films for Amitabh Bachchan, there was also the middle-class cinema of film-makers such as Hrishikesh Mukherjee, while the 'parallel cinema' also had a productive decade.

I have tried to include key figures – directors, stars, music directors, writers – throughout the selection, but I have also tried not to let any one of them dominate. If the list were of 'good' films or my favourites, there would have been more films by Raj Kapoor, Guru Dutt, Bimal Roy and Yash Chopra. Some key figures feature surprisingly infrequently, in particular those who have become important since the 1990s, while there is a disproportionate number of Salim–Javed films. The latter are foundational to the modern Hindi cinema, were huge hits, widely held to be 'good' films and set a standard which has rarely been equalled. Amitabh Bachchan starred in most of their films and, as he also acted in many of the middle-class films of Hrishikesh Mukherjee, he has by far the greatest number of entries in the volume. Yet I had to leave some of his films out and still regret missing some, such as *Coolie* (1983) and *Naseeb* (1981).

The 'parallel' or 'middle' cinema does not belong in this book, as it was produced, distributed and exhibited on different circuits from the others, and has hardly any connection with the mainstream cinema. Were I to pick films just for being 'good', this group would be more highly represented. Even Shyam Benegal, one of the most important film-makers and intellectuals in the Indian film industry, has only one film in this selection despite having made many 'good' films. Although Benegal's films are privately produced and many had theatrical releases, they are viewed as a separate form of cinema, a type of realist cinema that is close to that government-sponsored cinema of the National Film Development Corporation (NFDC). I have included only one NFDC-funded film, *Jaane bhi do yaaro* (1983) as it has reached wide audiences and is always cited as a landmark.

Satyajit Ray is internationally recognised as India's greatest film-maker and is certainly one of my favourite directors. He made only one Hindi film (apart from his film for television, *Sadgati* [1981]), which was *Shatranj ke khiladi* (1977). This is a great film but I have not included it here, as Ray's films belong to an entirely different tradition of film-making in terms of production and distribution. (I was amazed to find that many of the younger generation of Hindi film-makers who know their Hollywood movies have not seen a single film by Ray.)

I am not a connoisseur of Hindi B-movies, but they are not a part of the history of mainstream cinema. They have their own separate circuits of production, distribution and exhibition. In recent years, the horror movies of the Ramsay brothers have generated their own cult following, for films such as *Bandh darwaza* (1990), *Do gaz zamin ke neeche* (1972) and *Purana mandir* (1984). No one would call them 'good cinema', however.

I had thought of leaving out films that are not generally accessible, but I have included a couple (for example, *Phool* [1944] and *Khazanchi* [1941]), as these may soon join the others in becoming available on VCD and DVD. Most of the films in this book are available at least on VCD, with many on DVD (the latter have English subtitles and are more expensive). One of the great pleasures of writing this book was rewatching the films on DVD, as I had previously seen many of them only on low-quality VHS where the image was spoilt by advertising, the sound was poor and I saw them when my knowledge of Hindi was very limited.

'Bollywood'

There has been controversy over the name 'Bollywood' for some time now. Several voices in the industry have expressed a dislike for the term, as it implies that Hindi cinema is a derivation of Hollywood and thus an insulting term. The etymology of the word is clearly from 'Hollywood', the word that all round the world signifies 'cinema'. Hollywood is the centre of the largest film industry in the world in terms of distribution, budgets and global impact, and has created much of the world's cinema style. Indian cinema is not entirely indigenous (its supposed connections with Sanskrit drama and folk traditions are highly exaggerated) but it is a hybrid form that has been influenced heavily by other cinemas, in particular that of Hollywood, as well as by photography, painting, theatre, narrative forms and popular music, none of which can be described as 'purely' Indian. However, this hybridity does not mean that it is entirely derivative or imitative, but that it has evolved its own sense of style and form.

There is some dispute as to the origins of the term 'Bollywood'. It seems that the first use of 'Tollywood', to mean the cinema made in the Calcutta suburb of Tollygunge, dates back to 1932. (Madhava Prasad, 'This Thing Called Bollywood', <www.india-seminar.com/2003/525/525%20madhava%20prasad.htm>, viewed 8 March 2005.) Prasad suggests that it is unlikely that Bombay cinema would have become known as Bollywood without this detour via Tollywood. Perhaps it is after the word Bollywood was coined that we find terms like 'Nollywood' used to mean 'Nigerian cinema' and 'Lollywood' employed to describe 'cinema made in Lahore; Pakistani cinema'.

We can quibble with the 'B' in 'Bollywood'. This cinema is not made only in Bombay (or, since 1995, Mumbai). Much of it has been produced in other cities (for example, Prabhat Studios in Pune made bilingual films in Marathi and Hindi), so this restriction would exclude films such as *Aadmi* (1939), *Padosi* (1941) and *Duniya na mane*, and most of K. L. Saigal's films, as he made them in Calcutta with New Theatres (including the 1935 *Devdas*), along with several by Prithviraj Kapoor and P. C. Barua; it would also exclude the Hindi films made in the Madras studios (such as *Ram aur Shyam*), and those made in the Lahore studios before independence, such as *Khazanchi*.

If we discard the term 'Bollywood', then what do we call this cinema? Hindi cinema? This opens up another can of worms. Many films

are classed as Urdu films (right up to and including *Junglee* [1961]).
Should it be called the Hindi–Urdu cinema? Would anyone recognise that
term? If English continues to make inroads into Indian cinema, will it
become English cinema, even if it follows the style of the former? If the
actors say 'I love you' in English, is it still Hindi–Urdu cinema? What
about the fact that all the publicity and advertising is in English, along
with many of the film magazines? How would we then exclude forms of
Hindi cinema that are produced and distributed in a different circuit from
the cinema examined here? Do we call it 'commercial' cinema? Would I
call it 'art' cinema and 'commercial' cinema? But does that not mean
that one is creative and worthy of being called 'art', whereas the other is
interested in money at the expense of art?

So the appellation 'Bollywood' is problematic, but so are the other
terms. While some in the industry and outside think it is insulting, why
does it prevail? 'Bollywood' is a recognised term in the UK and US where
this book is to be distributed (though it may well be called Hindi in the
Indian edition). Indeed this may be part of the problem with the term
'Bollywood', as it is promoted by the NRIs (non-resident Indians) whose
culture is deeply problematic for many Indians. It has also been taken up
by westerners (with an entry in the *Oxford English Dictionary*), which also
causes cultural hand-wringing as to whether this is another form of neo-
colonialism.

'Bollywood' is not a term I use myself. I don't like its clichéd
humour, and to me it means *masala* film, a film that has some sense of
kitsch. Many of the films I have selected in this volume are by no means
'Bollywood' film in my understanding of the term.

However, I do not think the term is an insult. Hindi cinema is a
unique form, with its own structures of production and distribution, its
own audiences and its own narratives and style. It is a form of cinema
that has always had an international audience but is becoming truly
global, and it is one that is undergoing enormous changes. It is a cinema
that I prefer to most others, and one which I find intellectually engaging
as well as pleasurable. However, it is better that in 'Bollywood' it has a

brand name that is internationally recognized rather than continuing to struggle for recognition but missing the mark. I shall continue to call it Hindi cinema, even though that term itself is inaccurate. The term 'Bollywood' was not widely used when I began to study this cinema and I find habits hard to change. Whatever we call it, I hope this collection will add to other works in trying to define what makes this cinema.

I make no claim that the selection is entirely objective. I have included a few films I do not like because I think they have to be included by the criteria outlined above. Several other films fulfil these criteria but have not been included, because I have preferred others. There are new films appearing that mark a different kind of cinema, but time will only tell whether they are exceptions or are defining a trend.

Every reader will have another list of his or her own 100 films, and some will object to mine. I too shall probably wish to revise my selection in future. However, I have chosen this list carefully in conjunction with friends and colleagues. I hope it provokes debate and encourages people to see the films.

Note

The spelling of names varies greatly from film to film, so the same person will appear in several different versions in the book: for example, Nasir Hussain may appear as Nasir Husain. Also, many films have been released with the same name.

The length of films varies as they have often been re-edited and shortened after release, or the overseas version may have been re-edited for DVD release.

Most films have four writers: for the story, the screenplay, the dialogue (usually dialogues in Indian English) and lyrics. Film credits may simply say 'written by' or just give the writer of the dialogue; it is generally assumed that, if no other contributors are mentioned, the story and screenplay are by the director.

Aankhen
India, 1993 – 177 mins
David Dhawan

Aankhen deserves its place in this collection both in its own right as one of the most successful Hindi films of all time and as an example of one of the most popular comedy teams of the 1990s, the pairing of the star Govinda and the director David Dhawan. Few successful films sustain comedy throughout, generally relying on comic episodes enacted either by the star, or comedians (such as Johnnie Walker or Johnny Lever). Govinda, mostly in Dhawan's films, created his own style, often wacky, slapstick and somewhat downmarket, if not outright crude, in hits such as *Raja Babu* (1994), *Coolie No. 1* (1995) and *Hero No. 1* (1997). Dhawan made hit films with other stars throughout the 1990s, notably Anil Kapoor (*Andaaz* [1944], *Loafer* [1996]) and Salman Khan (*Judwaa* [1997], *Biwi No. 1* [1999]), which make him one of the decade's most successful directors, while Govinda has become a major star (and also an MP).

In his earlier films, Govinda came to be regarded as vulgar, not least for his own (bad) taste in dance, gesture and garish clothing. Shobhaa Dé called him 'an obscenity' on account of his hip-thrusting and suggestive dancing. However, he is popularly known as the 'Virar ka chokra', the lad from the Bombay (downmarket) suburb Virar, and has always had a loyal audience among the 'masses' rather than the 'classes' (as the cinema audience is popularly divided). It took some time for Govinda to be appreciated as a comic star and a dancer but now he is seen as a one-man show, one of the few stars capable of holding together an otherwise mediocre film, and is praised by many as a great star. He was undoubtedly the greatest dancer in Hindi films in the 1990s, one of only a few who possess natural rhythm and style.

Aankhen spotlights these elements of Govinda's work, from his vulgar yet impeccably timed dancing in hugely catchy songs, such as 'O lal duppatewali', to his mad fast-talking dialogues and excellent comic timing. Hindi films often use doubling (identical twins, lookalikes and so on), but *Aankhen* takes this device to its extremes. Govinda (Munnu) and Chunky Pandey (Bunnu) star as two good-for-nothing sons of a rich businessman, Hasmukh. They get caught up in a plot to replace the Chief Minister with his double, a villain transformed by plastic surgery; meanwhile Munnu's double, Gaurishankar (Govinda again), appears from a village to confuse Munnu's family and everyone in the town, while the real Munnu is mistaken for his double by the entire village. Hasmukh's long-lost identical twin appears and helps the others to catch the criminals. A monkey is another member of the Munnu–Bunnu comedy team, enjoying a more interesting and developed role than the female stars (Raageshwari, Ritu Shivpuri).

Dir.: David Dhawan; **Story/Scr./Dial.**: Anees Bazmee; **DOP**: Siba Mishra; **Music**: Bappi Lahiri; **Lyrics**: Indivar; **Selected Cast**: Govinda, Chunky Pandey, Raj Babbar, Shilpa Shirodkar, Raageshwari, Gulshan Grover; **Prod. Co.**: Chiragdeep International; Colour.

Abhimaan
India, 1973 – 125 mins
Hrishikesh Mukherjee

In some ways an Indian version of *A Star is Born* (1954), *Abhimaan* is the story of the famous singer Subir (Amitabh Bachchan), who is publicly acclaimed but has a fragile ego and is lonely apart from his one friend, Chandru (Asrani), and his girlfriend (or not – it is never quite clear) Chitra (Bindu). He receives late-night phone calls from his female fans. He drinks and works but his life is empty. When he visits his Mausi ('Aunt', played by Durga Khote), who has brought him up, he falls in love with a village girl Uma (Jaya Bhaduri), who has been taught to sing by her father (A. K. Hangal). She is a classically trained singer who even teases Subir about his popular style. He invites her to sing a duet at their wedding reception, where one of his friends (David) notices that she is the better singer. Uma begins her career as a recording artist by singing with him but soon producers want her to give solo performances at a higher fee than her husband, and fans mob her rather than him. This tension over work leads to tension at home, and he abuses her and drinks heavily even though she offers to stop singing. She returns to her father, while he picks up his relationship with Chitra. Only when she loses their unborn baby does he ask for forgiveness. However, her depression is so severe that she can no longer respond to him let alone sing. Subir sings their famous duet 'Tere mere milan ki yeh raina', and finally persuades her to sing it with him on stage.

A film about singers needs a special score, which this film certainly has. Composed by the elderly S. D. Burman, it contains some hugely popular songs, with lyrics by Majrooh Sultanpuri. Among the hits, favourites include the song Kishore sings for Amitabh, and songs like 'Meet na mila re man ka', which although sung in a happy mode, suggests he conceals an inner loneliness. Two of the duets are particularly outstanding: their first, 'Teri bindiya re', in which Mohammed Rafi sings for Amitabh, and their 'theme song', 'Tere mere'.

However, the story is also sustained throughout the film, with memorable dialogues by the Hindi writer Rajinder Singh Bedi, which, along with the songs, help maintain a steady pace in the realistic portrayal of the pain and suffering the couple go through despite their great love for each other.

This is one of several films by Hrishikesh Mukherjee that pairs Amitabh Bachchan and Jaya Bhaduri, who acted together in other major hit films including *Zanjeer* (1973), *Sholay* (1975), *Silsila* (1981) and *Kabhi khushi kabhie gham* (2001). They married in real life a few months before the release of this film. They were one of the most popular screen couples, and although he is undoubtedly the greatest star in Indian film history, she was initially the bigger attraction, and it was often said that she had to stand down because she would have outshone him, though, of course, that is entirely speculative. However, for this film, it was Bhaduri who won the National Award, in the category of Best Actress (shared with Dimple Kapadia for *Bobby*). None the less it was also a great performance from Amitabh, who brought his pain and anger to the role as he did to all his roles, whether in middle-class cinema or in the Angry Young Man fighting films. There was strong support from veterans such as Durga Khote, who made her name in the early Prabhat films, and A. K. Hangal, whose latest appearance was in *Lagaan*, having acted in films over many decades.

Dir./Story: Hrishikesh Mukherjee; **Scr.:** Nabendu Ghosh; **Dial.:** Rajinder Singh Bedi; **DOP:** Jaywant Pathare; **Music:** S. D. Burman; **Lyrics:** Majrooh Sultanpuri; **Selected Cast:** Amitabh Bachchan, Jaya Bhaduri, Durga Khote, A. K. Hangal, David; **Prod. Co.:** Amiya; Colour.

Achhut kanya
India, 1936 – 142 mins
Franz Osten

Bombay Talkies (1934–54), founded by the western-educated and
trained couple, Himanshu Rai and Devika Rani, nurtured major talents,
including Gyan Mukherjee, Manto, Ashok Kumar, Dev Anand, Kamal
Amrohi and Dilip Kumar. It was noted for its social films, including
Kangan (1939) and *Kismet* (1943). Rai and Rani had both worked with
film units in Germany before the Second World War and their studio
employed several German personnel, including Franz Osten (who
directed this film) and Joseph Wirsching (who was later the cameraman
on *Pakeezah* [1971]).

Devika Rani was a major star when this film was released, but Ashok
Kumar was just beginning his career (this was his second film). Although
Devika Rani dazzled as ever (looking nothing like a rural girl), Ashok
Kumar's appearance as the shy, awkward boy who falls in love with this
fearless girl is memorable. It was felt that he looked too urban and
sophisticated for the role (although it was clearly acceptable for Devika
Rani to wear lipstick and have plucked eyebrows), so he wore *kurtas* that
sparked a new trend among the young.

Kasturi (Devika Rani), the Dalit (so-called 'Untouchable') daughter
('Acchut kanya') of a railway signalman, falls in love with the Brahmin
Mohan (Ashok Kumar), the grocer's son. After protests and violence
from the villagers, they agree to marry others but ultimately Kasturi
sacrifices her life under a train. The train features regularly in Indian
cinema as a symbol of modernity and of the entrance of the new into
the seemingly unchanging village world.

It is very unusual for Hindi cinema to take up the issue of caste. It is
mentioned in passing in *Devdas*, where Paro and Devdas play different
types of Brahmin, and again in Bimal Roy's *Sujata*. Although Gandhi had
brought up the issue of the Harijans, as he called the Dalits, cinema did
not follow his lead, preferring to gloss over caste and untouchability, as

indeed it has often avoided other major issues, such as widow remarriage and underage marriage, looking rather at broader social problems such as westernisation, arranged marriage, abandoned children and so on.

The film's music was composed by one of the few female music directors in the history of Hindi cinema, Saraswati Devi. Khursheed Manchersher Minocher-Homji took this pseudonym because of protests from the Parsi community and specifically from Parsis within Bombay Talkies. The hit song was 'Main ban ki chidiya banke ban ban bolun re'.

Dir.: Franz Osten; **Story/Scr.**: Niranjan Pal; **Dial.**: J. S. Casshyap; **DOP**: Josef Wirsching; **Music**: Saraswati Devi; **Lyrics**: J. S. Casshyap; **Selected Cast**: Devika Rani, Ashok Kumar, P. F. Pithawala, Kamta Prasad; **Prod. Co.**: Bombay Talkies; Black and white.

Ashok Kumar and Devika Rani in *Achhut kanya*

Amar, Akbar, Anthony
India, 1977 – 186 mins
Manmohan Desai

This is one of the great *masala* films, a riotous blend of comedy, action and romance. Three boys are separated from their parents on Independence Day, when their father leaves them at the foot of a statue of Mahatma Gandhi; each one is subsequently brought up by different parents, one a Hindu (Amar – Vinod Khanna), one a Muslim (Akbar – Rishi Kapoor) and one a Christian (Anthony – Amitabh Bachchan). The family is separated although the mother (Nirupa Roy) knows Akbar and Anthony but, as she was blinded in an accident, does not realise they are her sons.

The fact that the boys' real parents are Hindus and the Hindu son is a policeman reinforces the underlying Hinduness of all Indians, although there is much lip-service to the religiosity of the Catholic priest and the sincere prayers of Akbar to Shirdi Sai Baba, whose devotees include Hindus and Muslims, which result in his blind mother's miraculous cure as two rays of light emanate from the eyes of the image. Thus begins the plot's denouement, but a great deal more must be untangled before the family can be reunited.

Romantic love remains divided by community (Amar falls for a Hindu girl, Lakshmi – Shabana Azmi; Akbar for Salma – Neetu Singh; and Anthony for Jenny – Parveen Babi), and while the Hindu's romance is sincere and reforming, the Muslim attracts the doctor by singing (camp) *qawwalis* ('Purdah re purdah') and bringing eunuchs to shame her father into permitting the romance ('Tayyab Ali, pyar ka dushman'). Amitabh Bachchan, in one of his greatest comic performances, takes on the role of the *tapori* or streetwise man, perfected in his stylised dialogue and his denim flares. His drunken scenes are much celebrated, but the wonderful moment during the Easter party at the Catholic gymkhana when he jumps out of an egg to sing 'My name is Anthony Gonsalves' is unforgettable.

The audience knows the whole story, while the characters only find out their origins later in the film: the credits roll as the three brothers are linked up to a machine unknown to medical science that transfuses blood from them directly to their mother, each unaware of the 'blood relationship'. The film's knowingness provides further fun: during the fight that restores order at the end of the film with Vinod Khanna, one of the great 1970s' heroes dressed as a 'one-man band', and the great Angry Young Man, Amitabh in a priest's costume, while Rishi Kapoor, the romantic hero of the 1970s, plays the accordion that is incorporated into the background score as 'fight' music. It also provides a song opportunity, with 'Anhonee ko honee'. A madcap, hilarious film, showing how much fun Hindi film comedy can be.

Manmohan Desai made some other wonderfully crazy films like *Naseeb* (1981) and *Coolie* (1983), which have some great moments, but *Amar, Akbar, Anthony* is one of my favourite films of all time.

Dir.: Manmohan Desai; **Story**: Mrs J. M. Desai; **Scr.**: Prayag Raj; **Dial.**: Kadar Khan; **DOP**: Peter Pereira; **Music**: Laxmikant–Pyarelal; **Lyrics**: Anand Bakshi; **Selected Cast**: Vinod Khanna, Rishi Kapoor, Amitabh Bachchan, Neetu Singh, Shabana Azmi, Parveen Babi, Nirupa Roy; **Prod. Co.**: MKD Films; Colour.

Anand
India, 1970 – 122 mins
Hrishikesh Mukherjee

Rajesh Khanna was at his peak as a superstar when he took this role in an altogether smaller budget, less commercial film. It proved to be a wise move, as this performance is widely regarded as his best.

Dr Bhaskar Banerjee (Amitabh Bachchan) wins a prize for *Anand*, the book he has written about his friendship with a dying man. In flashback we learn of Anand (Rajesh Khanna), who is dying of cancer but wants to enjoy every minute of what is left of his life. He and his doctor, Dr Bhaskar, become friends.

Amitabh Bachchan was an unknown actor at the time, and it was three years before *Zanjeer* launched him on his path to becoming Hindi film's greatest superstar. His emotional intensity and silence were a good foil to Rajesh Khanna's exuberance, and he won awards for Best Supporting Actor, although many feel that his performance eclipsed that of Rajesh Khanna. The film also features a range of other stars in smaller roles, including Durga Khote, Dara Singh, Lalita Pawar and Johnny Walker.

The film is said to be inspired by Hrishikesh Mukherjee's friendship with Raj Kapoor. Amitabh's role as Dr Bhaskar was modelled on the director (who was even called Babu moshai, which was based on Raj Kapoor's name for him), while Anand was based on Raj Kapoor. Certainly, Anand has many characteristics of the immature but exuberant males that Raj Kapoor (in *Andaaz*) and others, including Shah Rukh Khan in some of his earlier roles, have played.

The most popular of Salil Choudhury's songs for this film was 'Kahin door' (sung by Mukesh), which has remained a perennial favourite and has recently been released by Jagjit Singh. The other hit song was Manna Dey's 'Zindagi kaisi hai paheli'.

Hrishikesh Mukherjee took up this theme of friendship again in 1973 with *Namak haram*, in which Amitabh Bachchan and Rajesh Khanna once again star as close friends, but here the similarities end, as the later film charts the breakdown rather than the cementing of a friendship. This is one of many films by Hrishikesh Mukherjee that I would like to have included here; instead I have had to restrict myself to three that give a good idea of his range. *Anand* and *Abhimaan* are benchmark films with outstanding performances, while *Gol maal* is one of his many very popular comedies. Mukherjee worked with New Theatres in Calcutta before coming to Bombay with Bimal Roy where he was a writer on *Do bigha zamin*. He began directing his own films in 1957, enjoying hits from *Anari* (1959), with Raj Kapoor and Nutan, to *Anuradha* (1960) and right through the 1970s. All of his films engage with the issues and values of the middle and upper middle classes, yet employ the songs and stars of mainstream cinema in a way that few, if any, films have done in subsequent years. This kind of cinema may well prove popular in future with the multiplex audiences, as the days of the film that appeals to a national audience, across class divides, seem to be over.

Dir./Story/Co-scr.: Hrishikesh Mukherjee; **Co-scr./Dial./Co-lyrics**: Gulzar; **Co-scr.**: Bimal Dutt, D. N. Mukherjee; **DOP**: Jaywant Pathare; **Music**: Salil Choudhury; **Co-lyrics**: Yogesh; **Selected Cast**: Rajesh Khanna, Amitabh Bachchan, Sumita Sanyal, Johnny Walker, Dara Singh; **Prod. Co.**: Rupam Chitra; Colour.

Andaz
India, 1949 – 148 mins
Mehboob Khan

Mehboob Khan's *Andaz* opened the prestigious new Liberty cinema in
Bombay. Nargis plays the role of Neeta, a modern woman who mixes
freely with men, rides horses and wears western clothes. She seems to
be falling in love with her father's manager, Dilip Kumar, while we
ignore all the signs that become so apparent on a second viewing of the
film, namely that she has another man in her life. This is her fiancé,
Rajan, played by Raj Kapoor, with whom Nargis starred in many hit films
of the 1940s and 50s, and whose choice of an image of the pair
together as his company's logo supports the widely held belief that she
was his lover as well as his inspiration. Rajan is an infantile, spoilt brat of
a man, and many in the audience hope that she will change her mind
and end their relationship. However, the film's text seems to say that she
never loved Dilip, but that he misinterpreted their friendship. While the
text supports the latter, conservative argument, the film shows clearly
that Neeta has indeed fallen in love with the more sophisticated Dilip.
Neeta marries Rajan, and they have a child. Rajan begins to suspect an
affair and has a fight with Dilip, who is thoroughly beaten. Dilip seems to
go a little mad, and finally declares his love to Neeta, who responds by
shooting him dead. This is driven by the narrative, in that he has ignobly
threatened her family, but it is also part of the subtext that she loves him
and is punishing them both for this transgression. The justification for
murder is that the family can never be threatened, so Dilip is punished by
death, whereas Neeta, whose complicity is more dubious, is jailed for
murder. In many Hindi films, the law of the state is inadequate, and
Rajan's forgiveness of Neeta would be all that is required, but here the
state is in control and she is incarcerated. She does not regret her action,
but rather blames it on her westernised behaviour, protesting that
'Foreign flowers cannot flourish on Indian soil.' This rejection of
westernisation goes against much of the film, in which the viewer is

invited to enjoy the western décor of colonial-style houses, where lovers dressed in western clothes gather around pianos, and play tennis and other sports.

This is one of Mehboob's last black-and-white films, before he became one of the first in Bombay to experiment with colour, as he did in his 1951 film *Aan* ('Savage Princess'). His filming of Nargis is particularly striking, and she shines in this luminous performance as daughter, lover, wife, mother and modern woman. She did not act with Mehboob again until her last film, Mehboob's *Mother India* in which she played the eponymous heroine. During these intervening years, Nargis is best remembered for her roles with Raj Kapoor, in which they played some of the most memorable romantic characters, including in *Barsaat*, which was released in the same year as *Andaz*. Yet in this film, it is her partnership with the great tragic actor Dilip Kumar that is most remembered. The film also reverses norms, in that Mukesh sings for Dilip Kumar and Mohammed Rafi for Raj Kapoor. The romantic feel was

Nargis, Raj Kapoor and Dilip Kumar in *Andaz*

supported by Naushad's music (with lyrics by Majrooh Sultanpuri), which was a major hit, in particular the songs of Mukesh and Lata Mangeshkar.

Dir.: Mehboob Khan; **Story**: Shams Lucknowi; **Scr./Dial.**: Ali Raza; **DOP**: Faredoon Irani; **Music**: Naushad; **Lyrics**: Majrooh Sultanpuri; **Selected Cast**: Nargis, Dilip Kumar, Raj Kapoor, V. H. Desai, Sapru; **Prod. Co.**: Mehboob Productions; Black and white.

Angoor
India, 1982 – 170 mins
S. S. Gulzar

Gulzar has been a major presence in the film industry for over forty years as a writer of stories, lyrics and dialogues as well as a director (including *Mere apne* [1971], *Koshish* [1973] and *Maachis* [1996]). Although a Punjabi (real name, Sampooran Singh), he has been most closely associated with the Bengalis who have worked in the Bombay industry, mainly Bimal Roy (for whose *Bandini* he wrote his first song), Hrishikesh Mukherjee (he worked on *Anand*, *Namak haraam* [1974] and others) and Asit Sen (including *Khamoshi*).

Angoor, loosely based on Shakespeare's *Comedy of Errors*, is one of many stories of twins and doubles in this selection of films. A couple who have their own twins, both called Ashok, find another set of twins, each of whom they call Bahadur. They decide to take a trip by sea, but their ship is wrecked and one of each set of twins stays with one parent. Ashok (Sanjeev Kumar) is married to Sucha (Moushumi Chatterjee), while Bahudur (Deven Verma) is married to Prema (Aruna Irani). They live with Sudha's sister Tanu (Deepti Naval). One day the other Ashok (Sanjeev Kumar), who is obsessed with detective stories, and the other Bahadur, come to town to buy a vineyard ('angoor' meaning 'grape'). The families, the taxi drivers, the jeweller and the police do not realise that there are two sets of twins . . .

Comedy is usually just one element in the Hindi film and real comedies are quite rare. Among the best of these, *Chalti ka naam gaadi* uses visual and verbal comedy along with slapstick, while *Padosan* draws on romance and caricature and *Jaane bhi do yaaro* mixes up all forms. *Angoor* is entirely situational, as the characters end up in all sorts of complicated predicaments based on the mistaken identities of the two Ashoks and two Bahadurs. Everyone in the town thinks they are mad, while they, of course, think everyone else is crazy. The story gets more and more complicated and is only resolved towards the very end of the film. Surprisingly, given that Gulzar is also a lyricist, the film has few songs, although 'Preetam aan milo', with music by S. D. Burman was popular, and the comic song situations are not developed as in *Chalti ka naam gaadi* and *Padosan*.

The star of the film is Sanjeev Kumar, often held to be one of the best actors in Hindi cinema. Gulzar directed several films featuring him, including *Aandhi* (1975), *Koshish* and *Mausam* (1975). The two latter films were also strong contenders for inclusion in this selection, as the former features sensitive performances from Sanjeev Kumar and Jaya Bhaduri as a deaf and dumb couple, while the latter is the story of a doctor (Sanjeev Kumar) who comes back to Darjeeling after many years to find that his former lover is dead and that his illegitimate daughter, Sharmila Tagore, has become a prostitute.

Gulzar is still writing lyrics for many films, including *Dil se* (1998), *Satya* and *Saathiya* (2001), but after the success of his television series, *Mirza Ghalib* (1988), he has enjoyed working in the different medium, in particular bringing the literary classics of Premchand and others to the small screen.

Although adaptations from Shakespeare have been very popular in Indian theatre since the nineteenth century, they have been less so in Hindi cinema. While *Romeo and Juliet* is a major source (see *Ek duuje ke liye* and *Qayamat se qayamat tak*), other plays have been drawn on occasionally, such as *The Taming of the Shrew* for *Betaab* (1983). Direct adaptations are rare, a notable exception being *Maqbool* (2004), adapted from *Macbeth*.

Dir.: S. S. Gulzar; **Story**: William Shakespeare's *Comedy of Errors*; **Scr./Dial.**: Gulzar; **DOP**: M. Sampat; **Music**: R. D. Burman; **Lyrics**: Gulzar; **Selected Cast**: Sanjeev Kumar, Moushumi Chatterjee, Deven Verma, Aruna Irani, Deepti Naval; **Prod. Co.**: A. R. Movies; Colour.

Anmol ghadi
India, 1946 – 122 mins
Mehboob Khan

Mehboob's national epic, *Mother India*, has tended to eclipse his other work, but his films are all fascinating, from *Aurat* (1940) (an earlier version of *Mother India*, which, though less spectacular, has a realist edge) or *Al-Hilal* (1935), where, unfamiliar with sound, he reveals his debt to Parsi theatre, to his Muslim social *Elaan* (1947), where the woman chooses work over romance, or *Aan* (1952), his Ruritanian romance. However, my final choices were the three included here, *Mother India*, *Andaz* and *Anmol ghadi*. I have included the latter partly because it is simply such a good film, but also because it is by the famous playwright, Agha Hashr Kashmiri, and for its music, sung by two of India's greatest singing stars, Noor Jehan and Suraiya.

Lata and Chander are childhood friends but when her family moves to Bombay she gives Chander her father's watch (the *anmol ghadi*, 'valuable watch'). The grown-up Chander (Surendra) still pines for Lata, spending his time reading the novels of Renu, who seems to write about his life, and mending musical instruments. He is not well off, so when his wealthy friend Prakash (Zahur Raja) invites him and his mother to Bombay, so that Chander can run his musical instrument shop, he readily accepts. Basanti (Suraiya) comes into the shop and begins flirting with Chander. She is a friend of Lata (Noor Jehan), who has become a writer, and uses the pen name of Renu. When Lata decides to meet one of her fans – Chander – after reading his letter, Basanti talks to him, but he panics and rushes off, leaving his watch, which Lata recognises straight away. They finally meet, but Lata is engaged to Prakash and the situation must be resolved.

The music by Naushad (lyrics are by Tanvir Naqvi) is some of the most popular in the history of Hindi film. The already established Noor Jehan has 'Jawan hai mohabbat', 'Mere bachpan ke saathi' and a duet with Surendra, 'Aawaz de kahan hai' while Suraiya launched her career in this

film with her songs, 'Man leta hai angadaai' and 'Socha tha kya kya ho gaya', and Zohrabai and Shamshad have 'Udan khatole pe'. Mohammed Rafi, who was to dominate playback singing in Hindi films until the 1970s, enjoyed one of his first hits with the song 'Tera khilona toota', while Surendra sings 'Kyun yaad aa rahe hai' and 'Ab kaun hai mera'.

The film also has a great nostalgia value for the sumptuous interiors and the elegant clothes, but in particular for the outdoor shots, whose horse-drawn carriages seem somewhat out of place in front of shots of Bombay's corniche, the newly built art deco Marine Drive.

Dir: Mehboob Khan; **Story**: Anwar Batalvi; **Scr./Dial.**: Aga Jani Kashmiri; **DOP**: Faredoon Irani; **Music**: Naushad; **Lyrics**: Tanvir Naqvi, Anjum Pilibhiti; **Selected Cast**: Noor Jehan, Surendra, Suraiya, Zahur Raja, Leela Mishra, Anwari Begum; **Prod. Co.**: Mehboob Productions; Black and white.

(Opposite page) Song book cover from *Anmol ghadi*

Aradhana
India, 1969 – 169 mins
Shakti Samanta

Aradhana is one of Hindi cinema's most popular musical romances and established Rajesh Khanna as the great romantic hero of his generation.

Airforce pilot Arun (Rajesh Khanna) falls in love with Vandana (Sharmila Tagore) and they have a 'temple marriage' (where they are married 'in the eyes of God') ,which they consummate on a stormy night in a log cabin. He dies in a plane crash, leaving her pregnant and, in the eyes of the world, unmarried. She is forced to give their son up for adoption and then finds work as his nanny. She goes to jail to protect him from charges of murder when, as a young child, he kills her would-be rapist. On her release, she finds a position with the adoptive family of her grown-up son, Suraj (Rajesh Khanna), where his feelings towards her are finally proved true and he honours her as his mother in a public ceremony.

The film deals with a favourite theme of Hindi movies, namely society's cruelty to unmarried mothers. Although the couple here are 'married in the eyes of God', this is, of course, utterly bogus, being merely a plot device to show that the heroine has committed no 'fault' and putting the viewer in the position of knowing more than the other characters in the film. In another favourite plot device, the young 'husband', an airforce pilot, dies for his country leaving the young widow pregnant. As with other films, the heroine then undergoes penance for her transgression, here by working as a nanny for her son, whom she has given up for adoption, then going to jail for protecting him. It is very easy to read incest fantasies into the son's stabbing of the would-be rapist and in the fact that he is played by the actor who took the role of the husband, although there is no suggestion of anything other than pure, unselfish love in the film.

Sharmila Tagore began her career in Satyajit Ray's films, starring in the last of the Apu trilogy, *Apur sansar* (1958), before moving to glamorous roles in Hindi cinema, such as Shakti Samanta's *An Evening in Paris* (1967), in which she appeared water-skiing in a swimsuit. Playing the ageing mother of Rajesh Khanna in his second role in the film must have been something of a risk. The young Farida Jalal, now the choice of many in maternal roles (such as *DDLJ* and *Kuch kuch hota hai*), plays the love interest of Rajesh Khanna in his second role. Over the last few decades, the hero's mother, presumably aged only about forty, has changed from being shown as grey-haired and elderly into a much more glamorous figure. Ashok Kumar appears as the senior benevolent figure in the film, while the famed director and producer, Subhash Ghai (*Karz*, *Khalnayak*), has a small role as Rajesh Khanna's friend.

The film contains some of S. D. Burman's great songs, perhaps showing the youthful influence of his son, R. D. Burman. These include 'Kora kagaaz', 'Baaghon mein bahaar hai' (a humorous love song between Rajesh Khanna and Farida Jalal), the wonderfully shot 'Mere sapnon ki rani', as the hero's jeep drives alongside the heroine's

Rajesh Khanna and Sharmila Tagore during the song 'Roop tera mastana' from *Aradhana*

mountain train. The all-time classic is Kishore Kumar's rendition of 'Roop tera mastana', one of the most eroticised moments in Hindi cinema, as in a single take the camera circles the young couple, stranded by the weather in a log cabin, the heroine draped only in a blanket bewitching the hero as he gazes speechlessly, while in the next room a silhouetted couple sing 'Your beauty is intoxicating, my love is crazy; we should be careful lest we make a mistake'. The scene dissolves into the flames of the log fire and the result of the encounter is the heroine's pregnancy.

Dir.: Shakti Samanta; **Story/Scr.**: Sachin Bhowmick; **Dial.**: Ramesh Pant; **DOP**: Aloke Dasgupta; **Music**: S. D. Burman; **Lyrics**: Anand Bakshi; **Selected Cast**: Rajesh Khanna, Sharmila Tagore, Sujit Kumar, Pahadi Sanyal, Anita Dutt, Subhash Ghai; **Prod. Co.**: Shakti Films; Colour.

Ardh satya
India, 1983 – 130 mins
Govind Nihalani

One of the best police films of Indian cinema, whose realistic and gritty style and depiction of the links between the police, gangsters and politicians set the style for the whole genre of police and gangster films that became popular in the 1990s. Few have come close to it, apart from Ram Gopal Varma's *Satya* in its total achievement of direction, writing and performances.

Anant Welankar (Om Puri) has academic leanings but is made to join the police by his father (Amrish Puri). Welankar has a strong sense of right and is anti-corruption, but the personal trauma of his father's brutality, especially towards women, drives him to extreme violence in his treatment of men accused of assaulting women. His unfulfilled desires for poetry find their outlet in drink and in his romancing of college teacher, Jyotsna (Smita Patil).

Throughout the film, Welankar is locked in a struggle against Rama Shetty (Sadashiv Amrapurkar), the south Indian don with political aspirations. Following Welankar's arrest of three of Shetty's men for assaulting one of his colleagues, a phone call from Shetty has them released. As Welankar enters a downward spiral of drinking and personal problems as he agonises over the corruption in the force and in society, Shetty's star rises and eventually Welankar, in total despair, kills him and hands himself over to the police.

Om Puri's performance drives the film, as an ordinary man who cannot follow his beliefs and dreams because he is trapped by his family and by society. His only hope is for his love, Jyotsna, but even this romance is doomed. Om Puri's anger and passion burn throughout the film, relieved only in a few moments of romance. Smita Patil is in her element as the woman who cannot understand her gentle boyfriend's explosions of anger and drunken behaviour. Amrapurkar's performance as the south Indian don is superb and has been much imitated in later films. Naseeruddin Shah, who along with Puri is regarded as one of India's finest actors, has a few scenes as a drunken ex-cop.

Vijay Tendulkar's screenplay has sharp dialogues that are memorable but not too flamboyant or *filmi*. *Ardh satya*'s strengths include its structure, characters and dialogue, as well as the locations and the feel of the city. This film contains one of the best depictions of the city of Bombay, which has featured in very few films (Anurag Kashyap's *Black Friday* [2004] seems like something of a tribute to this film).

While we may think of it as 'art film', it was also a huge hit, being both commercially successful and critically acclaimed. Once again it shows that films in India can be appreciated by both the critics and the audiences and that there is no need for 'dumbing down' in the quest for box-office success.

Dir.: Govind Nihalani; **Story**: S. D. Panwalkar (short story); **Scr./Dial.**: Vijay Tendulkar, Vasant Dev; **DOP**: Govind Nihalani; **Music**: Ajit Varman; **Selected Cast**: Om Puri, Smita Patil, Amrish Puri, Naseeruddin Shah, Sadashiv Amrapurkar; **Prod. Co.**: Neo Film Associates; Colour.

Arth
India, 1982 – 143 mins
Mahesh Bhatt

Mahesh Bhatt, one of the Bhatt dynasty of film-makers, is known for his controversial themes and this film attracted notoriety right from the start, as it is said to draw closely on his own first marriage and his relationship with the star Parveen Babi (whose popular films include *Deewaar* and *Amar, Akbar, Anthony*), who suffered from schizophrenia. The film was one of the first to discuss an extra-marital affair and to show it in such realistic terms.

The film is shown mostly through the eyes of Pooja Malhotra (Shabana Azmi), an orphan whose great desire is for the security of having her own home. Her husband is a rising film-maker, Inder Malhotra (Kulbhushan Kharbanda), and he seems to be willing to help her achieve this dream but he is having an affair with an actress, Kavita Sanyal (Smita Patil). Although Inder is prepared to carry on with both relationships, Kavita delivers him an ultimatum and he leaves Pooja. After Pooja confronts Kavita at a cocktail party, Inder begins to see Kavita as a victim as she descends into mental illness. In the end, Pooja reassures Kavita that she forgives her and grants Inder a divorce. When Pooja finds her dream home is actually a gift from Kavita, she moves into a woman's hostel, where her room-mate tries to persuade her that she should exchange sexual favours for help from men. Although the singer Raj (Raj Kiran) falls in love with Pooja and she enjoys his company, she is unwilling to begin a new relationship. When her maid (Rohini Hattangadi) is convicted of killing her drunken and abusive husband, Pooja adopts her daughter and plans a new life for them. When Inder wants to return to her, she asks him whether he would have her back if she had had an affair. He admits that he would not and she refuses to take him back.

Although the film is based on the life of the director, Mahesh Bhatt does not paint a flattering portrait of himself. Inder is totally self-obsessed and only takes action when Kavita pressures him. He sees all his own problems but does not understand those of others, in particular Pooja's. His heartlessness is clear when he makes her sign the divorce papers and, although he has to recall the date, does not realise it is his wife's birthday. Kavita is also seen through his eyes, clearly mentally disturbed (she accuses Pooja of breaking her *mangal sutra* or wedding necklace, on the floor so that the beads will hurt her feet). The real focus of the film is Pooja, with much of the film shown from her point of view. Although she seems to be a victim at the beginning, weeping being her only reaction to her husband's infidelity, apart from an attempt to phone Kavita, she eventually accepts support from her friends (Geeta and Siddharth Kak) and summons the strength to break away, refusing reconciliation and a new relationship. The scene where she gets drunk and, with her sari falling off, abuses Kavita is one of the film's most memorable and shows that although it was meant to be a clash of the two great actresses, the film is Shabana's.

The feel of the film is given substance by Kaifi Azmi's poetry, which is set to Chitra and Jagjit Singh's music. All the songs are picturised on Raj Kiran, making him the romantic centre of the film and a commentator on the failed relationships, although his own romance is not given a chance to flourish.

Dir./Story/Co-scr. /Dial.: Mahesh Bhatt; **Co-scr.**: Sujit Sen; **DOP**: Pravin Bhatt; **Music**: Chitra Singh; Jagjit Singh; **Lyrics**: Kaifi Azmi; **Selected Cast**: Shabana Azmi, Smita Patil, Kulbhushan Kharbanda, Raj Kiran, Rohini Hattangadi; **Prod. Co.**: Anu Arts; Colour.

Awaara
In ıa, 1951 – 195 mins
¡ Kapoor

Awaara was the film that established Raj Kapoor as a major international film star; it also became one of the most popular Hindi films overseas (mainly in Asia and the former USSR) and was remade in many other national cinemas. It was also the first film Raj Kapoor made in his own studios and with his own team, from his stars (himself and Nargis) to his musicians (Shankar–Jaikishan) and singers (Lata Mangeshkar and Mukesh).

The wife (Leela Chitnis) of Judge Raghunath (Prithviraj Kapoor) is kidnapped by the evil Jagga. When the judge takes her back, he finds that she is pregnant, but does not believe the child is his. She brings up Raju (Raj Kapoor) in poverty and he falls into Jagga's company. When he falls in love with the lawyer, Rita (Nargis), Judge Raghunath's ward, the judge tries to forbid their relationship, convinced that the son of a thief will be a thief too. Rita defends Raju in court where all will be revealed . . .

This was the first film in which Raj Kapoor appeared as the Chaplinesque tramp. Unlike the usual Indian vagrant, Raj Kapoor is dressed as an American tramp, whose clothes Charlie Chaplin drew on in those famous oversized suits that appear to belong to someone else, thus undermining the suit's respectability and recalling, perhaps, the circus clown. In Raj Kapoor's case, the suit was too small, suggesting perhaps that he had outgrown what used to fit him. The western or colonial nature of the suit may also suggest an outfit discarded by a member of the ruling elite, and comically appropriated by a vagrant. Kapoor's tribute to Chaplin would not have been missed by many in the audience, for Chaplin's films had always found success in India. Raj Kapoor fans may be delighted to know that R. K. Studios have carefully preserved this outfit, shoes and hat, in their wardrobe department in Bombay.

(*Next page*) The dream sequence from *Awaara*

This film is also memorable for its presentation of Raj Kapoor and Nargis as the great romantic couple, passionately bound to one another. Nargis is presented as the idealised object of male fantasies, whether in a swimsuit on the beach or as a divine, celestial saviour in the dream sequence. The great Prithviraj Kapoor, Raj's real-life father, plays his on-screen father, often in moments of Oedipal drama. For despite the film's reference to mythology, notably in the rejection of the pregnant mother, recalling Ram's banishment of Sita in the *Ramayana*, this is a resolutely modern film, arguing that nurture, rather than nature, creates a person's moral character, inserting Raj Kapoor's quasi-Nehruvian or socialist views.

While almost every song in the film has become a classic – 'Awaara hoon', 'Dum bhar jo udhar mooh phere' – it is the nine-minute dream sequence that affords one of the most memorable set designs in Hindi cinema. The scene is not only stunning visually and aurally, but it also condenses into a dream many fears and anxieties about the film's key themes of love, religion, women, motherhood, punishment and crime, which it then projects onto Achrekar's sets themselves. The first shots show a spiral staircase surrounded by clouds, presumably in heaven. Dancers appear among statues of loops and swirls, singing and sliding down chutes. Rita stands at the top of a flight of stairs, dressed in fine fabric, sequins and shiny hair ornaments, dusted with glitter, singing a love song ('Tere bina aag yeh chaandni'). Raj, dressed in a black T-shirt and trousers, then appears in hell, where he sings of his desires for love and spring ('Yeh nahin, yeh nahin zindagi') as he is surrounded by flames, dancing skeletons and other monsters. In the last sequence, he emerges through clouds to the sound of 'Om namah Shivaya/Homage to Lord Shiva' at the bottom of a flight of stairs leading to a Trimurti (a composite image of Brahma–Shiva–Vishnu), when Nargis bends down to take him by the hand and lead him to heaven. Dressed in an embroidered bodice and skirt, she sings 'Ghar aaya mera pardesi' in front of a statue (of Devi, the goddess?) with flashing lights in the background. She begins to climb the spiral staircase and Raj follows her. They then climb more stairs towards a Nataraja (dancing Shiva) as Nargis appears in dancing clothes. As they begin to walk along a twisting road, a giant Jagga appears, holding a shining knife. Raj falls down yelling 'Rita' as she reaches over him but cannot save him. A montage of images, including one of Raj yelling as Rita appears superimposed, dissolves as Raj wakes up, shouting, 'Maa, mujhe bachao/Mother, save me!'

Dir./Scr.: Raj Kapoor; **Dial.**: K. A. Abbas; **DOP**: Radhu Karmakar; **Music**: Shankar–Jaikishan; **Lyrics**: Hasrat Jaipuri, Shailendra; **Selected Cast**: Raj Kapoor, Nargis, Prithviraj Kapoor, Leela Chitnis, Shashi Kapoor; **Prod. Co.**: R. K. Films; Black and white.

Baiju Bawra
India, 1952 – 168 mins
Vijay Bhatt

The greatest strength of this historical film about Baiju Bawra (Bharat Bhushan), the musician who challenged the court musician Tansen to a musical duel (a *jugalbandi*; performed here by Ustad Amir Khan and Pandit D. V. Paluskar) to avenge the murder of his father, is not surprisingly the outstanding music composed by one of Hindi cinema's most accomplished composers, Naushad Ali. Naushad, though one of the first composers to bring the western orchestra, in particular the large string section, to film music was able to move seamlessly between classical Indian *ragas* and western dramatic music in a way that no other composer has done. Although the subject matter of this film requires classical music, Naushad was able to blend this with light classical and contemporary music in a way that marks him as one of the finest exponents of the whole range of music essential for the Hindi film, a quality that can also be seen in his other scores for films such as *Mother India* and *Mughal-e Azam.* This film includes the popular songs, 'Tu Ganga ki mauj', 'Mohe bhool gaye sanwariya' and the *bhajan*, 'Man tarpat hari darshan'.

One sequence alone would ensure this film's inclusion in most lists of 100 best films. This is the astonishing depiction of the *ragas* or melodies, where they are embodied in a manner drawing on the classical paintings of *ragamalas* that illustrate the moods associated with *ragas*. The combination of visuals and music in this sequence overwhelms the viewer as much as it does Baiju Bawra himself in the film. Raga Lalita appears as a beautiful woman, while Gaur Malhar brings the rain; Shri is erotic, while Puriya is regal. This is one of several miracle sequences in the film, such as the statue that weeps when Baiju sings in sorrow 'O duniyaa ke rakhwaale'.

These miracles and the other strong religious elements of the film are not surprising, given Vijay Bhatt's earlier films of *Ramayana* stories. Baiju

Bawra, a disciple of Swami Haridas, lives in a pastoral idyll on the banks of the Jumna, where he sings to his beloved Gauri (Meena Kumari, in her first major screen role), who is seated on a swing in a bower of flowers. This reminds the viewer of Vrindavan, on the banks of the Jumna, where the young Krishna lived, playing his flute to enchant the world. There are many references to Krishna in the film, linking the innocent Baiju to him. There are striking location shots of the river, which also flows through the cities of the Mughal court (Delhi and Agra), thus linking these worlds of the Mughal, Muslim court and the Hindu Vrindavan, originally in revenge and anger, but after Tansen is defeated in music, in respect and the spirit of reconciliation.

Some have suggested that I should include K. L. Saigal's *Tansen* in this book. It certainly is a predecessor to this film and although Saigal's 'Diya jalao' is one of my favourite Hindi film songs, *Baiju Bawra* is simply an outstanding film and of significance in the history of Indian film music.

Dir.: Vijay Bhatt; **Story**: Ramchandra Thakur; **Scr.**: R. S. Choudhury; **Dial.**: Zia Sarhadi; **DOP**: V. N. Reddy; **Music**: Naushad; **Lyrics**: Shakeel Badayuni; **Selected Cast**: Bharat Bhushan, Meena Kumari, Surendra; **Prod. Co.**: Prakash Pictures; Black and white.

Bandini
India, 1963 – 120 mins
Bimal Roy

This was to be Bimal Roy's last film and is one of my favourites of his, with its fine cinematography, and beautiful and meaningful songs. A women-centred film, it has some fine acting and is the kind of Hindi film that can hold its own against any other cinema.

Bandini is set in the 1930s. The prisoner Kalyani (Nutan) looks after another prisoner who has tuberculosis and the handsome doctor (Dharmendra) falls in love with her. The jailer asks her to explain her past, which she does in writing, beginning with a flashback to the village where her father was a religious and learned man. She falls for freedom fighter Bikash (Ashok Kumar) and they pretend to be married to save him from the police, but he leaves and when her letters to him are returned, she flees the village where she is mocked as an abandoned woman. Kalyani remains an outcast but becomes a nurse, looking after a hysterical patient who turns out to be Bikash's wife. Driven to desperation by her incessant bullying, the death of her father and from seeing Bikash, Kalyani poisons her. The doctor's mother understands what Kalyani has been through and accepts her as a potential daughter-in-law, but on her release from jail, on the way to the doctor's home, Kalyani meets Bikash at the steamer port and finds out why he vanished from her life; now she has to choose between the two men . . .

The film is quite slow, and has some wonderful moments of melodrama but it also raises the serious issue of crime. It highlights different kinds of crime, from Kalyani's crime of passion to political crime that keeps the freedom fighters in jail along with common criminals. We do not know what the other women's crimes are or why they are incarcerated. The film also raises the issue of the crimes that society commits against women, and how women, even as they suffer themselves (as the song 'Ab ke baras bhej bhaiya ko babul' highlights), inflict suffering on other women, mostly through gossip and the imposition of social restrictions. These women – in jail and in the village – display a lack of sympathy for the suffering of others, where respectability means more than humanity. In this film, all the men – the doctor, the father, the jailer and the freedom fighter – act with compassion and humanity.

The performances of the actors are good throughout. Nutan is a fine actor, who, with minimal gesture, brings dignity and grace to the image of the suffering woman. Ashok Kumar displays his usual elegance and remoteness, while Dharmendra plays his role with a gentle and kind demeanour.

The film has beautiful cinematography by Kamal Bose for Bimal Roy. Like Roy himself, he uses black and white not for an empty intellectual show but to bring texture and form in simplicity mixed with richness. The images of the jail, including the memorable shots of the women at work, singing 'O paanchi pyaare', all serve the purpose of the film, and are never just for show. The film makes cuts to the watchtower where the guard cries, 'Sab thik hai!', to reinforce the feeling of surveillance. The shots of the moments before the poisoning uses Hitchcock-style discordant music, shots of the welders, flashing lights and rapid cutting to bring out the emotions in Kalyani's mind.

This cinematography is complemented by the use of songs. The two come together brilliantly for the shots of the execution of the freedom fighter, a sequence which for me encapsulates what the Hindi film is really about. The song 'Mat ro maata' has lyrics that explain the situation, dramatic shots of the man going to his death, and in the song about Mother (India) cuts to his mother to show her sacrifice as well as his, before we go to the starkness of the execution with close-ups of the noose and the lever.

The songs of S. D. Burman have a Bengali flavour, including 'O jaanewala ho sake to laut ke aana', sung by Mukesh when she leaves her natal home, driven out by rumours. Gulzar wrote his first song for this film, 'Mora gora ang lai le'. My own favourite is the song towards the end of the film, 'Mere saajan hai us paar', whose wonderful music is complemented by the images of the waiting room for the steamer made of thatch and the sand outside, which then shift to the drawing up of the anchor and casting away with shots of the pistons, the whistle and then the plume of smoke as the steamer moves off. The song expresses the emotion of the moment and, indeed, of the whole film.

Dir.: Bimal Roy; **Story**: Jarasandha (Charuchandra Chakraborty); **Scr.**: M. Ghosh; **Dial.**: Paul Mahendra; **DOP**: Kamal Bose; **Music**: S. D. Burman; **Lyrics**: Shailendra; **Selected Cast**: Nutan, Ashok Kumar, Dharmendra, Raja Paranjpe; **Prod. Co.**: Bimal Roy Productions; Black and white.

Bandit Queen
India, 1994 – 119 mins
Shekhar Kapur

Bandit Queen was one of the first Indian films to make an impact on the west and a rare example of a Hindi film that represented a real collaboration with an overseas producer (the UK's Channel Four Television). Hindi film rarely makes biopics but the story of Phoolan Devi (1968–2001), a Robin Hood figure, who was regarded as a fighter against gender and class oppression, seemed an ideal subject.

Shekhar Kapur, whose earlier films include *Masoom* and *Mr India* and who was later to win further international recognition for *Elizabeth* (1998), seems to have no single thread running through his work. This film was based on a real person but the story was controversially adapted for screen from a book by Mala Sen. In the film, the child Phoolan Devi (Sunita Bhatt) is married off in exchange for a cow and a bicycle. When she is 'raped' by her husband, she returns to her parents' home, where she is attacked by higher-caste men, Thakurs, and made to leave the village. Her cousin Kailash (Saurabh Shukla) takes her in but his family forces her to leave. Through Kailash she has already met Babu Gujjar (Anirudh Agrawal) and his bandits, who later kidnap her. One of the gang, Vikram Mallah (Nirmal Pandey), who is of the same caste, protects her, even killing the higher-caste Gujjar for raping her. Devi enjoys a happy time as an equal and lover of Mallah. However, the gang's main leader Sriram (Govind Namdeo), also higher-caste, is released from prison and, after Mallah's murder, Devi is stripped naked in public before being gang-raped by Thakurs. Her 'revenge' is the Behmai massacres of 1981, in which twenty-two men were killed. Although she acquires a Robin Hood status, she surrenders in 1983 and goes to prison.

Phoolan Devi objected to the film, which she said was inaccurate, in particular the rape scenes which she had never talked about. She was angry that the film-makers would not show her the film. Fierce debates raged about the depiction of the rapes and Devi's humiliation, as well as the simplistic telling of her story as a woman's murderous rampage in revenge for her rape while having a romantic fixation on her relationship with Mallah. The film was made at the time of Devi's release from jail, before she became an MP. She was murdered in 2001.

Although the film shows violence and oppression of gender and caste, it does not explore them in any way other than to favour a response through violence. Nor does it depict any attempts to go to the law or to take action through politics (although the 1990s saw the rise of lower castes in this area), or to look at any other form of resistance. The film is entirely fixated on rape, violence, anger and revenge. As a result, the character of Phoolan Devi becomes somewhat one-dimensional (however extraordinary Seema Biswas' performance is) and there is no

Seema Biswas in a still from *Bandit Queen*

attempt to show Devi's other emotions or inner feelings. The scene where she and Mallah first show their feelings to each other attempts to go beyond this, albeit clumsily, and there is one very clunky scene in which, after a raid, Devi gives a small girl some silver jewellery.

I am a great fan of Nusrat Fateh Ali Khan's music of pain and suffering, but it does not work here as a soundtrack. Perhaps it is too beautiful and too sophisticated for the brutality of this film.

Dir.: Shekhar Kapur; **Story/Scr.**: Mala Sen; **Dial.**: Ranjit Kapoor; **DOP**: Ashok Mehta; **Music**: Nusrat Fateh Ali Khan; **Selected Cast**: Seema Biswas, Nirmal Pandey; **Prod. Co.**: Kaleido- scope (India) and Channel Four Films (London); Colour.

Bhumika
India, 1976 – 142 mins
Shyam Benegal

This is the only film by Shyam Benegal in this selection (see Introduction). It is also one of the few films about the film industry, as it is very loosely modelled on the life of Hansa Wadkar (1923–71), a star of Prabhat Studios (see *Duniya na mane*). *Bhumika* has a strong central character, living in a difficult world. Although not an admirable person, her character is realistic and the film is told in a manner that allows us to feel sympathy for her dilemmas and her mostly poor decisions.

The film is told partly in flashbacks, most of which are in black and white, while the contemporary narrative is shown in colour. The young girl Usha (Baby Ruksana) is the granddaughter of a singer (courtesan?), while her mother (Sulabha Deshpande), struggling to break away from this existence and find a 'respectable' life, has married a Brahmin, even though she does not seem to be happy with him. Usha fights with her mother, sometimes over her mother's friend, Keshav Dalvi (Amol Palekar), whose relationships with the family members are unclear but rather disturbing. He seems to have some sort of hold on the mother but is interested in the daughter in a way she clearly finds threatening. He helps Usha enter the film world and she later marries him for reasons that again are unclear but amount to more than the fact that she is pregnant, rejecting her co-star, Rajan (Anant Nag), who is in love with her. Keshav continues to act as her manager even after marriage, living off her earnings and behaving more like a pimp than a husband. She leaves him and their daughter several times, having affairs but always returning to him. Her first affair is with director Sunil Verma (Naseeruddin Shah), with whom she plans an unsuccessful double-suicide, and then with Vinayak Kale (Amrish Puri), who keeps her as a traditional, secluded wife in his country house. Although she becomes close to his crippled first wife, his mother and his son, she arranges for Keshav to help her escape. She returns to find her daughter married, and although Rajan, still in love with her, wants to meet, she is unable to make a decision about her future.

Bhumika means 'role', and the film's main character, Usha, is always playing roles in films and in life, but never seems to find one that fits her. The emphasis on role-playing is underlined by her use of a stage name, Urvashi, showing that her identity is never fixed. Usha's quest in life is to find a fine balance between her desire for security and her wish for freedom. Keshav provides her with security and she keeps returning to him, but she can never stay with him for long before needing to leave to find her freedom.

Smita Patil shows off her talents in this film, as she acts with her entire body rather than just through dialogue delivery. Even though

Smita Patil in *Bhumika*

Smita could not carry a sexy song well in a mainstream film, she makes a good attempt here at the songs for the films within films. Amol Palekar is quite repulsive as Keshav, who is a very ambiguous character in the film. Usha's reliance on him and their relationship as a whole is shown as a major dilemma in the film. It is unclear whether his willingness to take Usha back several times and to help her out is based on his desire for her money or whether there is some real love in the strange bond between them. On one occasion, he takes her back but forces her to have an abortion when he does not believe he is the father of her child.

Dir./Co-scr.: Shyam Benegal, **Story**: Hansa Wadkar's 'Sangtye Aika' (1970); **Co-scr.**: Girish Karnad; **Dial.**: Satyadev Dubey; **DOP**: Govind Nihalani; **Music**: Vanraj Bhatia; **Lyrics**: Majrooh Sultanpuri, Vasant Dev; **Selected Cast**: Smita Patil, Anant Nag, Amrish Puri, Naseeruddin Shah; **Prod. Co.**: Blaze Film Ents; Colour.

Bobby
India, 1973 – 168 mins
Raj Kapoor

Although Raj Kapoor is now best remembered for the films he made with Nargis in the 1940s and 50s, such as *Awaara* and *Shree 420*, this late film is justifiably regarded as key to his oeuvre. After the box-office failure of *Mera naam joker (MNJ)* (1969), it seemed that Raj Kapoor's long career as star, producer and director was over. Having decided that he no longer wanted to act, he came up with the idea of making a teenage love story with his middle son, Rishi, who had already appeared in *MNJ*. Rishi was still a teenager, and Raj Kapoor presented a new heroine, Dimple Kapadia,

LOVE THAT DEFIED
ALL BARRIERS

Rishi Kapoor and Dimple Kapadia in publicity for *Bobby*

who bore more than a passing resemblance to Nargis.

Raj (Rishi Kapoor) has just finished school and returned to his rich but unloving parents. He meets Bobby (Dimple Kapadia), the granddaughter of his wet-nurse, Mrs Braganza (Durga Khote), and falls in love with her but his parents forbid the relationship . . .

K. A. Abbas, who had earlier worked with Raj Kapoor, wrote the Romeo and Juliet story, but with the addition of a happy ending to avoid the risk of box-office failure. Laxmikant-Pyarelal, with the lyricist Anand Bakshi, composed many hit songs, including among others an Ashkenazy wedding waltz ('Main shair to nahin'), a *qawwali* (Sufi-inspired devotional song), a Goan folk song ('Jhooth bole kauwa khaate') and the suggestive 'Hum tum ek kamre mein'. The young couple, in their outrageously fashionable clothes, ranging from hotpants, bikinis and miniskirts to leather suits and goggles, set a trend for all youngsters and sparked a host of teenage romances from *Love Story* (1981) to those of the 1990s.

Rishi Kapoor assumed the role of major romantic hero for the next twenty years, beginning his career during the reign of Amitabh Bachchan, and ending as the new generation of Khans dominated the box office in the early 1990s. Dimple, aged about sixteen when she made this film, married the reigning superstar, Rajesh Khanna, during the shooting of the film (the henna of her wedding decorations can be seen on her hand during the song 'Mujhe kuch kehna hai') and she was pregnant with Twinkle before the premier. Her comeback was with Rishi in 1985's *Saagar*, after which she became an iconic figure in the film industry, appearing in films such as Farhan Akhtar's *Dil chahta hai*.

One scene in particular stands out: when Raj visits Bobby's house, she is making *pakodas* and wipes the batter into her hair, as Nargis was said to have done when Raj Kapoor visited her house. Her line, 'Mujhse dosti karoge?/Will you be my friend?', has inspired a generation of younger film-makers to emphasise love as friendship, from Sooraj Barjatya, whose *Maine pyar kiya* quoted several scenes from *Bobby*, to Karan Johar's *Kuch*

kuch hota hai, where the teacher is called Miss Braganza (Bobby's surname), to Kunal Kohli's film *Mujhse dosti karoge* (2002).

Dir.: Raj Kapoor; **Story/Co-scr**.: K. A. Abbas; **Co-scr**.: V. P. Sathe; **Dial**.: Jainendra Jain; **DOP**: Radhu Karmakar; **Music**: Laxmikant-Pyarelal; **Lyrics**: Anand Bakshi, Vithalbhai Patel, Inderjit Singh Tulsi; **Selected Cast**: Rishi Kapoor, Dimple Kapadia, Pran, Premnath, Sonia Sahni, Durga Khote; **Prod**. **Co**.: R. K. Films; Colour.

Bombay
India, 1995 – 134 mins
Mani Ratnam

As with *Roja*, this is not strictly speaking a Hindi film, but once again its dubbed version and the re-recorded songs in Hindi have made it important in the history of Hindi film. It is one of the few films that refers to contemporary political events, in this case the communal riots that occurred in Bombay in 1992.

This is the second film in Mani Ratnam's 'trilogy' (see *Roja*), whose central narrative charts the intercommunal marriage between a south Indian Hindu male, Shekhar (Arvind Swamy), and Muslim girl, Shaila Bano (Manisha Koirala), who hope to escape communal tensions in Bombay. However, this is 1992, when the mobilisation of support for Hindutva via processions around India, which demanded the building of a temple at Rama's birthplace in Ayodhya on a site then occupied by a mosque, led to the demolition of the mosque and subsequent riots in Bombay in December 1992 and January 1993, leaving many dead, most of whom were Muslims. A film about such recent events, which seemed to threaten the future of India, was a bold move and one unlikely to pass the censors, who made many cuts, including references to the high number of Muslim deaths, images of the police shooting Muslims and actual footage of the mosque being demolished. The censors may have thought *Bombay* would not inflame communal sentiments, as it shows that Hindus and Muslims were equally culpable (whereas in fact the violence was disproportionately against Muslims) and that the violence was directed more at property than people. Mani Ratnam met the head of the Shiv Sena, Bal Thackeray, who acted as unofficial censor, authorising screening in Bombay without protest.

Bombay was the object of Muslim protests, and Mani Ratnam's home in Madras was attacked by a gunman. Muslims and secular objectors to the film argued that it shows the Hindu, secular male as the modern citizen, while his Muslim wife is a religious, domestic figure. The film enforces many stereotypical images of the Muslim, as aggressor (the girl's father) contrasted with the educated, peaceful Hindu (the boy's father), or images from the Muslim social. Again, while many objections to the film may be upheld, apart from the seal of approval from the Shiv Sena, which Mani Ratnam was obliged to obtain, there is no convincing argument that *Bombay* espoused Hindutva. In fact, in the film's final scenes, when the mob threatens to burn the hero alive, he claims he is an 'Indian', not a Hindu.

This film exemplifies how Mani Ratnam picturised the songs in such a way that every frame is carefully constructed, while also choosing some of A. R. Rehman's best songs. The first song of the film, 'Kehna hai kya', a *qawwali*, deploys some of the traditions of the Muslim social film as Shekhar seeks the elusive Shaila Bano, whom he has only glimpsed in the crowd at a wedding. While 'Humma humma' was one of the biggest dance songs of the year, the Bombay theme 'Tu hi re' is one of the most haunting tunes in Indian film music, and its picturisation, as Shekhar calls Shailo to the ruined seaside fort in the storm, is unforgettable.

Dir./Scr./Story: Mani Ratnam; **Dial.**: Umesh Sharma (Tamil original: Sujata); **DOP**: Rajiv Menon; **Music**: A. R. Rehman; **Lyrics**: Mehboob (Tamil original: Vairamuthu); **Selected Cast**: Arvind Swamy, Manisha Koirala; **Prod.Co.**: Aalayam; Colour.

Border
India, 1997 – 175 mins
J. P. Dutta

The Hindi film has not produced a war genre, even though India has gone to war several times since independence. Before this film, the most important was Chetan Anand's *Haqeeqat* set against India's defeat by China in the war of 1962.

Border looks back on India's last war with Pakistan, over the 1971 secession of East Pakistan. The narrative of the film is more focused than many Hindi films, closely following the conventions of the western war genre. The run-up to the war is taken as given, the film quickly introducing the main characters, three soldiers and one airforce pilot, bringing them to their posting on the western border in the Rajasthan desert. The stories of Major Kuldeep Singh (Sunny Deol), the brave Sikh whose duty comes before everything, even his family, and of the airforce pilot (Jackie Shroff) are established in the beginning of the film, with only a brief digression to the latter's wedding plans (cut from the version screened in the cinemas on release). The young Dharam Veer (Akshaye Khanna) is presented as the son of a 'martyr (*shaheed*)' of the 1965 war, whose mother has gone blind through weeping. Afraid to kill, he soon proves his mettle in despatching a Pakistani spy. He tells in flashback the story of his engagement, interrupted by the call to the border. The patriotic Rajput (Sunil Shetty) tells of his *suhaag raat* ('wedding night'), during which he too received the call.

Each of the two young heroes has a romantic song, while the film leads into the interval with the hit song, 'Sandese ate hain . . . Messages come, they disturb us, the letters ask: When are you coming home? The house is empty without you.' It illustrates how the characters miss the banality of daily civilian life, worry about how their families are coping in their absence, especially at important events such as deaths and births. In the song and the reading of the letters, each character is described by his family, along with his response to them. Some shed tears of sorrow and joy, while others reaffirm that they will come home soon. The song cuts to the families, showing that the soldiers' spirits are with them, touching them though they are far away. The song, which runs for over ten minutes, won awards for its music and also for its lyrics (by Javed Akhtar), which were emblematic of all those families and friends separated in duty.

The second half of the film is largely taken with the fighting, as most of the characters we have met die. We see the consequences for their families – the pregnant widow, the mother who has lost her son and her husband, the parents left without support. The state is criticised for supplying aircraft that cannot be used in night attacks and for the insufficient number of soldiers defending the post. The film's message seems to be that victory comes at a cost, but a cost worth paying. This rhetoric is underlined by the film's dedication to the director/producer's brother, who was killed in this war.

One of the strengths of the film is the attention to detail, for example the use of the right kind of military hardware for the time. This moving glimpse into the work, life and death of soldiers is resonant today, as tensions between India and Pakistan continue in what former President Clinton called 'the most dangerous area of the world'.

Dir./Story/Scr.: J. P. Dutta, **Dial.**: O. P. Dutta, **DOP**: Ishwar Bidri, Nirmal Jani; **Music**: Anu Malik; **Background Music**: Adesh Shrivastava; **Lyrics**: Javed Akhtar; **Selected Cast**: Raakhee, Sunny Deol, Jackie Shroff, Sunil Shetty, Akshaye Khanna, Pooja Bhatt, Tabu, Kulbhushan Kharbanda, Puneet Issar; **Prod. Co.**: J. P. Films; Colour.

Chalti ka naam gaadi
India, 1958 – 173 mins
Satyen Bose

In Hindi cinema, comedy is usually an essential ingredient of the omnibus social genre. While the main stars may perform comic turns – Amitabh Bachchan's many talents include great comic timing – there is also a separate group of comic actors who take these roles. Guru Dutt's light social comedies featured the popular comedian Johnny Walker, and even his later, more sombre films still had light-hearted moments in which Walker changed the mood. Often the comic roles in Hindi cinema are subaltern, often servants and lower classes, and the performances become one of the 'attractions' or 'items' in the films, disrupting the main narrative. The genre of comedy is much rarer, perhaps because it was felt to be too 'specialised' or possibly because there are very few comedians of sufficient star quality to carry a film. Today, one of the notable exceptions is Govinda (see *Aanken*), one of the most talented performers in Hindi cinema, who can also dance and enjoys star status. Although better known as a singer, one of the most prolific and popular in India, Kishore Kumar was also a great comedian, with excellent comic timing and the ability to perform physical comedy, deliver hilarious dialogues and sing funny songs. *CKNG* is one of the funniest films in Indian cinema and stands the test of time.

Perhaps India's answer to the Marx brothers, the Ganguly brothers play the part of three brothers who run a garage. The veteran Ashok Kumar plays the eldest, who hates women, while his two younger brothers (Kishore and Anoop Kumar) dream about romance despite their fear of their brother's boxing gloves. Kishore witnesses a murder, which brings in the crooks and underworld plot of the film, while he romances his real-life lover, Madhubala. The stories entwine and finally all three brothers enjoy a romantic episode.

Cars feature throughout the film, in particular the 1928 Chevrolet of the title, which is taken from a proverb and means something like 'It's

Anoop, Ashok and Kishore Kumar in *Chalti ka naam gaadi*

only called a car because it moves.' Cars appear in most scenes, not only because of the garage plot but also to allow jokes about women drivers (who must have been unusual at the time), for drives around Bombay and for a car race. While much of the film is shot in the studio and the car sequences usually have back projections, which can induce a sense of car-sickness in the viewer, the car race gives Kishore the opportunity for some good comic moments.

While the snappy dialogues are funny, it is really the songs which produce some of the best comedy in the film. Majrooh Sultanpuri's lyrics and S. D. Burman's catchy tunes, along with Kishore's flair for bringing comedy to them in his style of singing as well as gesture, have ensured the songs' enduring popularity. The song in which Kishore demands the garage fee from Madhubala ('Paanch rupaiya baarah anna') dressed in a series of 'regional' costumes, while her performance is Monroe-esque in its combination of sexiness and humour, still makes everyone smile whenever it is mentioned, even today. The more romantic songs, which are performed with comic aplomb in the film, have become popular even among those who are not so familiar with the film: 'Ek ladki bheegi bhaagi si' in which Kishore's total body comedy is marvellous, or 'Haal kaisa hai janab ka?' As a comedy, it remained unsurpassed, until Kishore appeared again in *Padosan* some years later.

Dir./Story/Scr.: Satyen Bose; **Dial.**: Ramesh Pant and Gobind Moonis; **DOP**: Aloke Dasgupta; **Music**: S. D. Burman; **Lyrics**: Majrooh Sultanpuri; **Selected Cast**: Kishore Kumar, Ashok Kumar, Anoop Kumar, Madhubala, Sajjan, K. N. Singh; **Prod. Co.**: K. H. Pictures; Black and white.

Chandni
India, 1989 – 186 mins
Yash Chopra

The huge box-office success of *Chandni* in 1989 marked an upturn in Yash Chopra's career, which had waned during the 1980s. This film is a personal favourite of mine, as it was one of the first to arouse my interest in Hindi films.

Chandni (Sridevi) meets Rohit (Rishi Kapoor) at a wedding in Delhi and they fall in love instantly. Rohit's family disapproves of Chandni as she is not from a wealthy background, but Rohit covers his wall with her photographs. While showering roses from a helicopter onto Chandni's roof terrace, Rohit falls from the helicopter and is paralysed. Although Chandni is keen to continue their relationship, he declares that he no longer loves her and his family abuses her. Chandni goes to Bombay, where she works as a secretary to Lalit (Vinod Khanna). Lalit has lived alone with his mother (Waheeda Rehman) since his partner (Juhi Chawla) died. With his mother's encouragement, Lalit proposes marriage to Chandni before going on a business trip to Switzerland. Meanwhile, Rohit has been cured in a Swiss sanatorium and by chance meets Lalit. While Rohit tells Lalit about his plans to try to marry his former lover, Lalit tells him about his life; neither of them realise that they are talking about the same woman. Although Rohit tells Chandni of his change of heart, she agrees to marry Lalit. At their wedding, Rohit arrives drunk and falls down the stairs. Lalit realises that Chandni loves Rohit and he helps them to get married.

The narrative of *Chandni* was typical of a Yash Raj Films' love triangle (or quadrangle), in which A loves B loves C, and so on. This plot device is common to many of Yash's films, since it rehearses the idea that love is not always reciprocated and that human relationships are founded on more than just romantic or sexual love. The film has many other typical features of a Yash Chopra romance, as it is set among the super-rich, where love is contained, prevented and encouraged by the family.

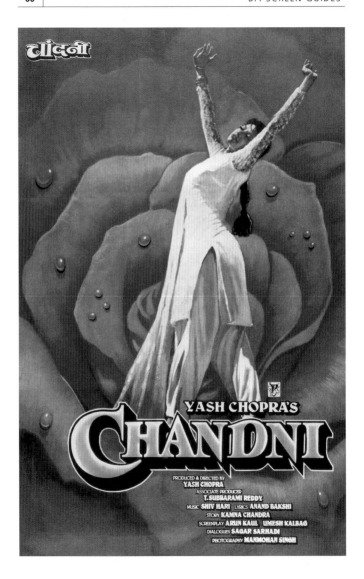

Switzerland once again represents healing (a high-tech cure combined with a miracle) and the location for romantic songs as well as a fantasy holiday destination (the theme of travel is reinforced by Lalit's travel agency). There are wedding songs (one of the best in any Hindi film – 'Mere haathon mein nau nau churiyaan hain'), a rain song, as well as other romantic songs (including the lilting 'Mitwa'), all of which were and remain very popular.

Chandni is unusual for its time, in that it is one of the great heroine-focused films, which came after the male-centred films of the 1980s, where macho men broke down over their *dosti* (friendship) with other men, for whom they were prepared to sacrifice their love and their lives (see *Qurbani*). Sridevi was one of the few women in recent times who could rival any male star in terms of box office and performance. While *Mr India* showcased her skills, her portrayal of Chandni represents one of her greatest moments. Chandni is the name of Yash Chopra's heroines in *Silsila* and *Faasle* (1985) and represents his ideal woman. In this film, she is a figure of idealised beauty, dressed in white outfits, occasionally in yellow, in a style that created a whole new fashion craze across India – the 'Chandni-look'. In her next Yash Chopra film, *Lamhe*, she plays the double role of mother and daughter, another great performance for which she also received widespread acclaim. While many prefer this film to *Chandni*, with its fascinating exploration of the life of diasporic Indians, UK locations and problematic theme, my vote is with *Chandni* for personal reasons, for the three main stars, the music and the Swiss element.

Dir.: Yash Chopra; **Story**: Kamna Chandra; **Scr.**: Umesh Kalbag, Arun Kaul; **Dial.**: Sagar Sarhadi; **DOP**: Manmohan Singh; **Music**: Shiv–Hari; **Lyrics**: Anand Bakshi; **Selected Cast**: Sridevi, Rishi Kapoor, Vinod Khanna, Juhi Chawla, Waheeda Rehman; **Prod. Co.**: Yash Raj Films; Colour.

(*Opposite page*) Poster for *Chandni*

CID
India, 1956 – 146 mins
Raj Khosla

This is one of Hindi cinema's few experiments with film noir. It engages with the genre fully, down to its rainy night street scenes and relentless emphasis on icons of modernity, such as telephones, cars, guns, newspapers and houses with sliding panels, trapdoors, etc. Inder Raj Anand took elements of film noir and mixed them with many other styles to form a total hybrid in the distinctive style of Hindi movies. The film's plot is not too exciting but the visuals and music are impressive.

After a network of phone calls, the editor of the *Times of India* is murdered and Inspector Shekhar (Dev Anand) of the CID brought in to investigate. He hijacks a car driven by a young woman, Rekha (Shakila) to chase the murderer but she throws away the car key. Aided by Master (Johnny Walker), Shekhar captures the murderer but is then taken to see a mysterious woman, Kamini (Waheeda Rehman), who warns him not to pursue his investigation further. Meanwhile, he finds out that Rekha is in fact his superintendent's daughter, and romance blossoms. Shekhar is framed for the killing of the murderer in jail but escapes, and is helped by Kamini to bring the story to a conclusion.

Although there are several of Dev Anand's films in this book, this one reveals how he early in his career established his style as 'Debonaire Dev', a persona which was later to become very mannered. This was Waheeda's debut and she is presented as an image of total female beauty. She would have a long career as a major star, first as a romantic heroine over two decades, then playing older characters. There is also a comic subplot focused on a lower-class couple, with the popular comedian Johnny Walker (who took his name from the whisky) as a tailor and petty crook.

The film's songs form a superb collection of music, and the collaboration between music director O. P. Nayyar and lyricist Majrooh Sultanpuri is ideally suited to the modern, urban nature of the movie. As well as having audio value outside the film as great songs, they are also employed skilfully to advance the action as well as being used as themes. The song picturisation is stunning too, whether they are shot as romance in the countryside, as village girls (in *filmi* costumes) fetch water from the river ('Nadi kinare gaam re'), or in the romantic duet 'Aankhon hi aankhon mein', or are shot in Bombay's public spaces. The city is also shown as boasting locations for romance, including the sea fronts, which have long been places where lovers meet. The question of romance is first raised with one of the most popular songs, 'Leke pehla pehla pyaar', during which Dev Anand walks along the sea front behind Shakila, accompanied by two professional singers. (This would become Dev Anand's trademark, walking rather than dancing through songs.) One of the most famous songs from the film is about the city of Bombay itself – 'E dil hai mushkil'.

These song picturisations reveal that Raj Khosla was very much a disciple of Guru Dutt and the style he took from the Anand brothers' Navketan banner. He had a rather uneven career in terms of success and genre, as his range included thrillers and cop films but also some huge hits, including *Mera gaon mera desh* and the 'woman's weepie' *Main tulsi tere aangan ki*.

Dir.: Raj Khosla; **Scr./Dial.**: Inder Raj Anand; **DOP**: V. K. Murthy; **Music**: O. P. Nayyar; **Lyrics**: Majrooh Sultanpuri, Jan Nissar Akhtar; **Selected Cast**: Dev Anand, Shakila, Waheeda Rehman, Johnny Walker, Kumkum, K. N. Singh; **Prod. Co.**: Guru Dutt Films; Black and white.

Deewaar
India, 1975 – 174 mins
Yash Chopra

Deewaar, produced by Gulshan Rai's Trimurti Films, ran in cinemas for over a hundred weeks and was soon recognised as a landmark Hindi film. Perhaps this was because it took so many risks. It has hardly any songs, the only two being the *qawwali* number and the title song; the hero is an anti-hero; there is little scope for romance, as the heroine has a very small role and is no innocent virgin; the lost father dies before there is a family reunion; and the hero dies at the hand of his brother.

The film's greatest strength is its script. The story draws in large measure on *Mother India*, and, to a lesser extent, *Gunga Jumna*, even in its structure, which is recounted in flashback by the suffering mother as the family's sacrifice is honoured by the state. The mother (Nirupa Roy), abandoned by her husband, struggles to bring up her two sons. Her good son, Ravi (Shashi Kapoor), conforms to the law, while her bad son, Vijay (Amitabh Bachchan), takes matters into his own hands, invoking the law of duty to one's family. The mother loves the bad son more but is compelled to choose the good son. The characters have the same mythic resonance as in *Mother India*, but they are given contemporary touches, so Vijay is 'cool', handsome and gives stylised speeches; Ravi is a young, idealistic police officer, thus embodying the law directly, who realises the corruption of the system yet will not take to crime. Nirupa Roy, though not such a great star as Nargis, plays the idealised mother, drawing on her earlier goddess roles, and acts as the focus for the film's emotion. She has to choose between the law of the state and that of kinship, so although she loves Vijay, she has to follow the law. Vijay rejects religion, but is superstitious about his armband with the number 786, regarded as lucky by many Muslims, which saves him from bullets. He finally goes to pray when his mother is ill, and his death takes place in the temple where he has long refused to worship.

Amitabh Bachchan in *Deewaar*

The connection with *Mother India* draws on elements of this mythical or epic film, setting it in a modern, urban context. It also draws on other films, notably *On the Waterfront* (1954), for the dockyard confrontations, and on the idiom of American urban cool that was becoming fashionable at this time. The character of Vijay clearly has the makings of a folk hero, as he supports traditional family values, although he criticises the 'system' or the state, fighting for righteous causes from outside its sphere of operation. There is no doubt that he is on the side of right, as his eloquent speeches reveal, but these values conflict with those of the state, a conflict that can only be resolved by his death, adding martyrdom to his cause.

In *Mother India* the bad son, Birju, dies at the hand of his mother, who was the principal actor in this film; whereas here Vijay is the central figure. *Deewaar* concentrates far more on the brothers' conflict, which is neatly stylised in the famous dialogue between the two men, in which Ravi acknowledges that, while he does not have any material goods, 'Mere paas maa hai/I have mummy'.

Dir.: Yash Chopra; **Story/Scr./Dial.**: Salim–Javed; **DOP**: Kay Gee; **Music**: R. D. Burman; **Lyrics**: Sahir Ludhianvi; **Selected Cast**: Amitabh Bachchan, Shashi Kapoor, Nirupa Roy, Neetu Singh, Parveen Babi; **Prod. Co.**: Trimurti Films; Colour.

Devdas
India, 1935 – 139 mins
P. C. Barua

There are many film versions charting the life of Devdas, the eponymous hero of Saratchandra Chatterjee's novel. Chatterjee wrote the novel as a teenager but it was published later in his career (1917), when he was already a popular novelist among the Bengali middle classes. Devdas, the proverbial romantic self-destructive hero, is from the rural landowning (*zamindari*) classes of Bengal. Although his childhood friend, Parvati (Paro), falls in love with him, he is unable to go against the wishes of his parents, who refuse to let him marry her because of a small difference in caste. So she is married to an older man with children almost her age. Devdas flees to Calcutta, but rather than finding refuge in modernity, takes up with a courtesan, a figure frequently associated with *zamindars* (as in *Sahib bibi aur ghulam* etc.). Once again he refuses a woman's sexual advances, but, true to the form of the Romantic hero, descends into alcoholism and contracts TB, returning to die on Paro's doorstep.

Among the many film accounts of this story, the most highly acclaimed are the Bengali version, starring P. C. Barua (1935), made at the same time as a Hindi film starring K. L. Saigal, the famous singing star, the Hindi version shot by Bimal Roy (the cameraman on these earlier versions) in 1955 and the 2002 film by Sanjay Leela Bhansali. The Saigal version has a great freshness, remains closest to the book and is the most convincing in terms of character, while the Bimal Roy film shows great restraint in its recounting of this maudlin story. The 2002 adaptation, although it has some wonderful musical and visual scenes, is a series of moments, where the story is spoilt by engineering Devdas' decline through the melodramatic device of a conniving sister-in-law and by the all too often kitsch quality of its visuals. The emphasis on the *mise en scène* overwhelmed the love story to the point at which it seemed to become almost irrelevant. The *zamindars* are presented as glamorous and supremely wealthy in the manner of bazaar art, whereas at this time (this version is set in the 1930s) they were in decline.

As one of the greatest and most popular of India's singing stars, K. L. Saigal effectively created a whole sound for the Hindi film song, though his acting skills were not so strong. The 1955 version features one of the most important actors of Hindi cinema, Dilip Kumar, whose understated style and elegance brought a new realistic way of acting into Hindi cinema. The extraordinary black-and-white photography of the films re-creates the ambience of Bengal around the turn of the century, as do the simple Bengali saris and style of the village women in contrast to the courtesan's glamorous outfits. These films also bring out in Devdas' childhood the romantic pastoral, typified in Indian culture by stories of Krishna and Radha, thus creating an ideal, eternal love for Devdas. Devdas' decline owes nothing to evil or the machinations of others but results from his own inability to deal appropriately with people and situations. He is no saint – his moments of nastiness and brutality, the rage of an impotent man – are graphically represented, the most appalling being when he assaults Paro with a stick and scars her forehead. The romantic view of the redemptive powers of women's love is emphasised, as Devdas assumes the role of child to these caring, maternal women.

Dir.: P. C. Barua; **Story**: Saratchandra Chatterjee's novel; **Scr.**: P. C. Barua; **Dial.**: Kidar Nath Sharma; **DOP**: Bimal Roy; **Music**: Rai Chand Boral, Pankaj Mullick; **Lyrics**: Kidar Nath Sharma; **Selected Cast**: K. L. Saigal, Jamuna, Rajkumari, K. C. Dey; **Prod. Co.**: New Theatres; Black and white.

Diamond Queen
India, 1940 – 155 mins
Homi Wadia

No book on Hindi films over the last century could omit 'Fearless' Nadia. Half Australian, half Greek, Mary Evans (1910–99) worked with Wadia Movietone, eventually marrying Homi Wadia in 1960. One of many foreigners who worked in the Indian film industry, she became a great star with a dedicated fan following. Riyad Wadia's documentary on his great-aunt, *Fearless* (1993), gives an idea of this fascinating and unusual woman.

Diamond Queen, though recognised as one of the first *masala* (spice) films, is quite different from many of the others in this book, as it more closely resembles the silent films in its use of gesture, its static camera (especially notable during the song sequences) and its reliance on visual gags. The usual thrills of the silent movie are all there – rescue from fire, jumping from moving horses, a race between a car and train (the former inevitably breaking down on the crossing), the fight in the waterfall, the saloon fight, and so on. The music is also reminiscent of the accompaniment of the silent period, entirely western in style, and mostly played on the piano, whether as the theme of the two clown-like figures, who evoke of Laurel and Hardy, or in the comic style used for the fight sequences, which are slapstick rather than realist. The Hollywood influence is visible at all times from the shots of the rural cabin of the '49er diamond miners, to Diamond Town itself, which resembles a Wild West town, complete with saloons with swing doors. However, this 'Western' also has distinctive Indian features and is very much part of the wider public culture of its time.

The story of the film's hero, Diler the bandit (John Cawas), is similar to that of many a western hero. As a child who has seen his family murdered by the villain, he is forced to live outside the law in order to pursue revenge, but is shown to be on the side of right and is ultimately forgiven through his other acts of bravery and good deeds. Madhurika (Nadia) is unlike any western heroine. Taller and bigger than the usual screen heroine of any cinema, as a stunt expert and fighter she is more convincing than many of the men. Her early circus training put in her good stead for her audience-pleasing stunts, with the horse, 'Son of Punjab', and her car, 'Daughter of Rolls Royce' are listed as cast members at the beginning. Nadia's physicality is also striking, in that she is blonde and blue-eyed, although there is never any reference to her foreignness. Her Hindi accent is a little better than she is usually credited with and does not detract from her speech. She does look slightly uncomfortable in her saris, seeming much more at home in her stylish western dress, which must have been quite shocking to many of her contemporary audiences. Her opening scene is the most resonant in the film and a classic of Hindi movies. A brawl which has broken out at a meeting of respectable social reformers is getting out of hand. Suddenly a fist at the end of a muscular arm comes into shot and the camera moves up it to reveal Nadia, who proceeds to take control of the situation before delivering a monologue about the rights of women. Often called 'Bombay-wali', the Bombay girl, she frequently brings ideas about equal rights for women from the metropolis to the provinces.

The film also contains specific references to its time, notably to social reforms such as women's rights and the advancement of literacy. A surprising amount is said about freedom, presumably from the British, who are not mentioned by name. The ruler of the princely state ultimately upholds social order, although justice is located in the courtroom (presumably recognised as a British institution), despite the corruption and incompetence of the police. The enormously popular work of Wadia Movietone, whose classic films also include *Hatim Tai* (1956), *Raj Nartaki* (1942) and *Toofani Tarzan* (1936), is now receiving the attention of several scholars, and the reassessment of the stunt film is essential to the history of Indian cinema.

Dir.: Homi Wadia; **Story/Scr.**: J. B. H. Wadia; **Dial./Lyrics**: Munshi Sham; **DOP**: R. P. Master; **Music**: Madhulal D. Master; **Selected Cast**: 'Fearless' Nadia, John Cawas, Radha Rani, Sayani; **Prod. Co.**: Wadia Movietone; Black and white.

Dil chahta hai
India, 2001 – 183 mins
Farhan Akhtar

Although this film was not a huge hit, its impact on the young middle
and upper classes of the Indian metropolises was enormous. It was the
first film that really focused on their lifestyle – or at least aspirations –
and showed friendships, romance and family relations as a way to
personal self-fulfilment. Unlike many other films, there is little emphasis
on family conflict, with parents shown as benevolent and understanding,
if somewhat baffled by their children's behaviour. Nor are the main
characters heroic; rather they are 'regular guys' at a crossroads in their
privileged lives. Very much a male-bonding or *dosti* theme, the three
friends, Akash (Aamir Khan), Sid (Siddharth) (Saif Ali Khan) and Sameer
(Akshaye Khanna), are at a loss as to what to do with their lives as they
leave college. Akash, who cannot take anything seriously, is given the
responsibility of running the family business in Sydney. He falls in love
with Shalini (Preity Zinta) but fools around, until he realises that to wait
any longer will mean she will marry another man (Ayub Khan). Sid is set
on becoming a painter, but falls in love with an older woman, Tara
(Dimple Kapadia), an alcoholic who has lost access to her daughter in her
divorce. Sameer is a total romantic but finally falls for Pooja (Sonali
Kulkarni), a girl his family introduce him to for an 'arranged marriage'.

It is not just the story that makes this film different. The main
characters are dressed like regular people who are part of the Bombay
club and party scene, with relaxed fashion and styling rather than the
glamorous style of the 1990s' film. The music, like the look, came from
and fed back into this scene and was a huge hit with this crowd. Some
of the songs, such as the title track, were picturised in a more western
style, with sharply edited sequences as a montage rather than playback.
The three perform a song together in a club on their graduation night
('Koi kahe kehta rahe'), then they each have their own song, which is
part of the careful delineation of character. Sid is given a 'new age'

romantic number ('Kaisi hai ye rut'); Akash sings a comic song about not believing in love ('Jaane kyun'), while Sameer performs a wonderful pastiche of Hindi film songs through the decades as part of a surrealist visit to the movies ('Woh ladki'). Perfectly paced and structured to bring out the characters and their quests, the film is tightly edited with sharply observed dialogues, great humour and wit.

Over the last few years there has been debate about the emergence of a new type of Indian cinema. Although many of these films do not fit the category for inclusion here, as they lie outside the mainstream Hindi cinema, *DCH* is very much within this genre, with its mainstream production and personnel, but new and different text. Although still too long to reach out to a western audience, this film, like Mani Ratnam's, would be the kind of movie that would appeal to an audience used to Hollywood but interested to know what a 'Bollywood' film could be like. *DCH* presents Bombay's urban culture as hybrid and complex, merging cultural specificities with wider youth subcultures. I believe that like *Lagaan*, to which there is little similarity except it is also a radical reshaping of the Hindi film, *DCH* is the film that may well herald a new trend in Indian cinema but one emerging from within the Hindi film mainstream.

Dir./Co-story/Scr./Dial: Farhan Akhtar; **Co-story**: Kassim Jagmagia; **DOP**: Ravi K. Chandran; **Music**: Shankar–Ehsaan–Loy; **Lyrics**: Javed Akhtar; **Selected cast**: Aamir Khan, Saif Ali Khan, Akshaye Khanna, Preity Zinta, Dimple Kapadia, Sonali Kulkarni; **Prod. Co.**: Excel Entertainment; Colour.

Dil to pagal hai
India, 1997 – 179 mins
Yash Chopra

I have included this film here partly for a personal reason, in that it was the first Hindi film whose sets I visited, spending a few months with the production unit. It is also a film that has grown on me since I first saw it. Its music has remained hugely popular, not least through its remixes, and the style it created has been much copied in recent years.

The major criticism of the film was that there was no real story and that most of the characters did not seem to have any family connections. The absence of family is not unusual in other cinemas outside of India, and the intention here was to create two modern, urban characters with no obligations to anyone but themselves. The story is that of the backstage Hollywood musical – and the film was, unusually, advertised as a 'musical' – where the hero's goal is to get his show on the road. In keeping with this genre, the second heroine is in love with the hero, while he is in love with the first heroine, who replaces her when she incurs an injury. These features were 'Indianised', as the first heroine is presented as a traditional Indian woman, largely signified by her dress, but also by her willingness to reconcile her own desires to family duties, while the second prefers sportswear and her family lives overseas.

The opening sequences were fast, establishing the film's dilemma – love is predestined: someone, somewhere is made for you – then cutting quickly to happy couples (including Yash and Pam Chopra), then straight into Karisma's big number 'Le gai', where she revels in her role as the 'top performer'. The film continued at this level, providing plenty of enjoyment with its glamour, froth, romantic intensity, jokes, strong performances and, of course, the songs and dances.

Yash Chopra took a gamble on a new music director, Uttam Singh, a violinist trained in western and Indian music, whose major success here was repeated later with *Gadar*. Yash was keen to modernise his unique visual aesthetic of 'glamorous realism', which he did through the set

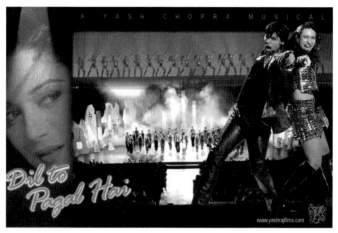

Publicity for *Dil to pagal hai*

designs of Sharmishta Roy and the costumes of designer Manish Malhotra. While Farah Khan worked as the dance director (choreographer) for several songs, Shiamak Davar added a new style to the 'staged' songs. Other regular favourites contributed to the film: Lata Mangeshkar with her songs and cameraman Manmohan Singh.

Shah Rukh was not criticised by the audience, but, although he gave a great performance, it was not his film. As Yash Chopra's alter ego, he is in charge, but mostly from a distance. Karisma's performance was acclaimed, but her costumes were thought too skimpy. They were cool, they were appropriate and the audience was kept at a distance, closing in only on her face. Madhuri was criticised for being too old and not as slim as usual, but she looked like a woman, not a girl, and her acting and dancing were excellent.

This film, which fans enjoyed but did not love as much as some of Yash Chopra's other work, will be seen in the future as a landmark film, with its depictions of love, friendship, its whole look, its music and its rapid editing. After almost fifty years in the industry, Yash Chopra has set the pace for a younger generation of film-makers who have to run to keep up with him.

It was with this film that Yash Raj began international distribution of their own films and selling VHS and then DVDs of films that they felt suited their banner, such as those of Guru Dutt, Bimal Roy and Raj Kapoor. This proved to be the beginning of a new era for the company which eight years later has expanded its distribution in India and overseas, set up a music business and constructed a purpose-built studio into which all their work will be integrated.

Dir.: Yash Chopra; **Story/Dial.**: Aditya Chopra; **Scr.**: Aditya Chopra, Pam Chopra, Yash Chopra, Tanuja Chandra; **DOP**: Manmohan Singh; **Music**: Uttam Singh; **Lyrics**: Anand Bakshi; **Selected Cast**: Shah Rukh Khan, Karisma Kapoor, Madhuri Dixit; **Prod. Co.**: Yash Raj Films; Colour.

Dilwale dulhaniya le jayenge
India, 1995 – 192 mins
Aditya Chopra

Aditya Chopra's directorial debut, *Dilwale dulhaniya le jayenge* (*DDLJ*), was one of the highest-grossing Hindi films of all time. While clearly resembling a Yash Chopra film in the romantic scenes, it was closer to the Barjatya's style in its more conservative deployment of the family in the couple's romance, and yet it displayed its own unique quality. All the hallmarks of a Yash Chopra romance were there – the gripping story, the visual beauty, the great locations, the unforgettable music. It would, however, be more accurate to see this as an affectionate tribute by an original film-maker, exploring his own cinematic vision while drawing on the visual vocabulary of romance created by his father for the Hindi cinema. This young couple does not challenge society's prohibitions and taboos as their passion unfolds, as Yash Chopra's lovers would; instead they persuade the harsh but well-meaning patriarchy to accept their love. Another difference is that Yash Chopra's cities are friendly homes for urban elites whereas here we have cold and anonymous London, an inappropriate location for romance, which flourishes in Swiss idylls but reaches a state of passion only in rural Punjab. The nuclear family is the norm in London, while Punjab has the extended family and traditional hospitality; its fields, which are full of yellow mustard also contain village girls, trailing their *dupattas* (the nostalgia for the *desh*, or 'homeland', perhaps increased by the distinctive voice of the director's own mother?); rather than a location for terrorism, as Punjab represented to many in the 1980s and 90s, it is a place appropriate for religious occasions – weddings and *karva chauth*. However, there is a significant change from earlier films, where foreign places were used only for spectacle. Here we see the beginning of the diaspora film, which had begun to emerge with Yash Chopra's

(*Opposite page*) Publicity for *DDLJ*

Lamhe (1991). The new transnational Indian middle-class nuclear family is the norm in London, but it still seems pale in comparison to Punjab's extended family and traditional hospitality.

The film's central theme is the hero's (Shah Rukh Khan as Raj) love for his heroine Simran (Kajol). It transforms him from brat to responsible adult, drives the story forward, gaining momentum as he wins over the whole of her family and friends through his relentless charm and good nature. Along the way it highlights the whole structuring of family friendships and emotions, bringing out tenderness and love in all the characters. The success of the film is due more to its driving logic and its emotional richness than its overseas locations and the subsequent return to the *desh*, reinforcing the belief that Indianness is not so much a question of citizenship as of sharing family values.

The great emotional highs of the scenes when the hero refuses the heroine's invitation to her wedding, or the scene when the heroine's mother urges her daughter to run away with her lover rather than sacrifice her happiness as she herself did, were among the high points of the movie. The exuberant and tender eroticism of Kajol which allows her to display her glorious sensuality as an innocent romp ('Mere khwabon mein') and the teasing of a wicked Shah Rukh, who pretends to have taken advantage of her while she was drunk, display a new relaxed attitude to sexuality within the constraints of a traditional morality. A critical factor is the dynamic pairing of Shah Rukh and Kajol, surely the greatest screen couple in India for decades. Shah Rukh was already a star after the success of *Baazigar* (1994) and Yash Chopra's *Darr* (1993) but he had played negative roles in these films. This was the first film to establish him as the top romantic hero, a position that he has held for a decade. Kajol was a newer face, but she too became a leading star with this film. The freshness and tenderness of their love, their negotiation of modernity and tradition, their ability to charm and love all around them touched the audience as much as the film's characters. Aditya Chopra's assistant on this film, Karan Johar – who appears as Shah Rukh's friend in several scenes –developed the magic of this film in his *Kuch kuch hota hai* (1998), itself a tribute to the Chopra family.

Dir./Story/Scr./**Co-dial**.: Aditya Chopra; **Co-dial**.: Javed Siddiqui; **DOP**: Manmohan Singh; **Music**: Jatin–Lalit; **Lyrics**: Anand Bakshi; **Selected Cast**: Shah Rukh Khan, Kajol, Amrish Puri, Anupam Kher, Farida Jalal; **Prod. Co.**: Yash Raj Films; Colour.

Disco Dancer
India, 1982 – 135 mins
Babbar Subhash

Disco Dancer is one of those films that I had known about for years
before I saw it. People often quoted it as a truly kitsch film and I had
heard the songs (by Bappi Lahiri, 'the R. D. Burman of the B-movies'
according to the *Encyclopaedia of Indian Cinema*) and seen them as clips
on television featuring Mithun Chakraborty, dressed in white trousers
and lamé, certainly a different image from that I knew from his work in
'art' cinema. He has subsequently become king of the B-movies, taking
only the occasional small role in mainstream films. The songs were catchy
enough but already dated when I heard them, the disco era being well
and truly over in London by the 1980s. Aware of the film's cult status as
a B-movie, I initially viewed it to consider it as one of the few items for
inclusion that are not from the A-list.

   The film's story is by the respected Dr Rahi Masoom Reza, whose
credits include B. R. Chopra's television serialisation of the great epic,
the *Mahabharata*, as well as several other films in this book. Following
the revenge theme of many post-1970s' movies, the child Anil, a
budding musician, and his mother are framed for stealing by a wealthy
neighbour, Mr Oberoi (Om Shivpuri). Anil vows to exact his revenge
through his music and as an adult (Mithun Chakraborty) soon displaces
Oberoi's son, Sam, as the King of Disco. He meanwhile falls in love
with Oberoi's daughter, Rita (Kim), with whom he played as a child. His
manager David (Om Puri) changes Anil's name to Jimmy and he
becomes a national phenomenon. Oberoi keeps trying to have Jimmy
killed but Jimmy is also a kung fu (if his moves can be called that)
expert. When Jimmy's mother dies, electrocuted by a guitar intended
for him, he gives up his music (he is said to be suffering from 'guitar
phobia'), but his uncle (a guest appearance by 1970s' superstar, Rajesh
Khanna) persuades him to take it up again and he and Rita dance into
the future.

After the titles play out on a glitter ball, the songs include Kishore Kumar's 'Ae oh aa zara mudke' and the memorable 'Auva auva koi yahaan nache' (sung by Usha Uthup and Bappi Lahiri), with Kalpana Iyer shimmering in shorts, ankle boots and what only can be described as Christmas-tree tinsel. The picturisations are nearly all set in discos with underlit floors and feature ungainly backing singers, while the lead dancers also make some odd moves. The title track, 'I am a Disco Dancer', is better seen than heard, with Mithun dressed in a very strange outfit (part-Donny Osmond, part-Elvis) performing fancy footwork. In 'Krishna dharti pe aa jaa tu', the male and female dancers appear to be dressed as angels for a school Christmas pantomime.

There are some strange touches, such as the depiction of the romance between Rita and Jimmy as a series of photomontages and the scene showing how, when Jimmy's mother dies, his photograph cracks and dissolves to the burning of her pyre.

So is this film more than just a piece of 1970s' (even though made in the 1980s) nostalgic kitsch? I think it typifies a move into the low-budget B-movie that finds its own audience during the 1980s, as the middle classes leave the cinema halls for the VHS and colour television. It is also worth watching for Mithun. Initially a serious actor, and one who could have pursued a successful career in A-grade Hindi movies (he landed major, though supporting, roles in films such as *Agneepath* [1989]), he chose instead to live in Ooty (Ootacamund, a hill station in south India) and appear in low-budget movies that produce good returns from the B-circuit. He turns in a good performance in the film and possesses a physique that makes him a convincing dancer and fighter.

Dir.: Babbar Subhash; **Story**: Balraj Deepak Vij; **Scr./Dial.**: Dr Rahi Masoom Reza; **Music**: Bappi Lahiri; **Lyrics**: Anjaan, Farooq Quaser; **Selected Cast**: Mithun Chakraborty, Kim, Kalpana Iyer, Om Puri; **Prod. Co.**: B. Subhash Movie Unit; Colour.

Do aankhen baarah haath
India, 1957 – 155 mins
V. Shantaram

Do aankhen baarah haath won many awards at international film festivals, including the Silver Bear in Berlin, and it remains the only Hindi mainstream film that has been screened at the London Film Festival to date. However, it was only post-1955 and the release of Satyajit Ray's *Pather Panchali* (1955) that 'art cinema' emerged in India. In the 1950s many films were produced within the mainstream that would now be regarded as 'middle class' or more 'realist' than movies produced today. The genre of *DABH*, the social problem film (rather than the social), emerged in the 1930s as the coming of sound encouraged the growth of a more literary cinema, with increased emphasis on the word rather than the spectacle. Shantaram's socials at Prabhat (including *Duniya na mane*) were outstanding examples of this genre. It flourished in the 1950s in the hands of film-makers such as Bimal Roy (*Bandini*, *Devdas*, *Do bigha zamin* and *Madhumati*) and B. R. Chopra (*Naya daur* and *Nikaah*) and is certainly the ancestor of the 1970s' middle-class cinema of Hrishikesh Mukherjee (*Abhimaan*, *Anand* and *Gol maal*) and others.

V. Shantaram was one of the founders of Poona's Prabhat Studios (see under *Duniya na mane*), but when he left Prabhat to found his own studio, Rajkamal Kalamandir, he continued to make films in this genre along with more mainstream colour films such as *Jhanak jhanak payal baje* (1955).

DABH argues that prisoners, even murderers, are human beings who can be redeemed if they are well treated, and is very different from B. R. Chopra's *Kanoon* (1960), which directly opposes the death penalty. Shantaram's father was a Jain, a member of a religious group known for its strict respect for all forms of life, and the character he plays in this film, Adinath, has a Jain name. Adinath is jailer who believes that

(*Opposite page*) Publicity still for *Do aankhen baarah haath*

prisoners are human beings too, and he takes six prisoners to his experimental farm, Azad Nagar (Freetown), where he demonstrates he can prompt them to reform by giving them trust and respect. He becomes their father figure, or Babuji, whose two eyes (*do aankhen*) watch their twelve hands (*baarah haath*), whose prints they give him in case he should need to report their escape, and which work the land in honest labour. His compassion and self-sacrifice are the qualities for which this film has been most celebrated. However, the film is not relentlessly preachy, and Sandhya, as the toy-seller, provides many light-hearted moments, although she is also the focus for discourses about sexuality and motherhood.

The film contains several haunting songs, notably 'Ae malik tere bande hum' (music by Vasant Desai and lyrics by Bharat Vyas), whose rendition by Lata Mangeshkar (picturised on Sandhya) at the death of Babuji is one of her most loved songs, and the catchy 'Tak tak dhoom dhoom' which is repeated several times. The black-and-white cinematography in an expressionist style that had been popular in earlier Indian cinema comes is outmoded by the 1960s, but this is a fine example of its last flourish.

Dir.: V. Shantaram; **Story/Scr./Dial.**: G. D. Madgulkar; **DOP**: G. Balakrishna; **Music**: Vasant Desai; **Lyrics**: Bharat Vyas; **Selected Cast**: V. Shantaram, Sandhya, Ulhas, B. M. Vyas, Baburao Pendharkar, Paul Sharma; **Prod. Co.**: Rajkamal Kalamandir; Black and white.

Do bigha zamin
India, 1953 – 142 mins
Bimal Roy

Bimal Roy, one of India's foremost film-makers, made many films that should be included in this volume but, given the numerical limits, I have had to select the very best of an outstanding oeuvre (*Bandini*, *Devdas* and *Madhumati*). Many will feel that I should not have left out *Sujata* (1959), but *Do bigha zamin* is one of Roy's best works and is a remarkable film by any standards. It brings together Roy's neo-realist form of Hindi cinema's melodrama with his deeply felt political concerns, to form a great study of human values and dignity among the poor.

Do bigha zamin explores the real impact of money-lending on the peasant farmer, as he becomes enslaved by his debts. Driven to try to raise money to pay off his loan, Shambu (Balraj Sahni) leaves his pregnant wife (Nirupa Roy) and elderly father to head for Calcutta. His young son smuggles himself onto the train and helps his father as a shoe-shiner. Robbed on their first day, the couple soon remake their village ties by finding surrogate families in the city: Dadi as their mother and Rani as an elder sister to the boy. Shambu's experience of helping a sick man leads him into rickshaw-pulling. While terrible accidents befall the family, the film avoids easy answers to the serious problems facing the urban migrant. Roy's melodrama is restrained, and he uses few devices of the Hindi film, with songs kept to a minimum, placing the emphasis instead on the black-and-white photography of realistic sets and wonderful footage of contemporary Calcutta.

The main strength of this film lies in the performance of Balraj Sahni as Shambhu. Sahni is regarded as one of the greatest actors of Indian cinema, both during his lifetime and with hindsight. (See also *Garam hawa* and *Waqt*.) He rarely appeared as the Hindi film hero but usually, as he said, as 'all those fathers and uncles', often taking roles in films dominated by the outstanding female stars such as Nargis and Meena Kumari. While Sahni's younger brother, Bhisham, became one of the

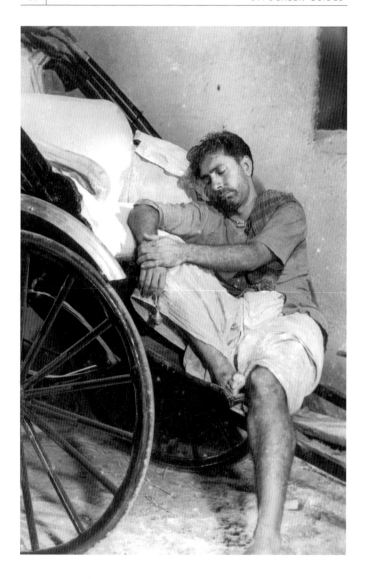

great figures of modern Hindi literature, Balraj had a variable career in theatre and cinema, as well as working for the BBC in London before independence. Despite his own elite and educated background, Sahni is totally plausible as the desperate but determined peasant, his physical movement accurately reproducing that of a labourer, while his facial expressions are restrained and powerful.

One scene in this film is particularly resonant, its images condensing the narrative of the invisibility of the poor and the way the rickshaw-pullers are seen as little more than draught animals. A middle-class woman, arguing with her lover, leaps into a rickshaw. The man follows her and they egg the pullers into a chase, where the pullers seem to be running after the extra money itself with no other sight in mind. The rapid editing by Hrishikesh Mukherjee adds to the speed of the chase and the desperate pursuit of a few extra coins. During the race, Shambu's rickshaw overturns and he is severely injured, but the couple pay no attention.

The setting of this film in the Bengali village and Calcutta of the 1950s inevitably invites comparison with Ray, and the differing merits of the Hindi film and the 'art' film.

Dir.: Bimal Roy; **Story**: Salil Choudhury; **Scr.**: Hrishikesh Mukherjee; **Dial.**: Paul Mahendra; **DOP**: Kamal Bose; **Music**: Salil Choudhury; **Lyrics**: Shailendra; **Selected Cast**: Balraj Sahni, Nirupa Roy, Rattan Kumar, Murad, Jagdeep; **Prod. Co.**: Bimal Roy Productions; Black and white.

(*Opposite page*) Balraj Sahni in *Do bigha zamin*

Don
India, 1978 – 166 mins
Chandra Barot

This was one of the Amitabh and Salim–Javed films that nearly missed the
list simply because there were too many examples of this type of movie.
However, *Don* eventually made it because it epitomises a style which was
often intended but rarely reached in Hindi films. Seemingly indebted to
Blaxploitation movies, *Don* is cool in a way that none of the other
Amitabh movies were, and is probably the most stylish of all Hindi films, at
least from the 1970s. It is perhaps the film that comes closest to being
'pure Bollywood' in terms of its implausible plot, its style, its use of song
and dance and its sheer exuberance. Hiding behind simple entertainment
is a series of moral dilemmas that the characters must address, and behind
them is a simple moral universe in which love and family count for all.

The Don (Amitabh Bachchan) falls into a trap, seduced by Kamini
(Helen), the greatest vamp of Indian cinema, in a stirring number, 'Yeh
mera dil pyaar ka deewana'. The police kill him but want to keep news
of his death quiet. The police commissioner (Iftikhar, nearly always the
good policeman) finds Bhola (Amitabh Bachchan), who bears an uncanny
resemblance to the Don. Amitabh, whose real-life family is closely
associated with Allahabad in Uttar Pradesh (UP), gives a hilarious
performance as a pan-chewing labourer from UP with a strong regional
accent, who sings about the strange ways of Bombay, 'Yeh hai Bambai
nagariya'. A significant number of Bombay's taxi drivers and other
workers are migrants from UP, while UP itself is one of the most
important markets for the Hindi film, and this seems calculated to delight
them. This element is played up later in one of the most celebrated songs
performed by Amitabh, 'Khaike paan banaraswala/Eat a Banarasi paan',
where the audience must have loved the megastar singing 'I'm just a boy
from the banks of the Ganges'.

Desperate to educate two children he has adopted, Bhola is willing to
learn how to pass as the Don, and to give up his rustic ways to

impersonate this urban cool guy. The ruse is that he has amnesia, which will pass once he grasps the scene. Meanwhile, Roma (Zeenat Aman) has infiltrated the Don's gang to avenge his murder of her brother. She helps the 'Don' to escape and is involved in his various escapades, during which they both eventually reveal their identities. Along the way they are helped by J. J. (Pran), a tightrope walker, shot by the police when attempting to steal in order to bring medicine to his wife, who later dies, leaving him with two children who are, of course, the two Bhola brings up. Although a number of innovative shots and the early use of hand-held cameras bring drama to the film, there are several dreadful car chases where the only attempt to thrill comes from speeding up the film. The final scene of a fight and shoot-out in a cemetery is filmed half as action and half as comedy, and the film ends as it begins to fall apart. (Zeenat Aman's body double is clearly male and rather dark and hairy . . .)

The film oozes 1970s' cool, often coming close to the style of the Blaxploitation genre, with its emphasis on funky music and style. The star, Amitabh Bachchan, is the master of control, silence and style, whether impassive in the face of sexual seduction or during a shoot-out. Zeenat Aman, the epitome of the chic babe, matches his style with her trousersuits and cropped hair that must have seemed shocking at the time. Most men remember the image of her in a very short nurse's uniform as iconic. The film's style is established with a blast in the opening credits, and this is maintained right through to the end. It is now being remade by Javed's son, Farhan Akhtar (see *Dil chahta hai*).

Dir.: Chandra Barot; **Story/Scr./Dial.**: Salim–Javed; **DOP**: Nariman Irani; **Music**: Kalyanji–Anandji; **Selected Cast**: Amitabh Bachchan, Zeenat Aman, Pran, Iftikhar, Om Shivpuri, Satyen Kappu, Helen; **Prod. Co.**: Nariman Films; Colour.

Duniya na mane/The Unexpected
India, 1937 – 166 mins
V. Shantaram

Prabhat Studios has enormous importance in the history of Indian cinema. It was founded in Kohlapur in 1929 by a group who had worked at Baburao Painter's Maharashtra Film Company and who then moved to Pune in 1933. It was famous for three genres: the devotional or 'sant' films about devotees (including *Sant Tukaram*) who practised the form of worship known as *bhakti*, or 'loving devotion'; the historical; and the social problem film that dealt with a single issue. Shantaram directed films in all genres, but also social films such as this one, as well as *Manoos/Admi* (1939) and *Shejari/Padosi* (1941). These socials were made in two versions, one in Marathi and one in Hindi. *DNM* is known as *Kunku* (the *kumkum* or vermillion powder that a married woman wears) in Marathi. Shantaram founded his own studio in Bombay in 1942, where he made films such as *Do aankhen baarah haath*.

The orphaned Nirmala (Shanta Apte) is brought up by her uncle and aunt, who want to marry her off for a substantial amount of money. Nirmala thinks she is marrying a young man but at the wedding ceremony she realises that her future husband, the lawyer Kakasaheb (Keshavrao Date), is old enough to be her father. Nirmala refuses to sleep with him and her husband realises that he has made a fool of himself through this marriage. Nirmala has to deal with the unwanted attentions of her stepson (Raja Nene) (who gets a good thrashing) and the interference of her husband's aunt (Vimala Vasishta), though she befriends the young girl in the house. However, she argues that suffering can be endured but injustice cannot. She makes friends with her stepdaughter, Sushila (Shakuntala Paranjpye), who is a widow and reformer. Kakasaheb repents his mistake as he comes to respect Nirmala and stops her from wearing her *kumkum* (as if she is a widow). He leaves a suicide note for Nirmala, in which he tells her that she is free at last.

Narayan Hari Apte (1889–1971), adapted his novel, *Na patnari goshta*, for this film. The novel had created a great stir when it came out, the orthodox voice objecting strongly to the wife's refusal to accept her husband. The eventual reconciliation between the couple looks as if it is going to lead to a happy ending but, although Nirmala is free at the end of the film, and Kakasaheb's note, signed 'From your father', instructs her to remarry, she is still a widow in the home of her unpleasant stepson.

Shanta Apte, as the woman who crusades against the injustice of old men marrying young women, and Keshavrao Date as the old man who repents, give well-matched performances. The film is mostly realistic, even when it comes to music. The songs are always explained by the film's text (festivals, singing to friends) and whenever Nirmala sings, she puts on a 78 for the backing music. The film has no background music, although animal noises are used to give realistic sound. One interesting feature is the inclusion of an English song, a version of 'The Psalm of Life' by H. W. Longfellow, which must be one of the first English songs in an Indian film.

The only break with realism is the heavy symbolism of the wall clock that is closely associated with Kakasaheb, and which he continually looks at when contemplating his mistake in marrying the young girl. Before he leaves the house for the last time, he removes the pendulum, which he uses as paperweight on his suicide note.

Dir.: V Shantaram; **Story**: N. H. Apte; **DOP**: V. Avadhoot; **Music**: Keshavrao Bhole; **Lyrics**: Shantaram Athavale; **Selected Cast**: Shanta Apte, Keshavrao Date, Shakuntala Paranjpye, Vasanti, Vimla Vasishta, Raja Nene; **Prod. Co.**: Prabhat Film Company; Black and white.

Ek duuje ke liye
India, 1981 – 167 mins
K. Balachander

The first film in Hindi of the great southern director, K. Balachander, it introduced Kamal Hassan to Hindi films, where more than two decades later he remains the only major southern male star. A remake of *Maro charithra* (1978), a love story between a Tamil and a Telugu couple, this film has Vasu (Kamal Hassan) as a Tamil and Sapna (Rati Agnihotri) as a Punjabi. The two neighbouring families' feud is likened to the Romeo and Juliet story by clear references to the play, where the famous 'a rose by any other name would smell as sweet' is discussed to show that language need not divide them. Yet the importance of language as a marker of cultural difference is a constant reference in the film, where the young couple are seen falling in love while learning the other's language – Vasu is so successful with his Hindi that he can speak in many north Indian dialects and registers by the end of the film. The film also keeps displaying written Hindi, first in Roman script and then, as Vasu's competence grows, in Devanagari, allowing him to write Sapna's name in the sand on the beach and later to compose love letters; she writes a love letter on his back and his name thousands of times on her bedroom wall. The other shibbolethes shown are the Brahmin Tamils' horror of the Punjabis' non-vegetarianism and the southerners' love of coffee.

Shot in Goa, which was just emerging as an attractive holiday destination for Indians, the action it is set outside the towns and the tourist resorts, focusing instead on the beaches. However, no Goan flavour is evoked through folk music or costume, as seen in Raj Kapoor's *Bobby*. The memorable songs include 'Kaisa hai yeh bandhan' and Vasu's attempt at Hindi poetry in a number made up of Hindi film song titles.

This film shows the parents to be blinded by their prejudice against romance and inter-caste marriage, and how they remain unrepentant even when they have alienated their children. The girl's mother is the particular villain of the piece, behaving more like the archetypal Hindi film stepmother.

No doubt it was the passion shown during the year-long separation of the couple that the audience loved the most: the idea of the testing of love, the pain of absence and the melodramatic gestures (notably the mother burning Vasu's photograph, then Sapna drinking the ashes in her tea), while Vasu turns his disco dancing into Bharat Natyam to express his feelings. Dramatic plot twists abound, such as when Vasu, misled into thinking that Sapna is getting married, decides to marry his widowed dance teacher, Sandhya. She discovers his true love and sends him back to Sapna at the end of the separation. However, it is too late to stop her brother ordering Vasu's murder, and at the climax of the film, when Sapna has been raped by an evil bookseller and Vasu has been beaten up and is near death, they leap off the cliff together. Their bodies are washed up on the beach, holding hands for eternity, an enduring symbol of doomed love in what has remained a benchmark film.

Dir./Story/Scr./Dial.: K. Balachander; **DOP**: B. S. Loknath; **Music**: Laxmikant–Pyarelal; **Lyrics**: Anand Bakshi; **Selected Cast**: Kamal Hassan, Rati Agnihotri; **Prod. Co.**: Prasad Productions; Colour.

Gadar – Ek prem katha
India, 2001 – 190 mins
Anil Sharma

This film became one of the highest-grossing movies of all time,
particularly in the Punjab, where 24-hour screenings were held to
accommodate the enormous crowds wanting to see this epic love story
of a Sikh and Muslim girl who are separated by the partition of India in
1947.

In pre-partition India, Sakina (Amisha Patel) is a rich Muslim girl at a
convent in Shimla, where truck driver Tara Singh (Sunny Deol) makes
deliveries and becomes smitten with 'Madamji'. Her family is then caught
up in the partition riots. The film has a twenty-minute sequence of the
horrors of partition, seen mostly through Sikh–Hindu eyes, as the
Muslims murder the departing refugees, which leads to counter-attacks
against Muslims. Separated from her family, Sakina is saved from a
rampaging groups of Sikhs by Tara, who pretends that she is his wife.
She stays with his family for a while, thinking her own to be dead, and
later she marries him and they have a child. Eventually she discovers that
her family is alive and living in Pakistan when she sees a picture of her
father (Amrish Puri), now the Mayor of Lahore, in the newspapers. She
visits them, but they refuse to let her return to her husband and her son,
insisting that she remarry and stay in Pakistan. Tara goes to find her and,
when the Mayor of Lahore calls out the Pakistani army and airforce, he
has to fight them single-handedly, mostly by shouting, to get her back.

This was only Amisha Patel's second film (after *Kaho na pyaar hai*)
and helped to establish her as a star. It restored Sunny as a major star,
and he gives a solid performance as the big-hearted Sikh who allows his
wife to remain a Muslim, and indicates that he is prepared to convert to
Islam himself. When tested by Sakina's father, he is willing to say '*Islam
zindabad*' ('Long live Islam'), '*Pakistan zindabad*' ('Long live Pakistan') (a
bit more reluctantly) but not '*India murdabad*' ('Down with India').
However, the film portrays Pakistan and Pakistanis in a negative light,

which undoubtedly partly explains its success. Although Pakistan was barely mentioned in Hindi films until fifty years after its creation, many films in the last decade have reversed this trend, whether war films (*Border*, *Lakshya* [2004]), movies about gangsters and terrorism (*Sarfarosh* [1999]) or Yash Chopra's last film, *Veer-Zaara* (2004), which tries to show that the borders between the countries are meaningless.

The other theme of the film is partition, a time when ten million people migrated and around a million people died at the founding of the modern Indian and Pakistani nations. Only a few films have been made about partition and its immediate aftermath (*Tamas* [1987], *Earth 1947*, *Train to Pakistan* [1997]), of which the best is *Garam hawa*.

Dir.: Anil Sharma; **Story/Scr./Dial.**: Shaktimaan; **DOP**: Najeeb Khan; **Music**: Uttam Singh; **Lyrics**: Anand Bakshi; **Selected Cast**: Sunny Deol, Amisha Patel, Amrish Puri, Lillette Dubey; **Prod. Co.**: Zee Television; Colour.

Garam hawa
India, 1973 – 146 mins
M. S. Sathyu

Many films have been made about the Partition, but they have mostly shown the unimaginable violence of that terrible time. This film is set in the aftermath of the partition, when the border between India and Pakistan was still open and Muslim families who had not thought of leaving their homes before began to wonder if they had made the right decision in the face of a social and political climate that had changed in ways they had not expected. This film focuses on the plight of families in Agra, the heartland of India, who were suddenly made to feel like strangers in their own homes. The suffering of these people, not through brutality but through the loss of their values and their human ties as their world moved under their feet, yet coupled with the hope of some final possible future, make this one of the most powerful films about the impact of Partition. I would include this film almost on the strength of just one shot: the image of Salim (Balraj Sahni) walking in front of the Taj Mahal, the symbol of love and of India but also a Muslim shrine and a part of everyday life to a person born and brought up in Agra, which shows so simply how the partition changed the subcontinent for ever.

While the film has few songs, there is a memorable *qawwali* ('Maulaa Salim Chisti, *aaqa* Salim Chisti' sung by Ustad Bahadur Khan), which is sung while the young couple, Shamshad and Amina, visit Fatehpur Sikri, not as tourists but as pilgrims to the tomb of Salim Chisti, demonstrating their religious attachment to their home city. The lyrics, as so often with Muslim devotional songs, outline not only the devotion of the pilgrims in the spiritual sense but also all earthly love and hopes.

The story by the Urdu writer, Ismat Chugtai, was adapted by the poet and writer, Kaifi Azmi. Salim Mirza runs the family shoe business in Agra. After partition, his friends and his family leave for the new country of Pakistan. Salim's brother, Halim, promises that his son Kazim will return to marry Salim's daughter, Amina (Gita Siddharth).

Balraj Sahni in *Garam hawa*

Since Halim is the elder, the *haveli* (ancestral home) is declared evacuee property and claimed by a Sindhi refugee, forcing Salim's family to move to a small house. Kazim arrives from Pakistan to marry Amina but the police force him to leave. Salim's brother-in-law leaves with his son Shamshad (Jalal Agha), whom Amina had hoped to marry. When he marries someone else, Amina commits suicide. With his business in difficulty, Salim is accused of starting a riot following an argument with a rickshaw-driver on the street, who tells him to go to Pakistan if he wants cheaper fares. When his factory is burnt down, Salim decides to leave, only to encounter a demonstration that includes his son Sikander (Farouque Sheikh); Salim changes his mind and joins the protesters.

The film is also visually stunning, with its locations in the old streets and *havelis* of Agra, and its exquisite costumes and furnishings. The acting is outstanding, with many of the actors, such as the veteran A. K. Hangal, associated with the IPTA (the Indian People's Theatre Association). The cast also includes some of the most talented young actors (Farouque Sheikh, Jalal Agha), alongside amateurs, one of whom is the old lady who plays Salim's mother, who was spotted in the area and hired even though she had never acted before.

We are informed before the film begins that this was Balraj Sahni's last film. Sahni had played the displaced person in many films (mostly with Bimal Roy, in, for example *Do bigha zamin*, as well as a smaller role in Yash Chopra's *Waqt*). The role also mirrored his own personal history (he lost his home in Lahore during the partition, and his brother, Bhisham Sahni, wrote the book, *Tamas*, which Govind Nihalani made into a television mini-series. The feeling of loss that this engendered in all those involved in the film and all those who knew Balraj Sahni's work makes this film even more elegiac.

The film was made on a total budget of eight lakh rupees (approximately £10,000) and won many awards, thus proving that a film of this quality could be made without a large budget and still be appreciated in India.

Dir.: M. S. Sathyu; **Story**: Kaifi Azmi (based on an unpublished short story by Ismat Chugtai); **Scr.**: Shama Zaidi, Kaifi Azmi; **Dial.**: Kaifi Azmi; **DOP**: Ishan Arya; **Music**: Ustad Bahadur Khan; **Lyrics**: Kaifi Azmi; **Selected cast**: Balraj Sahni, Farouque Sheikh, Gita Siddharth, A. K. Hangal, Shaukat Kaifi; **Prod. Co.**: Unit 3 MM; Colour.

Ghayal
India, 1990 – 163 mins
Raj Kumar Santoshi

Sunny (Ajay Singh) Deol, like his father, Dharmendra, is an actor who has often been overlooked by the critics despite enjoying a huge fan following, especially in the Punjab and north India. He is an action hero, muscular and macho, who often appears as a naïve, good-hearted country type.

He plays Pijay Mehra, the *Ghayal* ('The wounded') of the title living happily with his older brother Ashok (Raj Babbar) and his sister-in-law Indu (Moushumi Chatterjee). His boxing career is going well and he plans to marry his girlfriend Varsha (Meenakshi Seshadri). When he goes to Bangalore for training, he gets a strange phone call from his brother, and returns to find him missing. His investigations reveal police involvement with powerful criminals like Balwant Rai (Amrish Puri). When Ashok's body is found, Ajay is accused of killing him and having an affair with Indu. Ajay is imprisoned; Indu commits suicide. Ajay breaks out of jail to fight for justice . . .

The first half an hour of the film depicts happy family life, featuring slapstick jokes and a number of catchy songs that became hits, such as 'Maahiya teri kasam' (Lata Mangeshkar and Pankaj Udhas) and 'Sochna kya' (Asha Bhosle, Shabbir Kumar, Kumar Sanu). The atmosphere soon changes, however, the songs stop and the film finds its momentum, as Ajay begins his fight against Balwant Rai.

Although this selection includes more recent films starring Sunny Deol (*Gadar* and *Border*), it was in the 1980s that he created a new kind of hero. Rahul Rawail directed his first film, *Betaab* (1983), then *Arjun* (1985). In the former Sunny portrays a macho hero who could subdue a haughty woman (said to be adapted from *The Taming of the Shrew*), while the latter's excellent script (by Javed Akhtar) created a new kind of Angry Young Man for the 1980s; this film became something of a by-word for movies about unemployed young men. Although Deol and

Rawail have continued to work together, it was director Raj Kumar Santoshi, working under the Deols' banner, Vijayta Films, who made Sunny into the Rambo of India, an action hero who could ensure a good advance booking for a film. Sunny built up his muscles and came out fighting. Despite the rise of a new generation of male stars in the 1990s, it was not long before they too began to build up their bodies and take on action roles. However, Sunny Deol's popularity survived, with a few ups and downs, into the 2000s (notably with *Gadar*), as he represented an innocent, simple kind of all-male hero who would fight anyone and anything for honour and justice. *Ghayal* brought Sunny critical recognition for the first time, as it won many awards.

As well as *Ghayal*, Santoshi shot *Damini* (1993) and *Ghatak* (1996) with Sunny. Santoshi, who entered films as an assistant to Govind Nihalani, has never been associated with one genre. *Ghayal*, his debut, was an action movie, a genre in which he continues to work, with films such as *Khakhee* (2004), but he has also made *Damini* (1993) and *Lajja* (2001), which deal with women's issues, as well as a very popular comedy, *Andaz apna apna* (1994).

Dir.Story/Scr.: Raj Kumar Santoshi; **Dial**.: Dilip Shukla; **DOP**: Rajan Kothari; **Music**: Bappi Lahiri; **Lyrics**: Anjaan; **Selected Cast**: Sunny Deol, Meenakshi Seshadri, Amrish Puri, Raj Babbar, Moushumi Chatterjee; **Prod. Co**.: Vijayta Films; Colour.

Gol maal
India, 1979 – 175 mins
Hrishikesh Mukherjee

This is a film for the Hindi film connoisseur. The neophyte will not enjoy the slow opening or the ridiculous farce that ensues, but this remains one of the best-loved comedies among Hindi film fans. They delight in its affectionate parody of the mainstream cinema, and the wonderful performance of Amol Palekar, which relies not only on his exceptional acting talent but also on the subtleties of style, gesture and language that he brings to his performance of the dual role of the serious young intellectual and the fun-loving modern man, in which the central issue is a moustache – baffling to the uninitiated.

The story concerns a young graduate looking for work. Advised by his uncle of a winning strategy to join Bhavani Shankar's office, Ram Prasad (Palekar) disguises his true nature as a lover of sports and music by pretending to be a conservative, old-fashioned man. He does this by adopting an exaggerated form of 'pure' Hindi (that is, a non-colloquial or formal style of language encouraged by the government) and wearing khadi clothes (associated with Gandhi and hence with politics; latterly discredited, although still popular with the generation of intellectuals who were in their twenties at the time this film was made). Ram's deception is successful until he is seen by Bhavani at a sports game. When challenged, he invents an identical twin, Laxman, who is everything Bhavani despises, being modern and fashionable and, most importantly, not having a moustache. This double role is very much a commentary on the commercial film (see comment on *Ram aur Shyam*), which specialises in that device. An actor friend provides Ram with a false moustache and the plot thickens as Bhavani is constantly deceived by the 'twins' and their 'mother', who also has her own 'twin'. Bhavani's daughter falls in love with Laxman and the denouement begins as her father wants her to marry Ram. Once they are married, the deception is revealed and the film's final shot is of a clean-shaven Bhavani.

The music of R. D. Burman is exactly appropriate for the characters, reflecting a modern style these young professionals might enjoy. Hindi cinema has actors who specialise in comedy, several of whom appear in this film. Utpal Dutt's playing of Bhavani Shankar has been much appreciated, as has Dina Pathak's tongue-in-cheek performance as a *filmi*-mother. Amitabh Bachchan and Rekha make guest appearances, in which they send up their star personae. Deven Verma, who plays a mainstream actor in the film, makes several jokes about the course of events, including a much quoted remark that the story is getting so complicated that, were they to make a film, a commercial film director would be needed.

This film is very much in the style Madhava Prasad has identified as 'middle-class' cinema, which lies somewhere in between the commercial film and more realistic cinema. The main 'attractions' of the Hindi film are modified so that there is less stasis and spectacle and more use of characters than stars, with sets and locations that are explained diegetically, and more transparent editing. Hrishikesh Mukherjee was one of the leading figures in this type of cinema (see *Anand*), directing several hit films in the 1970s.

Dir.: Hrishikesh Mukherjee; **Story**: Sailesh Dey; **Scr**.: Sachin Bhowmick; **Dial**.: Dr Rahi Masoom Reza; **DOP**: Jaywant Pathare; **Music**: R. D. Burman; **Lyrics**: Gulzar; **Selected Cast**: Amol Palekar, Bindiya Goswami, Deven Verma, Utpal Dutt, Keshto Mukherjee, Om Prakash; **Prod**. **Co**.: N. C. Sippy and Hrishikesh Mukherjee; Colour.

Guide
India, 1965 – 183 mins
Vijay Anand

Guide is one of the handful of Hindi films adapted from a novel, in this case from R. K. Narayan's English novel of the same name, which won a national literary prize. Originally planned as an English film with a simultaneous Hindi version, the end result was very different once Vijay Anand was brought in to direct the Hindi film. I have not traced the English version, which sank without trace. While one would expect substantial differences in adapting an English novel to the requirements of a Hindi film, one of the most striking changes is that Narayan's ambiguity about the hero's mystical transformation is made much clearer in the film, which is surprising in the work of the Anand brothers, who are closely associated with some of the most secular and modern films. Religion is played down elsewhere in the film; for example, nothing is made of the Christian names of Rosie and Marco. A strong modern feel is discernible, nonetheless, not only in the narrative but also in its style (the expressivity of songs such as 'Kya se kya ho gaya' in which Raju is shown literally trapped by nets and webs), the costumes and in the use of Udaipur, a rising tourist destination (especially after the Kennedys' visit), as the place where Raju works as a guide.

Although the relationship between Rosie (Waheeda Rehman) and Raju (Dev Anand) is played down in the film, it is clear that she remains married to Marco (Kishore Sahu) despite living with Raju; this is underlined when Raju's mother leaves their house. Although Rosie's separation from Marco is presented sympathetically, in that he is more interested in sculptures and prostitutes than in his wife, whom he despises for coming from a family of *devadasis* (temple dancing girls associated with prostitution), this is very unusual in a Hindi film and I cannot think of another example of a wife singing a celebratory song ('Aaj phir jeene') on leaving her husband.

Raju is one of the early anti-heroes of Hindi cinema. A tourist guide, he also becomes a guide to love and life, to his lover's career and finally to God. Yet on the way he also becomes a criminal, through his careless forging of Rosie's signature; and his life's downward trajectory is emphasised through his drinking, his neglect of Rosie and his love of money. However, he is finally redeemed at the end of the film when his transformation through penance into a holy man brings rain to the drought-stricken village. Although Waheeda's brilliant dancing eclipses the rest of her acting, she does take on a variety of roles, from neglected wife, to rebellious woman, to dance star (where she excels), to abandoned lover and, at the end of the film a religious devotee, when she is touched by the spiritual experiences of Raju.

S. D. Burman, who wrote hits from the 1950s until the early 1970s, produced yet another group of successful songs with this film, ranging from virtual folk songs to the spectacular dance numbers and expressive laments of Raju and the great love duet 'Gaata rahe mera dil'. The 'item' songs could be incorporated in a relatively realistic manner, as the heroine of the film, Rosie, is a dancer who performs two dance numbers from a stage show, albeit highly elaborated, 'Piya tose naina laage re' and 'Saiyya beimaan', although in the latter, Raju, who is watching from the wings, suddenly apparently joins in the song in order to express his inner emotions. Two other songs are presented more in Hollywood conventions, one as a title song '(Wahaan kaun hai tera?') and the other as a folk song begging for rain ('Allah megh de'). The others are fine examples of typical song picturisation, more than fulfilling the usual dramatic and narrative functions of Hindi film songs. Rosie's assumption of her new life is expressed in song ('Aaj phir jeene ki tamanna hai'), and there are two typically romantic numbers, one of which is performed on the shore of Lake Pichchola in Udaipur ('Tere mere sapne') to express Raju's initial declaration of love, while the other takes place in the traditional landscape of hills ('Gaata rahe mera dil'). Two songs are used to express Raju's inner torment: 'Din dhal jaye' and 'Kya se kya ho gaya', both of which remain popular.

Dir./Story/Scr./Dial.: Vijay Anand; **Story**: R. K. Narayan's novel (1958); **DOP**: Fali Mistry; **Music**: S. D. Burman; **Lyrics**: Shailendra; **Selected Cast**: Dev Anand, Waheeda Rehman, Leela Chitnis, Kishore Sahu; **Prod**. **Co**.: Navketan Films; Colour.

Gunga Jumna
India, 1961 – 178 mins
Nitin Bose

Gunga Jumna is one of the finest examples of a popular theme of Indian
cinema, namely that of the good and bad brother. Gunga (Dilip Kumar),
framed for a crime by a landowner, becomes an outlaw, while his
younger brother, Jumna (Nasir Khan, Dilip Kumar's real-life brother),
whom he has educated, becomes a police officer. When Gunga and
Dhanno (Vyjayanthimala) are expecting a child, he returns to the village
but is killed by his brother acting on behalf of the law.

The theme of the good and bad brother was seen in *Mother India*
and later in *Deewaar*, where the bad brother is portrayed as a good
person who is forced to take the law into his own hands, often in search
of a higher form of justice, to protect his family or thwart a villain. His
good qualities are constantly emphasised and, although he is the true
hero of the film, because he has broken the law of society, his only
redemption is in death. This law of society is often embodied by a
policeman, particularly a younger brother.

The dialogues of Wajahat Mirza were highly acclaimed, with lines
like Dilip Kumar's, 'Mujhe ghar lautna hai, mere bhai ('I want to go
home, brother') being quoted even today. Like other dacoit (bandit)
films, this one employs the Bhojpuri dialect of eastern Uttar Pradesh (later
used by Gabbar Singh in *Sholay*) to given an authentic flavour to Gunga
and Dhanno, but Jumna speaks a more standard Hindi. Many have
commented on Vyjayanthimala's skill in mastering this dialect even
though she is a south Indian, and this may have helped her to win the
Filmfare Award for her role in the film. Dilip Kumar's death scene is often
shown as one of his best moments in cinema, though, like most death
scenes, it is milked for all it is worth. Gunga becomes the archetypal
victim of the feudal system, the helpless villager, who, if he fights back,
will be destroyed. There is no hope for the ordinary man who wants an
ordinary life for himself and his family.

Nitin Bose had earlier worked with New Theatres, but there is little obvious influence here, and it is often claimed that Dilip Kumar had more directorial input than Bose. Naushad's music was popular, though the score is not remembered as one of his greatest, despite popular songs like Asha Bhosle's 'Tora man bada paapi' and Hemant Kumar's 'Insaaf ki dagar pe', as well as those sung by Lata Mangeshkar and Mohammad Rafi.

Dir.: Nitin Bose; **Story/Scr**: Dilip Kumar; **Dial.**: Wajahat Mirza; **DOP**: V. Babasaheb; **Music**: Naushad; **Lyrics**: Shakeel Badayuni; **Selected Cast**: Dilip Kumar, Vyjayanthimala, Nasir Khan, Kanhaiyalal; **Prod. Co.**: Citizens Films; Colour.

Haqeeqat
India, 1964 – 184 mins
Chetan Anand

Haqeeqat deserves its status as the greatest war film made in India. The film's subject, India's defeat in 1962 by the Chinese, seems an unlikely topic, but here the viewers' sympathy lies with the heroic losers and martyrs. In many war films, the nobility of the enemy is highlighted, but here the Chinese are portrayed as cheating and dishonourable, from Zhou en Lai, who is seen in documentary footage accepting honours from Nehru, to the soldiers who are shown in close-up taking sadistic pleasure in torturing a woman.

It seems extraordinary that the success of this film did not make the war genre more popular in India, but only a handful of war films were made until after J. P. Dutta's *Border*. The Hindi film shows how it is able to transform itself to suit the demands of a Hollywood genre, without compromising its distinctive features. This film deploys melodrama, spectacle and song and dance to full effect, enriching the war genre rather than weakening it. The film's two hit songs are key moments in rousing the audience's sympathy and support for the army. Their success is due as much to the director's picturisation of the songs as to the wonderful music of Madan Mohan and the haunting lyrics of Kaifi Azmi. The first, 'Hoke majboor mujhe usne bulaya hoga', sung by the demoralised and exhausted soldiers, emphasises their plight and their longing for their wives and homes. The second, 'Kar chale hum fida jaan-o-tan saathiyon', is picturised on the young boy who finds his sister and Captain Bahadur (Dharmendra) dead, having fought off the Chinese on their own. The film then cuts to the many dead soldiers, before showing the Major (Balraj Sahni) breaking the news to the commanding officer (Jayant), who is also the captain's father. Nothing is said, but everything is conveyed through the images: a cut to the photograph of the captain's mother, in front of which lies a pile of unsent letters; a scene in which she and the other women remove their jewellery to sell for the war effort; and cuts to real footage of demonstrations through Delhi, and army parades. Everyone's sacrifice is stressed throughout the film, to create an atmosphere of martyrdom, in death and in life. The impact their service of their country has on their family lives is repeatedly brought home. Diwali is shown as the saddest time of all, the wives lacking the heart even to light lamps for the festival, while the soldiers listen to their leader attacking the Chinese in his speech while footage of Zhou's visit to Delhi is shown.

The landscape of Ladakh is beautifully shot and heightens the emotionality of the film, with its rugged and hostile elements. The film also includes love stories, as the soldiers are shown thinking about loved ones and waiting for letters, and it cuts to images of their homes. In one poignant moment, a soldier thinks his wife has sent him sweets ('mithai') but she has in fact sent him earth ('mitthi') from home and some seeds so that he can grow flowers to remind him of her. The main love story, between Captain Bahadur and the local girl (Priya Rajvansh), begins as a typical *filmi* romance, but ends with them both sacrificing their lives to save their country.

Rajvansh, brought from London to act in this film, was romantically linked to Chetan Anand, and acted in nearly all of his subsequent films. Her brutal murder by his sons, who were seeking the share of Anand's property bequeathed to her in his will, adds further pathos to her performance for today's viewers.

Dir./Story/Scr./Dial.: Chetan Anand; **DOP**: Sadanand Sengupta; **Music**: Madan Mohan; **Lyrics**: Kaifi Azmi; **Selected Cast**: Balraj Sahni, Dharmendra, Priya Rajvansh, Vijay Anand, Jayant; **Prod. Co.**: Himalaya Films; Black and white.

Hare Rama Hare Krishna
India, 1971 – 149 mins
Dev Anand

This is one of the few films that looked at the hippy view of eastern culture, pointing out its irreverence and shallowness. It was filmed in Nepal, perhaps because this was one of the major hippy destinations, but also perhaps to locate it on more neutral ground. A series of shots, supposedly views from a plane, introduces us to the tourist sites of Kathmandu, although we are subsequently shown very little of the landscape in the rest of the film.

As in *Purab aur pachhim*, the west is seen as a place lacking human warmth and familial love, where only material values matter. The film begins by cutting from 'real' devotees of Krishna across a map of the world to show 'Hare Krishnas' in London. We are then transported to Montreal, where it seems that this crisis of belief has infected even the Indians who live there. Prashant (Dev Anand) and his sister Jasbir (Zeenat Aman) are unhappy because their parents are always quarrelling. Eventually they divorce, and Prashant and his mother (Achala Sachdev) go back to India. Imbued with Indian values, Prashant becomes a pilot, that Hindi film icon of modernity, but he longs to be reunited with his sister once he discovers that she is alive and living in Nepal. Jasbir, brought up in the west by her father (Kishore Sahu) and her stepmother (Indrani Mukherjee), has joined the hippy trail and cut herself off from her past, even changing her name to Janice. Her crowd hangs out in a commune, the Bakery, where they get stoned and practise 'free love'. In something of a diversion from the main story of the broken family, Prashant soon falls in love with local girl Shanti (Mumtaz), before being framed for the theft of a golden statue from the temple. The true thief is Dronacharya (Prem), the local don who exploits the hippies and is also in pursuit of Shanti. Truth triumphs, of course, and the family is reconciled but not without tragedy.

(*Opposite page*) Zeenat Aman and Dev Anand in *Hare Ram Hare Krishna*

Zeenat Aman is ideally cast as the hippy chick who can look both Indian and western, while Mumtaz sparkles as the 'traditional' but spirited and independent girl. (It seems Mumtaz was initially offered the role of Janice but preferred to play the more typical heroine.) Dev Anand continues his usual walk through films, ever cool and stylish. The clothes are very fashionable for their time, from Zeenat's minis and maxis and huge sunglasses to the wool hair ornaments. Many of the clothes are saffron-coloured; these are often worn by the good characters, so Dev Anand wears a saffron *kurta* and Mumtaz a saffron shawl, but the thief is also dressed in a saffron silk robe, perhaps to mark his hypocrisy.

While undoubtedly Dev Anand's most accomplished film as a director, it is perhaps most famous for its song 'Dum maaro dum' (Asha Bhosle), a hippy song with a chorus about smoking a *chillum*. Although there were objections to using a religious chant in the song, the film shows Dev Anand singing that they should not take God's name in vain. Mumtaz features in a big dance sequence in the song 'Ghunghroo' and in the lilting, folkish 'Kanchi re, kanchi re', sung in a Tibetan wool mill, at the end of which she appears in a trendy trousersuit rather than her usual 'traditional' clothes. Another of the hit songs is the perennial ode to the love of a brother and sister, 'Phoolon ka taara ka sab ka kehna hai' (Lata Mangeshkar).

Dir./Story/Scr.: Dev Anand; **DOP**: Fali Mistry; **Music**: R. D. Burman; **Lyrics**: Anand Bakshi; **Selected Cast**: Dev Anand, Mumtaz, Zeenat Aman, Prem Chopra, Kishore Sahu; **Prod. Co.**: Navketan Films; Colour.

Hum aapke hain koun . . .!
India, 1994 – 206 mins
Sooraj Barjatya

The family film reached its apogee in 1994, with the release of Barjatya's *Hum aapke hain koun . . .!* ('What am I to you. . .!'), a film entirely plotted around the family-life events of engagement, marriage, childbirth and death. Despite being mocked as a wedding video, with its dozens of family members and its thirteen songs, it has been one of the biggest box-office grossers of all time.

Prem (Salman Khan) and Nisha (Madhuri Dixit) meet at the engagement of his brother Rajesh (Mohnish Behl) and her sister Pooja (Renuka Shahane), daughter of Professor Choudhary (Anupam Kher) and Kamladevi (Reema Lagoo). Prem and Rajesh's parents are dead but they have been brought up by their uncle Kailashnath (Alok Nath). The wedding is celebrated with all the usual rituals and ceremonies, and Prem and Nisha fall in love, spending time together when Nisha comes to stay for the birth of Pooja's baby. When Pooja dies in an accident, Nisha's father suggests she marries Rajesh, and Nisha and Prem are willing to sacrifice their love, but Fate/God intervenes, helped by Tuffy the dog, and the pair are reunited.

The younger generation is prepared to sacrifice love for the welfare of their loving and supportive families, who are the entire focus of the film. *HAHK* took this to its extreme, as the film has very little in the way of story, its focus being the celebration of the institution of the family. The film was popular for its depiction of family rituals, covering the entire spectrum from birth to death, each marked with a song. This takes up over two hours of the film, with the drama compressed into the last section. The song from the pregnancy ritual, 'Didi tera devar deewaana', was the biggest hit, while others, such as the wedding song about the ritual of the girl's family stealing the boy's family's shoes, 'Joote de do, paisa le lo', and 'Maai ni maaie' along with many others, have now become an integral part of Indian wedding celebrations.

Madhuri Dixit and Salman Khan in the song 'Didi tera devar deewaana' in *Hum aapke hain koun....!*

One of the greatest box-office hit of all time, the film is also important because its release brought about a crucial change in Hindi film-viewing when Barjatya introduced the policy of 'video holdback'. Initially, Barjatya released only one print, with seats selling at the then unheard of price of Rs 100. This publicity stunt aroused great curiosity and, as he gradually released the film at a few more theatres, demand exceeded supply. When the film came out on general release and was still not available on video, the audience thronged to the cinemas. The unprecedented success of this film meant that big-budget, family-oriented films were once again commercially viable.

Sooraj Barjatya, from a family known for its film distribution, made his debut film in 1989, with *Maine pyar kiya*, a huge hit that was very much part of the return to romance of the 1990s (see *Qayamat se qayamat tak*), in which the young couple begin their romance as friends, accompanied by catchy songs and a strong emphasis on family values.

Dir./Scr./Dial.: Sooraj Barjatya; **Story**: Keshav Prasad Mishra, S. H. Athavale; **DOP**: Rajan Kinagi; **Music**: Raamlaxman; **Lyrics**: Ravinder Rawal, Dev Kohli; **Selected Cast**: Madhuri Dixit, Salman Khan, Anupam Kher, Renuka Shahane, Mohnish Behl, Alok Nath, Reema Lagoo; **Prod. Co**.: Rajshri Productions; Colour.

Hum dil de chuke sanam
India, 1999 – 188 mins
Sanjay Leela Bhansali

Sanjay Leela Bhansali, whose films constitute a tour of various Indian communities (Goans in *Khamoshi*, Bengalis in *Devdas*), takes us to Gujarat. After Bhansali's first film, the critically acclaimed *Khamoshi – The Musical*, failed at the box office, he was approached by an elderly man, Pratap Karvat, with a story about a man who sends his wife to look for her lover. Apparently, Bhansali combined this with a story by the collector of Gujarati folk tales, Jhaverchand Meghani, in which the husband actually takes his wife to find her lover. The script was a collaboration between Karvat and others, with dialogue by Amrik Gill.

Nandini (Aishwarya Rai) is the daughter of a music teacher who lives in a vast, ethnically and lavishly appointed *haveli* (mansion or palace). Sameer Rossellini (Salman Khan), a half-Italian, comes to study music and inevitably he and Nandini fall in love. However, she is promised in marriage to Vanraj (Ajay Devgan), who falls in love with her when he sees her perform the song 'Nimbuda'. They marry but he sleeps separately when he realises that she does not love him. When she tells him about Sameer, Vanraj takes her to 'Italy' to find him. On their journey, she realises that her husband is a good man who is really in love with her and so, when she finally meets Sameer, she has to tell him that it is over. Sameer is left with his mother to rebuild his life, as marriage is upheld once again as inviolable.

The film's casting is excellent, with the notable inclusion of Salman Khan's real-life stepmother, the legendary dancer, Helen, playing his screen mother in the film. While this film marked the beginning of Aishwarya Rai's stardom, the real surprise was that Ajay Devgan as Vanraj, rather than the flatulent and foolish Sameer, is the hero of the piece, in a fine performance as the rejected and devoted husband.

Although the film boasts beautiful clothes, sets and locations, Bhansali is showing the beginnings of the excess that was to mar

Devdas. The location shooting is bizarre, as the main *haveli* seems to open onto different landscapes and climates in strange continuity breaks. The Italian connection – perhaps just a playful use of the name of the great Rossellini film family – is broken when the couple go to 'Italy', which is actually Hungary, where no effort is made to conceal either the famous buildings of Budapest or Hungarian names and script. The justification was that Indians would not have known where Hungary was! However, Bhansali once again shows his fine choice of music in the film, with a new composer, Ismail Darbar, providing several hit songs like 'Dholi taaro dhol', 'Aankhon ki gustakhiyan' and 'Nimbuda'.

Dir.: Sanjay Leela Bhansali; **Story**: Pratap Karvat; **Scr**.: Sanjay Leela Bhansali, Pratap Karvat, Kenneth Philips; **Dial**.: Amrik Gill; **DOP**: Anil Mehta; **Music**: Ismail Darbar; **Lyrics**: Mehboob; **Selected Cast**: Ajay Devgan, Salman Khan, Aishwarya Rai; **Prod. Co**.: Bhansali Productions; Colour.

Jaane bhi do yaaro
India, 1983 – 143 mins
Kundan Shah

I had to bend my selection criteria to include this film, as it is financed by the government's funding body (the National Film Development Corporation). It is a key Hindi film, though certainly not Bollywood. The younger generation of Hindi film-makers have grown up on this and always cite it as a significant influence. However, on rewatching it, I found much of the beginning rather dated with very theatrical comedy and too much buffoonery. Even though the film showcases some of India's leading actors, in a good story, which is also a political satire, the laboured style of farce, slapstick and other assorted shouting and grimacing initially detracts from the performances until the film really gets going with some inspired comic sequences.

Two hopeless young photographers, Vinod Chopra (Naseeruddin Shah) and Sudhir Mishra (Ravi Baswani), become entangled with Shobha (Bhakti Bharve), the editor of a magazine, *Khabardar*, which exposes corruption and scandals. They are commissioned to take photographs to provide evidence of corruption between builders Tarneja (Pankaj Kapoor) and Ahuja (Om Puri) and Commissioner D'Mello (Satish Shah). Their photos show a killer but many 'blow-ups' are needed (the reference to Antonioni's *Blow Up* [1966] is made explicit in that the body is left in Antonioni Park), before they find that D'Mello is the victim and Tarneja the murderer. They fell out over the contract for a flyover which collapsed but Tarneja, Ahuja and Shobha made a deal. The photographers take the corpse as evidence, to prove murder. This is where the comedy takes off. The first scene involves the coffin rolling away before it is found by Ahuja, who is so drunk that he thinks it is a man driving a sports car. The corpse is left at a guest house, to where our heroes return and put it on roller skates so that it can be moved around more easily. A chase ensues, involving the characters dressing up in *burqas*, followed by the best sequence in the film, in which they disrupt a theatrical performance of the episode of the *Draupadivastraharan* ('Disrobing of Draupadi') from the great Indian epic, the *Mahabharata*. This is very funny indeed, as the corpse is dressed as Draupadi and Vinod has to go against the story in refusing to disrobe her. The play is further disturbed when the Great Mughal Akbar appears from another play, ensuring that when the police finally arrive no one is sure if they are real or part of the chaos. Eventually the two photographers are framed for the murder.

A satire on many fronts – mocking the police, the municipal corporation, the press, etc., the film also refers to real-life incidents such as the notorious Byculla bridge collapse. It is also full of references to other films, such as naming the photographers after two young directors of the new cinema of the 1970s. While some of the references may seem obscure now, and some of the humour badly dated, gems such as the stage performance ensure this film its place in any list of Hindi films.

Dir.: Kundan Shah; **Story/Scr**.: Kundan Shah, Sudhir Mishra; **Dial**.: Ranjit Kapoor, Satish Kaushik; **DOP**: Binod Pradhan; **Music**: Vanraj Bhatia; **Selected Cast**: Naseeruddin Shah, Ravi Baswani, Bhakti Bharve, Om Puri; **Prod. Co**.: NFDC; Colour.

Jab jab phool khile
India, 1965 – 148 mins
Suraj Prakash

JJPK typifies the best of the 1960s' films, with its high fashion, catchy songs and its portrayal of a modern, wealthy Bombay woman falling in love with a poor boatman. Even after four decades and the film's 'remake' as *Raja Hindustani* (1996), *JJPK* remains as fresh as ever.

This was the first major hit for Shashi Kapoor playing the main hero. The youngest of the three sons of the great Prithviraj Kapoor, Shashi has not perhaps had the same impact on the Hindi film industry as his older brothers Shammi and Raj have. The handsome Shashi, with his beautiful eyes and crooked grin, was always regarded as the most westernised actor, in part for his work with Merchant–Ivory, but also because he was married to Jennifer Kendal (Felicity's sister) and pursued his father's interest in theatre, taking a major role in Bombay's Prithvi Theatre. Shashi, who played suave Indians for western audiences, was typecast as the sophisticated urbanite in Hindi films. (Yash Chopra told me that Shashi took a great deal of persuading to perform a song in *Dharamputra* [1961], as he considered this too frivolous.) Yet *JJPK* gave Shashi one of his most enduring images, against type, as the Kashmiri boatman, Raja, who, barefoot, dressed in a *salwar-khameez* and cap, sings 'Affoo Khuda!' as he runs through a pastoral landscape of trees, mountains and flocks of sheep. His declaration of love as he frantically paddles his *shikara*, his wide-eyed innocence and his revulsion at the sight of westernised behaviour are what made this character so endearing.

Nanda's great performance as Raja's 'Memsahib' is somewhat overshadowed by her amazing wardrobe. This is one of the earliest films in which western clothing and modern ways are not seen as 'bad', just different. The outfits range from slacks and tunics to two-tone dresses, op-art shirts and white satin nightgowns, as well as one that looks a little like a Father Christmas costume. Raja's ethnic outfit is changed briefly for a suit in a comic routine in the tailor's, but he soon sheds this new look.

Two other memorable features of the films are the classic songs
'Pardesiyon aankiyaan se na milaana' (whose equivalent in *Raja
Hindustani* was the hit 'Pardesi, pardesi, jaana nahin') and the romantic
'Yeh samaa'. Kalyanji–Anandji team up with Anand Bakshi, rather than
their preferred lyricist, Indeevar.

Most of the film is set in Kashmir, which was becoming established
during this decade as the great romantic film location, evoked as
paradise both for its beauty and for its status as a holiday destination for
the new consumerist classes. Its inhabitants include locals in their
regional dress and holiday-makers in their western fashions. It is
contrasted with Bombay, which is seen as a gateway to glamour and
modernity.

Dir.: Suraj Prakash; **Story/Scr./Dial**.: Brij Katyal; **DOP**: Taru Dutt; **Music**: Kalyanji–Anandji;
Lyrics: Anand Bakshi; **Selected Cast**: Nanda, Shashi Kapoor, Agha, Shammi;
Prod. **Co**.: Limelight Pictures; Colour.

Jai Santoshi Maa
India, 1975 – 145 mins
Vijay Sharma

Jai Santoshi Maa was a surprise hit film in 1975. It was one of the three biggest successes of the year, alongside *Sholay* and *Deewaar*, both of which starred Amitabh Bachchan, securing his subsequent domination of the box office and god-like status. Religious films have been made in India since the silent period, but they were seen largely as B-movies, or worse, by the 1960s. There were many popular mother goddess films made around this time, mostly about localised village goddesses, such as 'Maa' or, further south, 'Amma'. Most of these films contained numerous special effects, chiefly involving trident-hurling, but this type of religious film as family drama was more popular.

Santoshi Maa (Anita Guha) is the daughter of Ganesh, who is born to give her brothers a sister to tie *raakhi* (an auspicious thread tied by sisters to their brothers' wrists during an annual festival). Her devotee, Satyavati (Kanan Kaushal), is victimised and bullied by her in-laws and is helped by Santoshi Maa, a mother goddess for whom she performs *vrats* or particular fasts. However, three other goddesses (Brahmani, Laxmi and Parvati) are jealous of her devotion and make life difficult for Satyavati, who endures a series of misfortunes until she is finally restored to her husband (Ashish Kumar) and all the family become devotees.

Although the film is set in some vaguely north Indian village in roughly contemporary time, the cult of Santoshi Maa has also become strong in the cities, in particular for lower-middle-class women, who find the fast fairly easy to follow, as it requires only the avoidance of sour foods, and also because her story takes up the popular theme of *saas-bahu* (mother-in-law and daughter-in-law), a staple of television soap operas. It is often said that Santoshi Maa was a new or local goddess who became popular as a result of the film, but images of her seem to exist from the 1960s, produced by the well-known firm, Sharma Picture Publications.

Satyavati (Anita Guha) salutes the goddesses Brahmani, Laxmi and Parvati in *Jai Santoshi Maa*

The songs of *Jai Santoshi Maa* were a great success among college kids, for whom this became something of a cult film. The music by C. Arjun and lyrics by Kavi Pradeep made Usha Mangeshkar a star and even now many who were teenagers at the time of the release remember learning the songs and dances for the *aartis* (worship with lights), especially 'Main to aarti utaaroon re, Santoshi Mata ki/I raise the lamps to Santoshi Maa', a song that is often sung in rituals today.

The film is still shown on television during festivals, such as on the last day of Shravana (a month of the rainy season), so it is surprising that, subsequently, it did not spawn more successful copycat films. While there were many attempts, often with the same cast (Ashish Kumar, Anita Guha), or with more glamorous stars (Padma Khanna) or even the veterans of the old mythologicals, none of these worked at the box office. The lifting of restrictions on religious programming on Indian television in the late 1980s gave the genre a new lease of life as religious soap operas, which have been some of the most popular television programmes made anywhere in the world.

Dir.: Vijay Sharma; **Story/Scr./Dial.**: R. Priyadarshini; **DOP**: Sudhendu Roy; **Music**: C. Arjun; Lyrics: Kavi Pradeep; **Selected Cast**: Anita Guha, Ashish Kumar, Kanan Kaushal, Trilok Kapoor, Mahipal; **Prod. Co.**: Bhagyalakshmi Chitra Mandir; Colour.

Jewel Thief
India, 1967 – 186 mins
Vijay Anand

Vijay Anand, whose banner, Navketan Films, has produced many influential and popular films (including *Guide*, *CID*, *Johny mera naam*), is one director of Hindi cinema who really knows how to handle a story. The labyrinthine twists of this film mean it defies definition, as a tale of thieves and glamour leads us across the Himalayas to Sikkim with Dev Anand in a double role, meeting beautiful women (Tanuja, Vyjayanthimala, Helen) along the way, but crime thriller seems to be the nearest.

Vinay (Dev Anand), a police commissioner's son, is mistaken for the jewel thief, Amar. Accused of having made promises to marry a woman, he pretends to be Amar, while Amar is apparently pretending to be him. The plot takes many turns, but overall it is one of the best of its kind in Hindi film, where the narrative is so compelling that it does not need to end with a long lecture explaining to confused viewers what it was really about.

The weird gizmos and gadgets that abound in the film, contribute to it often seeming somewhat mad. It is full of surprises, notably the appearance of Ashok Kumar, the hero of Bombay Talkies (*Achhut kanya*, *Kismet*) and of comedies such as *Chalti ka naam gaadi*, who had become a staple father figure (*Aradhana* and many others) during this decade, here taking a change of direction, which gave the audience quite a shock.

S. D. Burman composed great songs for this film, which marks a transition between his own distinctive melodic mixtures of traditional and western sounds and the style that would be adopted by his son and assistant, R. D. Burman, who created a funky fusion of music that still sounds cool today. The songs range from the soulful 'Dil pukaare' to the raunchy number 'Raat akeli hai' (the dance performed with panache by Tanuja, of the female dynasty that included Shobhana Samarth, Nutan and Tanuja's daughter Kajol). Kishore Kumar's free and easy style in 'Yeh dil na hota bechaara' is well suited to this song, which accompanies the natty Dev Anand as he strolls along, carrying a fishing rod complete with a fake fish hanging from it, blocking the road for a group of glamorous ladies in an enormous car. All stops are pulled for the item number, 'Hothon pe aisi baat', with Vyjayanthimala's stunning dancing, its Sikkim-influenced costumes and sets, the great rhythmic style of the younger Burman's music and Lata Mangeshkar's skilful performance of a dramatic dance song. One of my all-time favourite film songs is 'Dil pukare', which exemplifies the hybrid style of film music at its best, in which Indian instruments such as the flute, sitar and percussions are orchestrated in a western style, seamlessly blending with a western orchestra. Today it sounds completely 'Indian', but at the time it must have seemed radically new. Rafi and Lata match one another's styles effortlessly, demonstrating the perfect style of singing for Hindi film.

Other song picturisations are stunning. The costume designer has a few strange moments such as Helen's outrageous outfit for the cabaret song, 'Baithe hain kya us ke paas', which cannot be described better than on the box of my Shemaroo DVD as a 'costume with jewel-dripping tights and a rooster tail', and she turns in yet another zinging performance. Vyjayanthimala's bizarre red sari with small patches of white fur or cotton wool brings an unexpected and probably unintentional Christmas feel to the 'Dil pukaare' duet.

Dir./Scr./Dial.: Vijay Anand; **Story**: K. A. Narayan; **DOP**: V. Ratra; **Music**: S. D. Burman; **Lyrics**: Majrooh Sultanpuri; **Selected Cast**: Ashok Kumar, Dev Anand, Vyjayanthimala, Tanuja, Helen; **Prod. Co.**: Navketan Films; Colour.

Johny mera naam
India, 1970 – 159 mins
Vijay Anand

Famous for the typical slickness of producer Gulshan Rai's Trimurti Films and its rich mix of *masala*, or spice, rather than the Navketan style, this film develops a popular theme of Hindi cinema, namely that of good and bad brothers' adventures in a series of disguises and masquerades. After seeing their father murdered by Ranjit (Premnath), Mohan (Pran), disguised as Moti, becomes a member of Ranjit's gang without realising that he is the murderer, while his brother Sohan (Dev Anand) becomes a policeman, Johny. Johny infiltrates Ranjit's gang along with Rekha (Hema Malini), whose father is held by Ranjit. The brothers eventually discover one another's true identity and reunite to defeat the villain.

Gulshan Rai had been a film financier in pre-partition days and was closely associated with B. R. Chopra and later Yash Chopra. He helped Yash Chopra finance his early films and when he began his own productions, hired Yash Chopra to direct some of his classic (notably *Deewaar*). He only produced a dozen or so films, almost all huge blockbusters, working with established directors like Vijay Anand and Yash Chopra, before concentrating on the films of his son Rajeev Rai (including *Tridev* [1989] and *Gupt* [1997]), who began his career as an assistant director to Yash Chopra.

Johny mera naam is remembered for its songs by Kalyanji–Anandji and for its dance 'items', including Hema Malini's 'Vaada to nibhaya', but, most famously, for the overtly sexual 'Husn ke lakhon rang', as Tara (Padma Khanna) seduces Ranjit, which must be cited as a counter-example of the censorship of sexuality in the Hindi film, as its imagery is still rather shocking today. Comedian I. S. Johar, who played three parts, won the Filmfare Award for his send-up of multiple roles in the film.

The film is important for its presentation of Hema Malini, who was to go on to be one of the top female stars of the 1970s, as well as for setting the pace for many of the crime films of the decade, whether Pran and Hema's fake preachers or the style of its dialogues.

Dir./Scr.: Vijay Anand; **Story**: K. A. Narayan; **DOP**: Fali Mistry; **Music**: Kalyanji–Anandji; **Lyrics**: Rajinder Krishen, Indivar; **Selected Cast**: Dev Anand, Hema Malini, Premnath, Jeevan, I. S. Johar, **Prod. Co.**: Trimurti Films; Colour.

Junglee
India, 1961 – 150 mins
Subodh Mukherji

Shammi Kapoor yelled 'Yahoo!' and became a new kind of hero for the 1960s. Raj Kapoor's younger brother had shaved off his trademark pencil moustache in the 1950s and created a new Elvis-style image for the Indian hero as he danced to western-style songs in nightclubs and discos. His physical presence dominated the screen, with his height, striking fairness and endless energy as he danced and pulled comic faces while wooing the new style of heroine, leading a whole generation of young men to imitate his style. Raj Kapoor never found a hero's role for his younger brother in his films, and Shammi was linked with the Filmistan 'film factory', with directors such as Subodh Mukherji and Nasir Hussain, as well as Shakti Samanta, who followed their style. Shammi worked with the most glamorous of a new generation of actresses – Asha Parekh, Saira Banu and Sharmila Tagore.

Mohammed Rafi sang Shammi's songs with a panache and flair suited to the dancing hero, perhaps surprising those who knew the gravitas and dignity he bestowed on romantic heroes, such as Dilip Kumar and Guru Dutt in the 1950s. Few other singers have the range he displayed in this film, from the dance numbers to the ever popular *ghazal,* 'Ehsaan tera hoga mujh par'.

Junglee was one of the first of the decade's light romances to be shot in colour, which it used to great advantage on locations in snowy mountains and on elaborate sets, such as for Suku Suku, which has an MGM-style set of a giant artist's palette and an unexplained troupe of Russian dancers. Shammi plays the businessman returned from foreign climes, whose mother is intent on keeping the family away from love and laughter and focused instead on the business and accumulating wealth. Shammi's seriousness is presented as ridiculous and makes him a figure of fun, a 'stuffed shirt'. When he falls in love with Rajkumari (Saira Banu), his world is turned upside down and, although his realisation of

Shammi Kapoor yells 'Yahoo!' in *Junglee*

love begins with Urdu poetry, the real epiphany occurs when he leaps
around the snow yelling 'Yahoo!'('Chahe koi mujhe junglee kahe'). The
newly romantic hero resists his mother's attempts to marry him off to a
princess (a rajkumari) by pretending to be mad. Although he will not
marry Rajkumari without his mother's permission, he reveals the princess
to be a fraud put forward by her scheming family, before he and his
sister, who elopes with her lover, persuade the mother to become more
loving and give up her 'patriarchal' role. The theme of young lovers
obeying their parents, while persuading them that love is the answer, is a
regular theme of Hindi films even up to the present.

Dir./Story/Scr.: Subodh Mukherji; **Dial**. Agha Jani Kashmiri; **DOP:** N. V. Srinivas,
Music: Shankar–Jaikishen; **Lyrics**: Shailendra, Hasrat Jaipuri; **Selected Cast**: Shammi Kapoor,
Saira Banu, Shashikala, Anup Kumar, Lalita Pawar; **Prod**. **Co**.: Subodh Mukherji Productions;
Colour.

Kaagaz ke phool
India, 1959 – 153 mins
Guru Dutt

This is often said to the be the film that marked Guru Dutt's mental decline towards suicide, as its failure at the box office led to his refusal to direct another film. Many believe that he actually directed *Sahib bibi aur ghulam* (1961) and *Chaudhvin ka chand* (1960), in which he starred, but that he did not want to be named as the director. However, this seems to have much to do with the confusion between the author, Guru Dutt, and the character he plays in this film, Suresh Sinha. A further echo of 'real life' was the fact that, just as the married Suresh Sinha was in love with Shanti (Waheeda Rehman), so Guru Dutt was said to be in love with his leading actress, with his marriage to playback singer Geeta Dutt breaking down. This whole feel of the film, which exposed too much about the director and the film industry, is sometimes cited to explain why the film did poorly on release but became a classic in subsequent years. It seems more likely that the film's dark mood was not initially appealing, but that its other qualities led to its subsequent appreciation.

The film traces the fall of the film director, Sinha, who, as the maker of *Devdas*, is presumably loosely based on P. C. Barua. His decline is both personal and professional, ending in his death in his director's chair. *Kaagaz ke phool* is an unusual film, in that the hero's marriage has broken down beyond repair. He is separated from his wife, Bina (Veena), at least in part because her snobbish upper-class family look down on his work in the film industry. The relationship between the two is ambiguous. Suresh falls in love with another woman, Shanti (hired to play Paro in the film), who is presented as pure and good. While she seems willing to enter into a relationship with him, even though he is married, his daughter from his first marriage persuades her that this relationship is damaging his family. When she withdraws from the film world to take solace in teaching, Suresh falls into a downward spiral of

alcoholism and self-hatred, and his professional life collapses.

It is said that Sahir Ludhianvi had fallen out with S. D. Burman after they both worked on Guru Dutt's *Pyaasa*, so the pairing could not be repeated. The lyrics of Kaifi Azmi include some happy numbers, but its main songs foreground the betrayal of relationships ('Dekhi zamaane ki yaari') and the impermanence of the self and of love ('Waqt ne kiya').

The first Indian film to be shot in CinemaScope, it is notable, like most of Guru Dutt's films, for the superb black-and-white photography of V. K. Murthy. The use of lighting and shots creates an atmosphere of beauty, half in love with death, that is very much in the Romantic tradition as well as that of Urdu poetry.

Dir.: Guru Dutt; **Scr./Dial**.: Abrar Alvi; **DOP**: V. K. Murthy; **Music**: S. D. Burman; **Lyrics**: Kaifi Azmi; **Selected Cast**: Guru Dutt, Waheeda Rehman, Baby Naaz, Johnny Walker, Mahesh Kaul, Veena, Minoo Mumtaz; **Prod. Co**.: Guru Dutt Films; Black and white.

(*Opposite page*) Guru Dutt in *Kaagaz ke phool*

Kabhi kabhie
India, 1976 – 177 mins
Yash Chopra

Yash Chopra was making *Deewaar* at the same time as *Kabhi kabhie* and was working with some of the same cast. In *Kabhi kabhie*, this included actors who had worked across several decades, from the veteran (Waheeda Rehman) to the very young (Rishi Kapoor and Neetu Singh), with some actors like Amitabh Bachchan and Raakhee playing young lovers and then an older generation.

Amit Malhotra (Amitabh Bachchan) woos Pooja (Raakhee) with his poetry but, in accordance with their parents' wishes, she marries an architect Vijay Khanna (Shashi Kapoor) while Amit goes into the family business. Pooja and Vijay form a happy family with their son, Vicki (Rishi Kapoor), who falls in love with Pinky (Neetu Singh), the daughter of Dr and Mrs Kapoor (Parikshit Sahni and Simi Garewal). The Kapoors and the Khannas discuss the dilemma they face in telling Pinky that she is adopted. Pinky finds her birth-mother, Anjali (Waheeda Rehman), who pretends to her husband, Amit, and their daughter, Sweetie (Naseem), that she is her niece. When Vicki arrives, he hides his connection with Pinky and works in Amit's quarry; Sweetie falls in love with him. Vijay brings Pooja with him on a business trip to build a hotel. When he realises that Pooja and Amit were lovers, he laughs it off, but when Amit finds out that Pinky is the illegitimate child of Anjali and an airforce pilot who died before their marriage, he rejects Anjali. Events come to a head when Sweetie, on discovering that Vicki and Pinky are lovers, tries to commit suicide by heading for the part of the quarry where the blasting is about to begin. She is saved by the concerted efforts of all. Amit suddenly remembers Anjali and rushes back to the house to find her about to leave. The film ends with the marriage of Vicki and Pinky, where the three sets of parents perform the rites and Sweetie is the bridesmaid.

Kabhi kabhie weaves together two different stories, contrasting romantic love over two generations in the context of love in the nuclear family unit. The first story, the Romantic poet who cannot free himself from the past, was inspired by the life of the film's lyricist, Sahir Ludhianvi, while the second is about adoption and its impact on families.

The theme of family love is very strongly developed here and is used to establish a generational contrast. The happy families are those who place an emphasis on trust and love. The norm is the nuclear family, characterised by great love between husbands and wives, parents and children, whether natural or adopted, the joking relationships of in-laws and the love of friends for each other. The final scene allows Pinky's adopted parents, her natural parents and her new husband's parents to take an equal part in the *kanyadaan* or the giving away of the bride.

Dir./Co-scr.: Yash Chopra; **Story**: Pamela Chopra; **Co-scr./Dial.**: Sagar Sarhadi; **DOP**: Kay Gee, Romesh Bhalla; **Music**: Khayyam, **Lyrics**: Sahir Ludhianvi; **Selected Cast**: Amitabh Bachchan, Shashi Kapoor, Waheeda Rehman, Raakhee, Neetu Singh, Rishi Kapoor, Naseem; **Prod. Co.**: Yash Raj Films; Colour.

Kaho na pyaar hai
India, 2000 – 172 mins
Rakesh Roshan

Although there was much hype around the debut of Rakesh Roshan's son, Hrithik Roshan, no one anticipated the hysteria that would ensue from this film. Rakesh Roshan had made films that did well at the box office but was never seen as a major film-maker. This film was to have starred Shah Rukh Khan, who had been hugely popular, along with Salman Khan, in Roshan's previous film, *Karan Arjun* (1995). However, as he was unable to appear, Roshan decided to launch his son's career.

The story was largely forgettable – or, at least, was memorable only for the strange device of having Hrithik's character die at the end of the first half, only for him to reappear as a totally unrelated double in the second half, joining forces with the heroine to avenge the first hero's death.

While the film was shot in beautiful locations of Thailand and New Zealand, and Amisha Patel was fine as the heroine, the film's success rested entirely on Hrithik's shoulders. Hindi cinema had not produced a new male star since the early 1990s when the three Khans (Shah Rukh, Aamir and Salman, none of whom is related) had dominated the box office. Although much was made by some political groups of the fact that Hrithik was a Hindu, this was not even a point of discussion among his fans. Hrithik looked different from the other stars: he was taller, thinner, muscled and fair-skinned with green eyes. He was also an extraordinary dancer, with a rubber-limbed ability that none of the other stars could match. He seemed able to master complicated routines with no effort. In the months following the release of *KNPH*, it was as if the other film stars no longer existed. Even King Khan (Shah Rukh) seemed to have fallen from his number one slot. However, although Hrithik was appreciated in several films after this, he did not have another major box-office success until the multi-starrer *Kabhi khushi kabhie gham*, while his next solo hit was another film made by his father, *Koi mil gaya* (2003).

The songs, composed by Hrithik's uncle, Rajesh Roshan, were catchy and fresh, and became all the rage, from the title song, 'Chand sitare', and 'Pyar ki kashti mein', to two by the popular young singer Lucky Ali, 'Na tum jaano na hum' and 'Ek pal ka jeena'.

However, the success of the film and Hrithik's debut was marred by the underworld attack on Rakesh Roshan, who was shot and seriously wounded, though he later made a full recovery. This was one of the few cases of the underworld actually carrying out the threats it is said to have made against several producers who made hugely successful films, highlighting the very real dangers faced by the film world.

Dir./Story: Rakesh Roshan; **Scr.**: Honey Irani, Ravi Kapoor; **Dial.**: Sagar Sarhadi; **DOP**: Kabir Lal; **Music**: Rajesh Roshan; **Lyrics**: Vijay Akela, Ibrahim Ashq, Sawan Kumar; **Selected Cast**: Hrithik Roshan, Amisha Patel, Anupam Kher, Dalip Tahil; **Prod. Co.**: Filmcraft; Colour.

Karz
India, 1980 – 160 mins
Subhash Ghai

One of the most popular films dealing with reincarnation (see also *Madhumati*), in Hindi cinema, *Karz* is closely based on an American film, *The Reincarnation of Peter Proud* (1974), and differs in some respects from the norm, which would have, for example, the same actor playing the person who is reincarnated.

Ravi Varma (Raj Kiran) marries Kamini (Simi Garewal). However, she is after his fortune and murders him according to a plan hatched with her late father's business partner, Sir Judas (Premnath). She then evicts Ravi's widowed mother (Durga Khote) and sister from the family house, so that Sir Judas can take over the whole estate. Twenty years later, a young singing star, Monty (Rishi Kapoor), falls into a trance when he plays a particular song and then imagines he sees a woman killing a man. He falls in love with Tina (Tina Munim), whom he pursues to Ooty. Her uncle Kabir (Pran), a friend of Ravi's father, starts to realise that Monty is an incarnation of Ravi and that Kamini is a murderer. Monty meets Ravi's mother, who is blind but senses that her son has come back, and his sister then sets out to avenge the debt (*karz*) of his own murder in a previous life . . .

One of the many religious elements is the association of murder and revenge with the image of Kali: Kamini kills Raj in front of a shrine of Kali, and this is the location where Monty eventually takes his revenge on Kamini. Wendy Doniger has traced the mythological elements in this film, which include the role of the mother, who is the paragon of virtue typical of the hero's mother in a Hindi film. She invokes Kali in the film, while Kamini's evil is contrasted with a picture of the Virgin Mary and child that hangs in her room. Doniger also notes the mythic resonances of the two 'rapes' (one staged by the uncle's friends to test the hero; another by the hero's friends so he can 'rescue' her) and of Kamini's similarities to other demons. She also notices the image of the mare-

Songbook showing Rishi Kapoor performing 'Om shanti om' in *Karz*

headed goddess of classical mythology, which rarely appeared after the medieval period but which features the exorcism sequence. Doniger shows how some of these mythological references may have been used deliberately, while others are probably subconscious.

Rishi Kapoor was no longer the teenager he was in *Bobby* seven years earlier, but Tina Munim looks very young and innocent in the film. Among the several memorable songs ('Dard-e dil', 'Ek haseena thi') is 'Om shanti om', a disco number, in which Rishi Kapoor, in a white satin suit, dances on a giant record turntable, backed by dancers dressed in 'tribal' outfits.

Dir.: Subhash Ghai; **Story**: Mukta Films Story Department; **Scr.**: Sachin Bhowmick; **Dial.**: Dr Rahi Masoom Raza; **DOP**: Kamalakar Rao; **Music**: Laxmikant–Pyarelal; **Lyrics**: Anand Bakshi; **Selected Cast**: Rishi Kapoor, Tina Munim, Simi Garewal, Raj Kiran, Premnath, Pran, Durga Khote; **Prod. Co.**: Mukta Films; Colour.

Khalnayak
India, 1993 – 190 mins
Subhash Ghai

This film was mired in controversy on release, over the supposed relationship between the two main stars and the alleged obscene lyrics of one of the songs, but mostly about Sanjay Dutt's arrest on suspected terrorism. A still from the film of Balu Balram (Sanjay Dutt) in captivity was used in the press as if it were a photograph of Dutt himself. In retrospect, despite the gaping holes in the story and the strange characterisation of the heroine, this film is enjoyable for its stars, its songs and its glamour.

Balu Balram assassinates a politician and is caught at the scene by police officer Ram (Jackie Shroff). Sentenced to twenty years, he keeps attacking people, including Ram. When Ram visits his girlfriend Ganga (Madhuri Dixit), a prison warden, Balu escapes and Ram is discredited. To redeem his honour, Ganga plans to capture Balu by going undercover as a dancer. On their journey, pursued by Ram, Balu, although he knows Ganga's true identity, falls in love with her and she develops a soft spot for him. Ram, who was a childhood friend of Balu, gets Balu's mother (Raakhee) involved and we learn how Balu became pulled into the criminal world. Ganga lets Balu escape and she is put on trial and sentenced to seven years. When Balu appears in court to confirm that she is 'pavitra' (that is, she did not have sex with him), she is acquitted and walks free with Ram.

Madhuri Dixit is one of the outstanding heroines of Hindi film. Beautiful, a good actress and an excellent dancer, she brings elegance to dances that would otherwise look tacky. Sanjay Dutt uses his overwhelming presence and decadent face, along with a highly toned body, to advantage to show both anger and sadness in the typical manner of a Hindi film hero. Jackie Shroff has surprisingly little to do for a senior actor and one of Subhash Ghai's favourites.

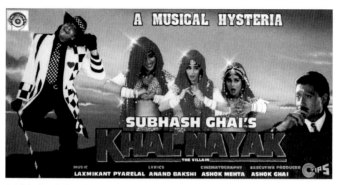

Publicity for *Khalnayak*

The film is most famous, if not notorious, for the song 'Choli ke peeche' ('Underneath My Blouse'), whose risqué lyrics, erotic choreography by Saroj Khan, catchy music and Madhuri's dancing make it a gem of Indian cinema. This far outshines any other item songs, notably one where Sophie (Ramya), Balu's girlfriend and a club dancer, performs 'Khalnayak' in a tacky and unfortunate outfit. Sanjay Dutt also does a version of the same song in another bizarre outfit that is part Batman's Joker, part Michael Jackson. However, Subhash Ghai is one of the masters of shooting Hindi film songs, and here he shows how they can be used to provide spectacle and emotion rather than any narrative function. For example, in 'Palkhi pe hoke sawaar chali re', during which she is travelling along a road, Madhuri goes through numerous costume changes and encounters with strangely dressed people, but its effect is such that one willingly suspends the criteria of realism.

The religious overtones of the film are often laboured. The comparison by the mother of her son, a murderer, to Jesus is unfortunate, but many well-known references to Hindu mythology are also made. Ganga, the Ganges, is pure, and Ram, Lord Ram, is righteous. Balram is the younger brother of Krishna and an incarnation of Vishnu. Balu's mother compares her naughty son to Lord Krishna, famed for his childhood pranks, and the drama over Ganga's purity draws on the story of the return of Sita after having been held captive by Ravan.

Dir.: Subhash Ghai; **Scr**.: Ram Kelkar; **Dial**.: Kamlesh Pandey; **DOP**: Ashok Mehta; **Music**: Laxmikant–Pyarelal; **Lyrics**: Anand Bakshi; **Selected Cast**: Sanjay Dutt, Jackie Shroff, Madhuri Dixit, Raakhee, Anupam Kher; **Prod. Co**.: Mukta Arts; Colour.

Khazanchi
India, 1941 – 171 mins
Moti B. Gidwani

This is an example of the work of the studio in Lahore that was a centre of the Indian film industry before partition and is now the home of 'Lollywood' or the Pakistani film industry. A huge hit, it is one of the films that helped to establish the musical style of the Hindi film industry in subsequent years.

Shadilal (M. Ismail), the *khazanchi* (cashier) must take some jewellery to Bombay. His son Kanwal (S. D. Narang) wants to marry Madhuri (Ramola), the daughter of the rich Durgadas (Durga Mota), but the wicked Ramesh (Ajmal) is determined to marry her to get his hands on her wealth. The news comes from Bombay that Shadilal has murdered an actress and stolen her jewellery, although it seems that Ramesh was involved in hiring a vamp and putting powder in his drink . . .

The film puts great emphasis on the modern, with shots of clocks, banks, bicycles, train and phones. It uses many outdoor locations, and its stars, who are mostly fairly ordinary-looking, though well dressed, give strong performances. (Pran, who goes on to play a villain, then also a hero's friend in Hindi films, has a small role in the film.)

The outstanding feature of this film is its music composed by Ghulam Haider, especially 'Saawan ke nazaare hain', 'Ek kali naazon ki pali' and 'Nainon ke baan'. Originally a dentist from Sind, Haider had previously worked in Calcutta but his first hits were those he composed for Pancholi, introducing the young Noor Jehan, although Shamshad Begum was the main Pancholi singer. In this film, he uses Noor Jehan as a playback singer, though she does not act. *Khazanchi* was Haider's biggest hit, his music drawing on Punjabi and light classical styles; using Punjabi rhythms and instruments like the *dholak* (a kind of drum), it became a huge craze across the country. After this he moved to Bombay, where he had several hits and famously 'discovered' Lata Mangeshkar, before moving back to Lahore after partition, leaving the field open for Naushad, the other music director who, with him, shaped the history of Hindi film music.

Dir.: Moti B. Gidwani; **Story/Scr./Dial**.: Dalsukh M. Pancholi; **DOP**: Badri Dass; **Music**: Ghulam Haider; **Lyrics**: Walli; **Selected Cast**: M. Ismail, Ramola, S. D. Narang, Manorama, Durga Mota; **Prod. Co**.: Pancholi Art Pictures; Black and white.

Kismet
India, 1943 – 143 mins
Gyan Mukherjee

One of the most popular films of all time, *Kismet* ran for several years. It was the last of a long string of successes for Bombay Talkies (including *Achhut kanya*), when, after Himanshu Rai's death, a group, including Ashok Kumar, broke away to form Filmistan before coming back to Bombay Talkies after Devika Rani's departure, for one great swansong with *Mahal* (1949).

As soon as Shekhar (Ashok Kumar) is released from jail, he returns to stealing. Chased by the police, he hides in a house which turns out to be the home of Rani (Mumtaz Shanti), an actress who was disabled after an accident. Her father used to be a theatre-owner but the villainous new owner, Indrajit, is chasing them for a debt. Shekhar pays this off and he and Rani fall in love, but he continues to steal, giving her a stolen necklace and robbing Indrajit of the money needed for Rani's treatment. After another spell in jail, he is reunited with his wealthy parents.

This film was criticised at the time of its release for promoting crime, even in this Robin-Hood style of theft. However, this became the most famous role for Ashok Kumar, who was previously paired with Devika Rani (for example, in *Achhut kanya*) and with Leela Chitnis (for example, in *Kangan* [1939]) as a romantic hero. He became a cult figure for this anti-hero role of a smooth-talking, cigarette-smoking thief. It is said that a whole generation imitated his style of smoking.

The music for *Kismet* was composed by Anil Biswas, who worked at Sagar and National Studios before joining Bombay Talkies. The hits from the film included 'Ghar ghar mein Diwali' and 'Dheere dheere aa'. One of the most memorable sequences in the film is the song 'Dur hato o duniyawalon', in which a staged (theatrical) patriotic number presents the emblems of the Indian nation – from military images and the appearance of several soldiers, the map of (as yet undivided) India, several prominent buildings (the Qutb Minar, the Taj) and a variety of

The famous song 'Dur hato o duniyawalon' in *Kismet*

ethnic and regional costumes, to a static image of Mother India, the goddess created by Indian nationalism, who blesses the audience (both in the theatre as well as in the cinema hall). While it is surprising that these images got past the British censors, the words were even clearer. With a chorus partly comprised of soldiers, the song describes India's unity, declaring that it would be wrong for anyone to lay claim to this country because 'India is ours'. The chorus sings 'Foreigners keep out' several times until we are finally told that the foreigners in question are Germans or Japanese, rather than the British we might have expected.

Kismet was one of the first films to have a 'lost and found' theme, in which families were divided and reunited, where family members are often acquainted and develop close bonds for one another without realising they are related. Many successful films like *Waqt* and *Amar, Akbar, Anthony* took up this theme, albeit in more elaborate forms.

Dir.: Gyan Mukherjee; **Story/Scr./Dial.**: P. L. Santoshi, Shaheed Latif, **DOP**: R. D. Pareenja; **Music**: Anil Biswas, Lyrics: Pradeep; **Selected Cast**: Ashok Kumar, Mumtaz Shanti, Shah Nawaz, Moti, P. F. Pithawala; **Prod. Co.**: Bombay Talkies; Black and white.

Kuch kuch hota hai
India, 1998 – 177 mins
Karan Johar

Karan Johar established himself among the A-list in Hindi cinema with his debut film. Son of producer Yash Johar and former assistant to Aditya Chopra, Karan brought his flamboyant and emotional style to the Yash Raj school of film-making. Starring the Yash Raj couple, Shah Rukh and Kajol, who had been such a success in *DDLJ*, the film developed around a college romance, with the hero, Rahul (Shah Rukh Khan), forsaking his tomboy of a best friend Anjali (Kajol), with whom he has never associated any romantic notions, for the more sophisticated Tina (Rani Mukherjee). After Tina's death, he brings up their daughter (Sana Saeed), who is the focus of his whole life. Unbeknown to him, Tina left their daughter, named after Anjali, eight letters, one to be given to her each year on her birthday by Rahul's mother (Farida Jalal). The letters reveal that Tina realised that Anjali was in love with Rahul, who could have fallen in love with her, and she asks her daughter to reunite her father with Anjali, which becomes her life goal, in which she is supported by her grandmother.

Karan talks freely about how he was inspired by various other films in the making of *KKHH*, including the theme of the legacy of the eight letters. The film does not aim to depict lifestyles in a realistic manner but in an aspirational and glamorous way. The college was supposedly Bombay's St Xavier's College but these scenes were actually filmed in Mauritius, where the students wear American designer sportswear, play basketball and have wild dance parties. The children go to an American-style summer camp, albeit one fused with a surfeit of Indian nationalist spirit. The protagonists all live the sumptuous lifestyles created by the Yash Raj production house.

Key to Karan's work is the occasional strong sentimentality and emotional intensity of the script, such as when the young girl has to speak on the subject of *Maa* ('Mum') at a speech competition, or when

Rahul tells Anjali that he is in love and she is devastated to find out that he means Tina and not her, or in the final reunion of the couple. Karan cast the two premier actors for weepies, Kajol and Shah Rukh, combining this with a strong script and good use of music to focus the audience's emotions. Also, there is much laughter in the film and there is much self-sacrifice, from Anjali's intended (Salman Khan) to Tina's last desire that her absence in the family should be filled by their friend Anjali. Farah Khan's choreography is ideally suited to the characters, while the music is highly situational, with song picturisations that intensify the emotionality of the film.

Karan continued this style in his next film, the multi-starrer, *Kabhi khushi kabhie gham*, where it became almost a self-parody, and in the film he produced but did not direct, the weepie *Kal ho na ho* (2003), but he has recently experimented with a new genre in *Kaal* (2005), which is a thriller.

Dir./Story/Scr./Dial.: Karan Johar; **DOP**: Santosh C. Thundiiayil; **Music**: Jatin–Lalit; **Lyrics**: Sameer; **Selected Cast**: Shahrukh Khan, Kajol, Rani Mukherjee, Farida Jalal, Salman Khan; **Prod. Co.**: Dharma Productions; Colour.

Lagaan/Once Upon a Time in India
India, 2001 – 224 mins
Ashutosh Gowariker

Lagaan became internationally known when it was nominated for an Oscar for best foreign film, one of the very few times an Indian film has been recognised in this way. It was not a huge box-office success internationally but has become a benchmark against which Indian films must measure themselves in the hope of gaining further recognition.

The year 1893, Champaner village, north India. As in the other princely states of British India, the villagers have to pay an agricultural tax, *lagaan*. The Raja pleads with Captain Russell (Paul Blackthorne) to lower the tax as the rains have failed and the villagers will starve, but he is ordered instead to raise double tax, *dugna lagaan*. Annoyed by the villagers' rebellious nature, in particular Bhuvan's (Aamir Khan) comparison of cricket to their game *gulli-danda*, Russell says he will excuse them tax for three years if the villagers beat the British at cricket. If they lose, they will have to pay extra tax. The villagers are unwilling to take the risk, but Bhuvan encourages them one by one to join him in his fight against British injustice. Bhuvan tries to teach the villagers what he thinks are the rules of cricket, but they are clearly in need of help. This comes in the form of Russell's sister, Elizabeth (Rachel Shelley), whose sense of fair play and enthusiasm for India (she masters Hindi in a matter of days) persuade her to oppose her brother by coaching the village XI. Gauri (Gracy Singh), the village girl who dreams of marrying Bhuvan, realises that Elizabeth is in love with him, but Bhuvan has no delusions about his future. The other villagers unite against the enemy, Hindu, Muslim and Sikh, high and low caste. During the three-day match (which lasts longer on screen than the average Hollywood movie), the villagers face many setbacks, not least Lakha's treachery, but Bhuvan wins against all odds and the villagers are relieved from their taxation. Gauri and Bhuvan are now ready to marry, while the other villagers return to their daily routine. Elizabeth returns to England, while her brother is posted to Africa.

Aamir Khan, a pin-up as college kid and streetwise rough, abandons his jeans and leather jackets for a *dhoti* and bare chest, portraying the heroic nineteenth-century village leader with style. The eight main village men are clearly depicted as individuals, each with his own strengths and weaknesses. Bhuvan uses their traditional skills in the cricket match, deploying the farmer's ability with stone and sling as idiosyncratic bowling, while another's dexterity in catching chickens strengthens his fielding. The disabled Dalit, in an excellent twist, invents spin bowling and allows Bhuvan to make his final bid for village unity in a reformist speech about caste. Gauri is charming as the traditional village beauty, while the surprisingly convincing British actors make a brave stab at the Hindi dialogues.

The sets, locations and costumes are superb. The bleak landscape of Bhuj and its palaces (later devastated in the 2001 earthquake) are supplemented with meticulous sets, while the villagers are dressed in appropriate style rather than presented as glamorous city girls. A. R. Rahman's score is superlative, with many of the songs becoming major hits in their own right. The dance sequences are choreographed by different dance directors to bring out rural or British styles, or romance, which is very different from the MTV-style routines popular elsewhere.

In 2001, two other new historical films (*Asoka* [2001] and *Gadar*) were released. Despite the critical success of *Lagaan* and the huge box-office success of *Gadar*, there have been surprisingly few others (unless one counts remakes of films such as *Devdas* and *Parineeta*, which are set in the past). It remains to be seen if others will follow.

Dir.: Ashutosh Gowariker; **Story**: Ashutosh Gowariker; **Scr.**: Kumar Dave, Sanjay Dayma, Ashutosh Gowariker; **Dial.**: K. P. Saxena; **DOP**: Anil Mehta; **Music**: A. R. Rahman; **Lyrics**: Javed Akhtar; **Selected Cast**: Aamir Khan, Gracy Singh, Rachel Shelley, Paul Blackthorne, Suhasini Mulay; **Prod. Co.**: Aamir Khan Productions; Colour.

Madhumati
India, 1958 – 179 mins
Bimal Roy

Madhumati was the biggest hit of director Bimal Roy. His hallmark neo-realist images and social concern are evident in this unusual reincarnation/ghost story scripted by Ritwik Ghatak, later acclaimed as one of India's greatest directors. Two of the top stars of Hindi cinema, Dilip Kumar and Vyjayanthimala, take multiple roles in this complex narrative.

Devendra (Dilip Kumar) is on his way to collect his wife and child from the station when he and his friend are forced to take shelter from the storm in an old mansion. Devendra has a sense of déjà vu and tells the story of his previous birth. Anand (Dilip Kumar) was a manager of a timber estate who fell in love with a tribal girl, Madhumati (Vyjayanthimala) he met during his walks in the forest. The owner of the timber concern is Ugranarayan (Pran), who comes to hate Anand. When Anand confronts Ugranarayan about his connection with Madhumati's disappearance, he is beaten up. He meets a girl in the forest called Madhavi (Vyjayanthimala), who looks identical to Madhumati. He gets her to pretend to be Madhumati's ghost, whose appearance so frightens Ugranarayan that he confesses to her murder and is arrested. However, Anand realises that Madhavi really is Madhumati's ghost when she shows him where she fell to her death running away from Ugranarayan. Just as Devendra reveals that his present wife is Madhumati, news arrives that her train has crashed. However, when he reaches the station, his wife Radha (Vyjayanthimala) appears, unhurt, with their child.

Although the story was much criticised as melodramatic and unconvincing, it is gripping and well told. The film depicts negotiations in a transitional society between powerful social groups of *zamindars* (landowners), tribal rulers and new middle-class professionals. Bimal Roy creates an atmosphere to suit the uncanny in this almost gothic ghost story, which he connects to the theme of reincarnation.

Dilip Kumar is as charming as ever as the middle-class professional with a passion for art and nature, while Vyjayanthimala, besides looking stunning in the Hindi-film idea of tribal clothes, shines in both her acting and dancing. Pran is wonderfully villainous and it was films like *Madhumati* that established him as India's top villain.

Salil Choudhury composed a set of songs for this film that I think constitute one of the best scores of any Hindi film. Many people (including Lata Mangeshkar) would choose 'Aa ja re pardesi' as one of their favourite Hindi film songs, but there is also the ever popular 'Suhana safar' and the catchy 'Dil tadap tadap' or 'Ghadi ghadi mera dil dhadke' as well as the sad 'Toote hue khwabon ne'. With the exception of the latter, the songs are mostly joyful and happy, which may seem surprising in view of the uncanny, romantic atmosphere of the film, but they work wonderfully within the film itself too.

Dir.: Bimal Roy; **Story/Scr.**: Ritwik Ghatak; **Dial.**: Rajinder Singh Bedi; **DOP**: Dilip Gupta; **Music**: Salil Choudhury; **Lyrics**: Shailendra; **Selected Cast**: Dilip Kumar, Vyjayanthimala, Johnny Walker, Jayant, Tarun Bose, Pran; **Prod. Co.**: Bimal Roy Films; Black and white.

Maine pyar kiya
India, 1989 – 192 mins
Sooraj Barjatya

Maine pyar kiya is a landmark film, partly because it was the debut of
Sooraj Barjatya (who later made *Hum aapke hain koun . . .!*), partly
because it marked a revival in the popularity of young romances which
began with *Qayamat se qayamat tak*. There are discontinuities with these
romances, and *MPK* stands apart. Yash Chopra's earlier romances, in
which the eroticism and romanticism are carried as much by words
(dialogues and lyrics) as visuals, seem now an elegy to Urdu poetry and
its imagery. In *MPK*, eroticism has almost vanished, apart from the
monochrome opening sequences, where a modern dance is performed

Salman Khan and Bhagyashree in *Maine pyar kiya*

to a Hindi version of Stevie Wonder's 'I Just Called'. The female body is not presented for display – the heroine's appearance in a sexy dress is for the hero's eyes only as she seems to 'flash' him from behind a raincoat. Even her most romantic song, the gorgeous 'Dil deewana', is replete with her prayers for the beloved and a reminder of her procreative abilities made real by the presence of children. This is no girl with a past, with a life, but a sweet and innocent traditional girl who certainly knows 'how to shell peas'. In this film there is no doubt that the loving relationships offered by family ties and friendship are valued more highly than erotic love. Friendship occurs not only among men but also between men and women, in the *devar-bhabhi* (younger brother and older brother's wife) relationship seen here across two generations, which will later be serenaded so famously in *HAHK*, and in the romantic couple bound more by *dosti* ('friendship') than passion. The vamp is not sexy, just brazen, while the focus of the viewer's desiring eye is on the male body of the young, sexy Salman Khan, shown performing exercise and physical labour, shaved smoothly for a dance number in red sequins. The music was very popular and the *antakshari* (a competitive game where verses of songs are connected by their first and last syllables) sequence is a stunning piece of visual and aural nostalgia. The story refers to the young romance seen earlier in *Junglee* and *Bobby*, the conservative ideology being updated by the new features of the camp servants and the bejewelled maid, the 'Friends' baseball cap, the car-hopping pigeon and the need for the characters to say 'I love you' in English – when 'Maine pyar kiya' can no longer express their feelings.

Dir./Co-story/Scr./Dial.: Sooraj Barjatya; **Co-story**: S. M. Ahale; **DOP**: Arvind Laad; **Music**: Ramlaxman; **Lyrics**: Asad Bhopali, Dev Kohli; **Selected Cast**: Salman Khan, Bhagyashree, Alok Nath, Rajiv Verma, Rima Lagoo; **Prod. Co.**: Rajshri Productions; Colour.

Main tulsi tere aangan ki
India, 1978 – 151 mins
Raj Khosla

This is one of several films by Raj Khosla, who had an uneven career in Hindi cinema, during which he directed several outstanding films including *CID* and *Mera gaon mera desh*. His style was closely associated with that of Guru Dutt and of the Anand brothers' Naveketan films.

This film takes the theme of the Thakurs (approximately, landowning gentry) and dancing girls seen in many other films, but here the sympathy lies with both parties rather than the emphasis being on the decadence of the former. The dancing girl here is called Tulsi, evoking the sacred basil who is wedded to Vishnu, but the story highlights the story of Vrinda, a prostitute who fell in love with Krishna (an incarnation of Vishnu), but could not marry him, so remained, like the *tulsi*, outside in his *aangan* (courtyard), the public area of the house.

In this total melodrama or 'woman's weepie', we see Tulsi (Asha Parekh), a dancing girl, being saved from rape by a client in her brothel by Thakur (Vijay Anand), who installs her in a safe house before falling in love with her. He wants to marry her but when his mother suffers a heart attack at the news, Tulsi makes him promise her that he will marry a suitable girl, Sanjukta (Nutan). Tulsi and Thakur have a son, Ajay, but when Sanjukta orders her to leave, Tulsi drinks poison. Sanjukta is as grief-stricken as her husband and, even after Thakur dies, promises to bring Ajay up as an equal to her own son. Ajay is sent to study in a convent and comes home as an adult (Vinod Khanna), although no one knows who he is. The rest of the film concentrates on the mother's relationship with her good stepson, Ajay, and the bad son, her own son, Pratap (Deb Mukherjee). Pratap has to deal with his jealousy of Ajay, who, every bit as saintly as his mother, finds his place in the family.

The music by Laxmikant–Pyarelal includes the theme song, 'Main tulsi', which is played again and again, every line packed with meaning about a woman who cannot join the family but is loving and self-sacrificing. The film finds justification in a religious story for an illicit relationship. Its argument is that love and sin have become confused and the sin is the family's restrictions on such relationships, whereas love, the most important value, cannot be a sin. While Tulsi is totally devoted and self-sacrificing, Sanjukta, whose reaction to finding out about her husband's mistress and her demand for her to leave seem quite reasonable (she could not have anticipated Tulsi's suicide), atones for her rejection of her 'co-wife' by her penance as a widow and her recognition of Ajay as her husband's son, demonstrating that a child deserves to be loved and acknowledged whatever the circumstances of his or her birth.

Although a rather tubby Vijay Anand with a peculiar haircut is less than romantic or heroic, the Thakur element is emphasised in Vinod Khanna's macho image and in his polo-playing (which he seems to have learnt at the convent). Khanna had appeared as a villain in Khosla's earlier *Mera gaon mera desh*, but here takes the role of the long-suffering hero that he played in many of his films (notably *Qurbani*). The women are very weepy but also strong-minded, whether the saintly Tulsi (former glamour queen Asha Parekh) or the penitent Sanjukta (Nutan, best remembered for her roles in Bimal Roy films such as *Bandini*).

Dir.: Raj Khosla; **Story/Scr.**: G. R. Kamat; **Dial.**: Dr Rahi Masoom Reza; **DOP**: Pratap Sinha; **Music**: Laxmikant–Pyarelal; **Lyrics**: Anand Bakshi; **Selected Cast**: Nutan, Vinod Khanna, Vijay Anand, Asha Parekh, Deb Mukherjee, Neeta Mehta; **Prod. Co.**: Raj Khosla Films; Colour.

Masoom
India, 1982 – 143 mins
Shekhar Kapur

This story of an illegitimate child is a real weepie, which picks up the
theme of forgiveness that runs through so many Hindi movies. It is said
to be based on *Man, Woman and Child* (1982), a film adapted from the
book of the same name by Erich Segal of *Love Story* fame, although, in a
seeming reversal of trends, this version by Gulzar seems less
melodramatic than the western one.

D. K. Malhotra (Naseeruddin Shah) lives a seemingly idyllic life with his
beautiful wife Indu (Shabana Azmi) and their two little girls, Twinkle (the
young Urmila Matondkar, who later became a star in *Rangeela*) and Minni
(Aradhana, a true star who, I believe, died soon after the film was made).
However, it emerges that he had had an affair with Bhavna (Supriya
Pathak), a desperately lonely women, at his college reunion and a son,
Rahul (the young Jugal Hansraj), was born. After Bhavna's death, D. K. is
told about Rahul, who comes to live with D. K.'s family in Delhi. Indu
cannot forgive her husband, whom she now rejects, and refuses to accept
Rahul. Indu uses harsh words to Rahul but occasionally moves towards him,
only to draw away again. The girls welcome Rahul immediately and D. K.
and Rahul develop a close relationship, although D. K. cannot bring himself
to tell his son that he is his father whom he hopes one day will come to find
him. Rahul finds a letter that reveals his parentage and runs away. Indu
tries to accept him but cannot until the ultimate moment of the film.

The theme of forgiveness runs throughout. Even Bhavna's 'sin' is
forgiven by the narrative, as her affair with D. K. is explained as the
action of someone deprived of all affection. The girls and Rahul are
shown to be naturally forgiving and accepting of others, and are clearly
the model to follow. Both the protagonists are in need of forgiveness:
D. K. needs Indu to forgive him for his affair, while she needs to be
forgiven for her refusal to let herself love an innocent (*masoom*) child
because of her husband's actions.

The pain of the two adult protagonists and Rahul is dwelt on at great length. It is occasionally verbalised, but the film uses gesture and performance, as well as song, to convey the emotions of the characters. The skill of the film-maker is to make us understand Indu's treatment of Rahul, even while we sympathise with him. There is only one solution, namely the reunion of all the family, but the route to this is shown to be realistically difficult.

Masoom reveals a great upper-middle-class sensibility in its characters, their occupations and lifestyle. The women's saris have an almost nostalgic value for a certain kind of elegance associated with the Delhi elite. The music is the light classical type, with haunting melodies by R. D. Burman and lyrics by Gulzar, including 'Tujhse naaraz nahin zindagi' (Lata Mangeshkar).

Naseeruddin Shah, one of India's major acting talents, delivers an outstanding performance as the errant husband and devoted father, as does Shabana Azmi, who manages to portray her deep ambivalence to the child. Saeed Jaffrey, as always, provides strong support and the children are excellent.

Shekhar Kapur has made few Hindi films but all of them have been significant, including *Mr India* and *Bandit Queen*.

Dir.: Shekhar Kapur; **Scr./Dial.**: Gulzar; **Music**: R. D. Burman; **Lyrics**: Gulzar; **DOP**: Pravin Bhatt; **Selected Cast**: Shabana Azmi, Naseeruddin Shah, Jugal Hansraj, Saeed Jaffrey, Supriya Pathak, Urmila Matondkar, Aradhana; **Prod. Co.**: Krsna Movies Ents; Colour.

Mera gaon mera desh
India, 1971 – 165 mins
Raj Khosla

While a fascinating film in its own right, *Mera gaon mera desh* is also of interest in the history of the dacoit film, especially as it clearly anticipates *Sholay*. Many elements of the latter are present in this film, from the star (Dharmendra), who is a reformed criminal, the Thakur with his gun arm missing, the name of the villain (Jabbar Singh here, later Gabbar Singh), the determining of fate by tossing a coin, and even the torture of the heroine. However, these are mostly details, this being much more like other dacoit films than a stylish spectacular like *Sholay*.

When Ajit (Dharmendra), a petty crook, leaves jail, a Thakur (Jayant), who has retired from the army, invites him to his village, which is terrorised by dacoits (rural bandits). Ajit spends his time getting drunk, and falling in love with Anju (Asha Parekh), but he keeps his distance from the villagers, just poking fun at them, until a young boy he has befriended and Anju's father are killed by dacoits, led by Jabbar Singh (Vinod Khanna). Jabbar's girlfriend, Munni (Laxmi Chhaya), flirts with Ajit and offers to help him. Ajit and Jabbar fight and Anju is captured. When Ajit comes to her rescue, he is also captured, but Munni helps them escape and defeat the dacoits.

Dharmendra and Asha Parekh were already major stars, but this film added Vinod Khanna to their number. Although he gave a good performance and looked very dashing as an evil dacoit, he moved on from villainous roles to become one of the top heroes of the 1970s, before giving up his career to follow the spiritual guru Ranjeesh/Osho. Although Laxmi Chhaya is not a well-known name in Hindi film today, it was one of her dance sequences from *Gumnaam* (1965) that was chosen to depict 'Bollywood' in Terry Zwigoff's *Ghost World* (2001).

The film was mostly shot on location around Udaipur, which is usually shown as a tourist destination (as in *Guide*, for example), with most dacoit films being set in Madhya Pradesh and Uttar Pradesh.

Two images from the film linger, both of them representations of women that may well make the viewer uneasy. One is the scene of Ajit beating up Munni in the river when he thinks she has betrayed him. It is quite graphic and the sight of a hero hitting a woman so forcefully may shock some audiences. In another scene, the vamp Munni sings the hit song 'Maar diya jaaye ya chod diya jaaye', waving a knife as she dances around the hero and heroine, who are tied up while Jabbar watches. Although she eventually cuts their ropes, before that she cuts the strings that hold Anju's bodice together and draws blood from Ajit. Again the pleasures of this scene seem somewhat transgressive and tend towards the sado-masochistic.

The music of this film remains popular, other hits including the song at the *mela* (fair), the romantic duet, 'Kuch kehta hai yeh sawan', 'Sona lei ja re, chandi lei ja re' and 'Hai sharmaoon kis kis ko bataoon', among others.

Dir.: Raj Khosla; **Scr**.: G. R. Kamat; **Dial**.: Akhtar Romani; **DOP**: Pratap Sinha; **Music**: Laxmikant–Pyarelal; **Lyrics**: Anand Bakshi; **Selected Cast**: Asha Parekh, Dharmendra, Vinod Khanna, Laxmi Chhaya, Jayant; **Prod. Co**: Khosla Enterprises; Colour.

Mother India
India, 1957 – 168 mins
Mehboob Khan

Mother India has come to be regarded as the quintessential Indian film, a new national epic, in particular in its treatment of the essence of the Indian woman. It remains hugely popular and was the only Indian film to receive an Oscar nomination as Best Foreign Film until *Salaam Bombay!* (1988) and *Lagaan*. It has a powerful storyline, top stars and great music by Naushad, as well as spectacular visuals, especially the shots of Radha and sons with a plough, taken in the style of Soviet realism.

Among his many hits, Mehboob made a film called *Aurat* ('Woman'), of which *Mother India* was a remake. The film presents the nation as woman, but it also presents the woman as nation. Mother India was a goddess created by the nationalist movement in the nineteenth century, who, like Mother Earth, is a 'secular' goddess. Radha (Nargis) is also associated with other goddesses, and the film abounds in mythological references to Krishna, Ram and other deities. Although many of those involved in the film were Muslim (including Nargis, Mehboob and Naushad), the film refers only to Hindus, with Muslim residents notably absent from the village.

The film presents viewers with a deep ambivalence, which is never resolved, between the traditional Indian village, where life is grim but lightened by moments of pleasure, and a utopian modern India of dams, machinery and the state itself, where life's needs are provided for but at the cost of enormous human sacrifice and misery.

Mother India concentrates on the life span of one woman, Radha, whose honour is central to the prestige of family and the whole village, and who realises her duty to uphold this in all the struggles she has to face. At the beginning of the film she is a young bride, happily married to Shyam (Raaj Kumar) and mother to several sons. However, debt and floods leave them homeless and they have to rebuild their lives. Her sons choose two different paths: the older, Ramu (Rajendra Kumar), is law-abiding and obedient, whereas Birju (Sunil Dutt) is a rebel who wants to take the law into his own hands and set the world to rights. When his conduct threatens the village's honour, Radha has no choice but to kill him. The village (or nation) is more important than the individual or the family.

Nargis' performance in this film is regarded as one of the great moments of Indian cinema. She dominates the film totally and it is regrettable that she only appeared in two or three more films after this, as she retired after marrying Sunil Dutt.

The film was also Mehboob Khan's last great hit. His was a rags-to-riches story. Said to be illiterate, he began his career in the industry as an extra and ended up as an acclaimed director, a wealthy producer and studio owner. His films (*Anmol ghadi* and *Andaz* are included in this book) featured strong stories, top stars and excellent musical scores,

Sunil Dutt, Nargis and Rajendra Kumar in *Mother India*

whichever genre he worked in. Many of the songs that Naushad composed for this film (lyrics by Shakeel Badayuni) remain popular today, especially at weddings and festivals, notably 'Pi ke ghar aaj', 'Holi aayi' and the lament 'Duniya mein hum aaye hain to jeena hi padega'.

Dir./Story/Scr.: Mehboob Khan; **Dial.**: Wajahat Mirza, Ali Raza; **DOP**: Faredoon Irani; **Music**: Naushad; **Lyrics**: Shakeel Badayuni; **Selected Cast**: Nargis, Sunil Dutt, Raaj Kumar, Rajendra Kumar, Master Sajid; **Prod. Co.**: Mehboob Productions; Colour.

Mr India
India, 1987 – 179 mins
Shekhar Kapur

Mr India is the only real 'Bollywood' film made by Shekhar Kapur, whose earlier film *Masoom* was more in the style of the parallel Hindi cinema, while his later works, *Bandit Queen* and *Elizabeth* (1998), are made in a western style. This was the last film that Salim–Javed ever worked on together, and featured their usual mix of social issues (food adulteration), populism (the moment where Mr India removes the groaning table of the decadent rich to give it to the beggars on the street) and pastiche of, and quotes from, other Hindi films, notably in a song medley.

Anil Kapoor and Sridevi were well cast in their roles in the film. Anil Kapoor (whose outfit of a tweed jacket and a canvas hat is somewhat baffling) is excellent as Arun, the son out to avenge his father's death at the hands of the evil Mogambo (Amrish Puri in a very silly blond wig, with plenty of gadgets, a pink acid pit and a great catchphrase: 'Mogambo khush hua!/Mobambo is pleased!'), who is hell-bent on taking over the world. Arun's father has left him a wristband that makes him invisible and allows him to carry out heroic acts as 'Mr India'. His chaotic life includes running a small orphanage from his house. Into this world comes Seema (Sridevi), an investigative journalist, who falls in love with the invisible Mr India, finding out later that it is the man she knows. Although she despises children, they win her over and help the couple break Mogambo's crime ring, so in the end she and Mr India become their adopted parents.

The songs by Laxmikant–Pyarelal (lyrics by Javed Akhtar) are among the film's high spots. The famous 'Hawa hawaii' song, quoted in Mira Nair's *Salaam Bombay!* (1988), is a pastiche of all nightclub songs, as Sridevi dons a bewildering change of costumes to divert the gang's attention, while she dances and performs comic turns to nonsense and silly lyrics, appearing with a motley crew of variously 'blacked-up' and camp male dancers. 'Kaate nahi katate' is one of the defining 'wet sari' sequences of Hindi cinema, when Sridevi's now iconic blue chiffon sari is soaked during an erotic encounter with an invisible man. The songs pulsating chorus 'I love you' was also much imitated on the streets. Alongside the children's performance of a medley of songs, 'Karte hai hum pyaar Mr India se' affectionately mocks film-style romance and marriage.

During this period, Sridevi was one of the few female stars whose name was a box-office attraction. After her early days in south Indian films, she soon became a major star in Hindi films, where her sexy dancing, acting skills and comic turns made her one of the last great divas. She became a Yash Chopra heroine in *Chandni* (1991) and *Lamhe*, repeating her star pairing with Anil Kapoor in the latter. Sridevi retired after her marriage to Anil Kapoor's producer brother, Boney Kapoor, but there are still rumours that she may return to cinema.

Shekhar Kapur made *Mr India* perhaps as a knowing pastiche of Hollywood and the Hindi movie. There is much in this film for the cinephile, with its many references to Hollywood films, as Arun/Mr India, blends the Invisible Man with Indiana Jones, in his struggle against a villain worthy of a Bond movie, in this blend of fantasy and detective film with *The Sound of Music*. The heroine even appears as Charlie Chaplin and performs a cabaret number when not working as a journalist on the local rag. The full *masala*, or spice, of the Hindi movie is also present throughout the film, in its narrative, song and dance. After several disastrous attempts from outside India to make pastiches or tributes to Hindi cinema, this is a reminder that it takes great skill to make this kind of film.

Dir.: Shekhar Kapur; **Story/Scr./Dia**l.: Salim–Javed; **DOP**: Baba Azmi; **Music**: Laxmikant–Pyarelal; **Lyrics**: Javed Akhtar; **Selected Cast**: Anil Kapoor, Sridevi, Amrish Puri; **Prod. Co**.: Narsimha Ents; Colour.

Mughal-e Azam
India, 1960 – 173 mins
K. Asif

Mughal-e Azam tells the story of the Great Mughal, Akbar
(r. 1556–1605). The film's making was itself something of an epic, as it
took over fifteen years to shoot, and involved a complete change of cast
(the original included Chandramohan, who played Jehangir in *Pukar*
[1939], Nargis and Sapru), several writers and so on. It had the largest
budget of any film of its day, Rs 15m, of which a large proportion was
spent on costumes, sets and extras. The cinematography is superb,
mostly black and white, with some songs shot in colour, including
Anarkali's defiant 'Pyar kiya to darna kya?', which was shot in the Sheesh
Mahal or Mirror Palace. The film has recently been coloured by computer
but I have no inclination to see it.

The story concerns Anarkali (Madhubala), a dancing girl in the
Mughal court. Prince Salim (later Emperor Jehangir) (Dilip Kumar) falls in
love with Anarkali but his father, Emperor Akbar (Prithviraj Kapoor),
forbids him to continue this affair. Salim leads a campaign against his
father, is defeated and sentenced to death. Anarkali offers to sacrifice
her life to save Salim and is buried alive, although Akbar allows her to
escape through a tunnel unknown to Salim.

It is not clear whether Anarkali was a historical person, but she was
certainly a legendary figure. A favourite story for Indian theatre, the first
film version of her life was a silent shot in 1928 by the Great Eastern
Corporation of Lahore: *The Loves of a Mogul Prince* (1928), based on
Syed Imtiaz Ali Taj's play, *Anarkali*. The Imperial Film Company of
Bombay made its own version of the film with Sulochana, and in 1952
Filmistan made *Anarkali* with Bina Rai and Pradeep Kumar, but *Mughal-e
Azam* outshone them all.

Mughal-e Azam tells Mughal history in the context of the new
nation, emphasised by the voiceover at the beginning and the depiction
of the Muslim sites of India, yet it relates family history rather than social

Madhubala dances to 'Pyar kiya to darna kya?' in *Mughal-e Azam*

history. The film brings out themes that are popular in Hindi film, notably the struggle between the father and son, and between public duty and private desires and the self-sacrificing woman. It evades issue of Hindu–Muslim relations, despite the Mughal's reputation for even-handedness, although it suggests religious tolerance in the court, as Queen Jodhabai (Durga Khote) was a Hindu and Anarkali sings a Hindu devotional song on the occasion of the birth of Krishna, Janmashtami, 'Mohe panghat pe', with Akbar participating in his wife's Hindu rituals.

Mughal-e Azam is greatly enhanced by Naushad's music (and Shakeel Badayuni's lyrics), in particular, two numbers sung by Bade

Ghulam Ali Khan ('Shubh din aayo' and 'Prem jogan banke'). As well as the two Anarki songs mentioned earlier, there is a *qawwali* and the thrillingly dramatic 'Mohabbat ki jhooti kahaani pe roye', which Anarkali sings when she is in the dungeons, bound in chains. One of the most popular songs is the wonderful *qawwali* competitions between Anarkali and Bahaar (Nigar Sultana), 'Teri mehfil mein kismat aazmaakar hum bhi dekhenge.'

The film contains perhaps the most erotic sequence of Hindi cinema, where Dilip Kumar and Madhubala, said to be off-screen lovers, are shot in close-up, Madhubala's beautiful and iconic face motionless in ecstasy as Dilip Kumar watches in adoration. From time to time they tease the viewers by hiding their faces from the camera with a white (?) feather, forbidding the audience's look but inviting their speculation.

Dir./Co-scr.: K Asif; **Co-scr./Co-dial**.: Aman; **Co-dial**.: Kamal Amrohi, Ehsan Rizvi, Wajahat Mirza; **DOP**: R. D. Mathur; **Music**: Naushad; **Lyrics**: Shakeel Badayuni; **Selected Cast**: Prithviraj Kapoor, Dilip Kumar, Madhubala, Nigar Sultana, Ajit, Durga Khote; **Prod. Co**.: Sterling Investment Corp; Black and white/colour.

Munnabhai MBBS
India, 2004 – 168 mins
Rajkumar Hirani

This is one of the rare films in recent years to have been both a critical and a commercial success, acclaimed by all its viewers, from Delhi academics to the urban 'masses' and the *mofussil* circuits. Whenever the film is mentioned, it usually produces a smile. It is unusual for a comedy to have such a wide appeal, but it was also striking that it did not do particularly well in the overseas markets, where the big romances (such as those of Yash Chopra and Karan Johar) remain the most successful.

This film is the story of a failure, Munnabhai (Sanjay Dutt), the son whose parents wanted him to become a doctor but who ended up a small-time crook. However, to keep them happy, he and his friends convert their den into a 'hospital' when his parents make their annual visit to Bombay. However, Dr Asthana (Boman Irani), a family friend and a doctor at a teaching hospital, discovers this fraud and, after his parents are humiliated by this exposure, Munnabhai is forced to keep face by registering as a student for the MBBS medical degree. Of course, he has to fake his entrance exam and fails to keep up with the studies. During this time, he falls in love with Dr Asthana's daughter, Suman or Chinki (Gracy Singh), also a doctor at the same hospital. Munnabhai shows himself to be a truly caring person, for all his rough and unorthodox ways, and brings the patients great comfort with his magic hugs ('jaadu ki jhappi'). In one case, Zaheer (Jimmy Shergill), who is dying of cancer, has not had the chance for fun and romance, so Munnabhai brings in a dancing girl to perform an item song to cheer him up. In the end, Munnabhai, realising that he cannot continue with this fraud, gives up and attempts to resolve his relationships with his parents and with Dr Asthana . . .

Sanjay Dutt brings his powerful screen presence to the title role, revelling in Munnabhai's complex mixture of thuggery, stupidity, kindness, humour and conscience. Sanjay's real-life father, Sunil Dutt

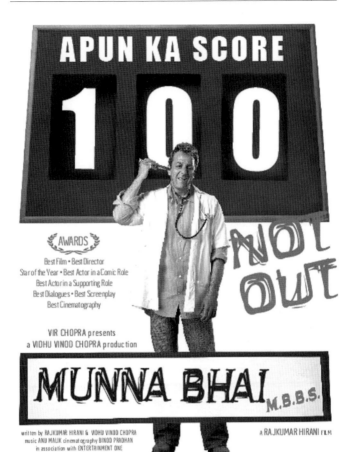

Munnabhai MBBS celebrates its run of 100 days

(who had starred in many films, including *Mother India* with Sanjay's mother, Nargis), plays his screen father in an immensely popular pairing. Arshad Warsi revived a flagging career with his hilarious performance as Munnabhai's friend, Circuit, whose use of Bambaiyaa (Bombay street slang) was much imitated following the film's release, with people repeating 'Bole to' (which functions somewhat as 'like' in colloquial forms of English). Boman Irani has rapidly become one of the most popular character actors in Hindi film, sometimes in serious roles, although his performance here makes it hard to believe that he could play anything other than a comedian. Jimmy Shergill's convincing portrayal of the innocent victim adds pathos to the film.

The songs were not great in themselves but they worked well in context, with the picturisation of the title song particularly excellent, displaying, as do many other scenes in the film, a real Bombay feel in language as well as its images. 'Dekh le', the song sung to the dying Zaheer, has become quite popular on the club scene.

Munnabhai is a comedy with a moral, showing that while children may not live up to expectations, human qualities should be valued more than material success. Everyone learns in the film how to be a better person and to be happier. It is hardly surprising that this fairytale told as comedy should be so successful or that it has been popular in a Tamil remake (*Vasool Raja, MBBS* [2004], with Kamal Hassan) and that Mira Nair (of *Salaam Bombay!* [1988] and *Monsoon Wedding* [2001] fame) has bought the rights to an English version.

Dir.: Rajkumar Hirani; **Story/Scr.**: Vidhu Vinod Chopra, Rajkumar Hirani, Lajan Joseph; **Dial.**: Abbas Tyrewala; **DOP**: Binod Pradhan; **Music**: Anu Malik; **Lyrics**: Rahat Indori, Abbas Tyrewala; **Selected Cast**: Sanjay Dutt, Sunil Dutt, Arshad Warsi, Gracy Singh, Boman Irani, Jimmy Shergill; **Prod. Co.**: Vidhu Vinod Chopra Productions; Colour.

Muqaddar ka Sikandar
India, 1978 – 189 mins
Prakash Mehra

One of Amitabh Bachchan's definitive Angry Young Man films, *MKS* sees him endlessly wronged and misunderstood, his passion marked out as doomed from its beginnings in his childhood. An orphaned Hindu, he is brought up by a Muslim foster-mother, Fatima (Nirupa Roy), who gives him a 'Muslim' name, Sikandar. A Servant in Ramnath's house, she finds him work but he falls in love with Ramnath's daughter, Kaamna, whose mother has died. Wrongly accused of stealing, he is thrown out of the house but never forgets his love. Kaamna, however, believes him to be a thief and wants nothing to do with him again.

Sikandar (Amitabh Bachchan) bursts onto the screen as a young man, on a motorbike driving around Mumbai, singing the theme song 'Muqaddar ka Sikandar' ('Man of Destiny'), apparently in control of the city though not of his own destiny. He remains in love with Kaamna (Raakhee) and anonymously pays her father's bills when he is ill.

The theme of doomed love and passion reaches out beyond Sikandar to all the other characters, played by an all-star cast. Everyone is in love with someone who rejects them – the gangster Bilawal (Amjad Khan) loves the courtesan Zohrabai (Rekha), who loves Sikandar, who loves Kaamna, who finds mutual love with the lawyer Vikas (Vinod Khanna). Kaamna does not realise that Sikandar loves her, and he cannot declare his love, as Vikas is his close friend who had earlier saved his life. Zohra kills herself to ensure that Sikandar is not tainted by his association with her (his sister's eligibility is at stake). Bilwal thinks she has killed herself because Sikandar abandoned her and they fight to the death.

The extravagant song picturisations of Kalyanji–Anandji's delightfully hybrid music more than compensates for some of the rather poor cinematic quality of the film itself. The great songs include the recurring theme, 'O saathi re', with its 1970s' sound dominated by wah-wah pedals and the fabulously outrageous rhymes of Anjaan Prakash Mehra.

This theme is first sung by the child Kaamna and later by Sikandar. The image of Zohra writhing on the floor and swinging her hips to 'Salaam-e ishq' in a shocking pink and silver dress, while Sikandar, in a funky white trousersuit watches, open-mouthed in astonishment, predates Rekha's exquisitely tasteful role as the courtesan in the eponymous *Umrao Jaan*. Vikas and Kaamna do not have a traditional love song but instead dance to 'Pyaar zindagi hai' in a grotto-like nightclub decorated with red hearts.

Prakash Mehra was one of several directors (notably Ramesh Sippy and Yash Chopra) to film Salim–Javed's scripts for Amitabh Bachchan's Angry Young Man, shooting the first of these films, *Zanjeer* (1973). Mehra's later films, including *MKS*, though not written by Salim–Javed (their dialogues are by Kader Khan), reprise this role for Amitabh, notably in *Laawaris* (1981), *Namak halal* (1982), and *Sharaabi* (1984).

Dir.: Prakash Mehra; **Story**: Lakshmikant Sharma; **Scr.**: Vijay Kaul; **Dial.**: Kader Khan; **DOP**: N. Satyen; **Music**: Kalyanji–Anandji; **Lyrics**: Anjaan Prakash Mehra; **Selected Cast**: Amitabh Bachchan, Vinod Khanna, Raakhee, Rekha, Amjad Khan; **Prod. Co.**: Prakash Mehra Productions; Colour.

Naya daur
India, 1957 – 173 mins
B. R. Chopra

Akhtar Mirza (father of the directors Saeed and Aziz Mirza) wrote the story for *Naya daur* ('New Era'). In a village, whose main economy depends on a sawmill, many workers face unemployment when the ruthless Kundan (Jeevan) modernises his mill with the introduction of electricity. Two drivers of *tongas* (horse-drawn taxis), Shankar (Dilip Kumar) and Krishna (Ajit), are rivals for the love of Rajni (Vyjayanthimala). They decide that, according to the flowers she chooses for the temple, one will give up his pursuit. Shankar's sister Manju (Chand Usmani), who loves Krishna, changes the flowers and Krishna is convinced that Shankar made her. They fall out and Krishna sides with Kundan, who buys a bus that threatens the livelihood of the *tongawallas*. Kundan agrees to withdraw the bus if a *tonga* can beat the bus in a race. The villagers, led by Shankar, build a road along which the race can be held . . .

The story argues for a new humanism over both modernity and feudalism and for a collectivist approach to the new technology. Mehboob Khan, S. Mukherji and S. S. Vasan had all rejected this story, claiming that it would make a good documentary but not a feature film. When B. R. Chopra went to discuss the story with Dilip Kumar, he refused even to listen to him, let alone sign up for it. B. R. then approached Ashok Kumar, who felt that he looked too urbane for the role of a villager, but did speak to Dilip Kumar on B. R.'s behalf. Dilip Kumar was eventually persuaded to take the role but, by doing so, inadvertently contributed to the film's great notoriety.

After shooting for a couple of weeks at Kardar Studios, the unit, comprising several hundred people, was preparing to leave for a two-month location shoot near Bhopal, when Madhubala's father refused to allow his daughter to go. Apparently, he disapproved of the alleged relationship that had developed between his daughter and Dilip Kumar. The Chopras took Madhubala and her father to court, arguing that the film needed to be shot outdoors, which was still not always the practice in Bombay films of the 1950s. Dilip Kumar supported the Chopras, even appearing in court as a witness, where he had to declare his love for Madhubala. The Chopras won the case, but asked for it to be withdrawn so that Madhubala would not face criminal charges. Madhubala was replaced with Vyjayanthimala.

The film's songs are still played today, with hits like 'Ude jab jab zulfein teri' (Mohammed Rafi and Asha Bhosle), 'Reshmi salwaar' (Shamshad Begum and Asha Bhosle) and socialist numbers like 'Saathi haath badhaana' and the song that sounds like a *tonga* trotting, 'Maang ke saath tumhara' (Mohammed Rafi and Asha Bhosle). This is an example of a film with a very Punjabi soundtrack. Lyricist Sahir Ludhianvi worked with the brothers, B. R. and Yash Chopra, until his death in 1981.

B. R. Chopra (1912–) is a director and producer whose work is not as well known today as that of some of his contemporaries, even though his films were very popular for about four decades. It may be that the issue-based nature of his work is no longer so attractive or that he is now known to the younger generation as the producer of the television series, *The Mahabharata* (1989), which ran for nearly a hundred weeks to the largest audiences ever seen. He still produces hit films like *Baghban* (2004).

B. R. Chopra is highly esteemed in the film industry. Mehboob Khan kindly gave ten weeks he had booked at Liberty Cinema for *Mother India*, whose release was late, to what he called B. R.'s 'Taangewaala ki kahaani/Story of a *tonga*-driver'. He was worried that B. R. would lose money, so advised him to book this prestigious cinema for just five weeks. When the film had its Silver Jubilee (that is, ran for twenty-five weeks), he telephoned B. R. and asked if he could be the chief guest at the celebrations.

Dir.: B. R. Chopra; **Story/Scr.**: Akhtar Mirza; **Dial.**: Kamil Rashid; **DOP**: M. N. Malhotra; **Music**: O. P. Nayyar; **Lyrics**: Sahir Ludhianvi; **Selected Cast**: Dilip Kumar, Vyjayanthimala, Ajit, Chand Usmani, Jeevan; **Prod. Co.**: B. R. Films; Black and white.

Nikaah
India, 1982 – 145 mins
B. R. Chopra

This film is a particular favourite of mine, as the music was all the rage when I was a student. Twenty years later, it still sounds as good as ever, and the songs by Ravi, with lyrics by Hasan Kamaal, are well placed in the film. The famous *qawwali* ('Chehra chupa liya hai'), Salma Agha's own rendition of her song ('Dil ke armaan aansuon mein beh gaye') and the song given to Raj Babbar are all well picturised, but my favourite is still the weeping Nawab, Wasim, listening to an old gramophone recording of Ghulam Ali's rendition of Hasrat Mohani's Urdu *ghazal* ('lyric poem') 'Chupke chupke'. This song encapsulates the decadence of the film, for Wasim is being punished for his own actions, and yet his genuine sorrow is expressed in the images and the words, and the music.

Each of B. R. Chopra's films addresses a serious topic, but they are always entertaining. *Nikaah* looks at the issue of Muslim divorce, arguing that to be able to get a divorce merely by uttering the three words 'Talaq, talaq, talaq' is not in the interests of women or even of men. To address this topic, B. R. Chopra has made a Muslim social, a genre that was rare during the 1980s, and even the success of this film did not lead to its revival. As is typical of this genre, all the characters are Muslims, speak and read Urdu and live an aristocratic life that is rare among Muslims in modern India but was certainly known before partition. The 'Islamicate' nature of the film is constantly exaggerated in gesture, seen in the elaborate greetings of 'aadaab', in the language, which is always flowery and Persianate, and in the spectacular sets and neo-traditional costumes. The contrast between the traditional nawabi house and the glamorous, modern world of Bombay is carefully underlined, as is the difference in lifestyle and customs between the world of the Muslim elite and the educated middle classes. The Nawab seems part of the decadence associated with Islamic cultures in film and literature, but he does not participate in the arts and learning of the old world.

As one expects of B. R. Chopra, the story is told in a gripping way, avoiding didacticism and excess while focusing at all times on the social message. The only exception, perhaps, is the final denouement, which is very stagey and wordy. The dialogues are well written and the film moves at a steady pace.

The film is surprisingly frank about sexual matters, from the depiction of the female nude at the beginning, as 'Woman' talks about the suffering and sacrifice she has undergone in history, to the married relationships of Niloufer (Salma Agha). The Nawabi Wasim (Deepak Parashar), Niloufer's first husband, makes it clear that his love for her is based not on companionship but on sexual pleasure. His lack of any empathy for her is clear when he divorces her in a fit of temper but cannot see why she should be unwilling to take him back. Haider (Raj Babbar), Niloufer's second husband, by contrast, sees companionship as central to their relationship, although the physical side also plays a key part.

Even though B. R. Chopra consulted with an adviser on Muslim religious law, the film caused some controversy among the Muslim population, who thought it portrayed them as backward in their gender politics, with their hot-headed men willing to throw their women out onto the street; however, it apparently found a major audience among *burqa*-clad Muslim women, who wept with the heroine and enjoyed her questioning of the divorce law, and her decision to leave both men until they admitted that they have misunderstood and wronged her.

Dir.: B. R. Chopra; **Story/Scr./Dial.**: Achala Nagar; **Prologue**: Ram Kumar; **DOP**: Dharam Chopra; **Music**: Ravi; **Lyrics**: Hasan Kamaal, Hasrat Mohani; **Selected Cast**: Salma Agha, Raj Babbar, Deepak Parashar, Asrani, **Prod. Co.**: B. R. Films; Colour.

Padosan
India, 1968 – 157 mins
Jyoti Swaroop

This is one of the great comedies of Hindi cinema and one that remains funny today. It is full of visual jokes such as the opening scene where Thakur Kunwarji is having a massage and the position of his body makes it looks as though he has a tiger's head; but most of the comedy is based around regional accents and stereotypes, especially south Indians, who seem to find the film particularly amusing.

Bhola (Sunil Dutt) is the innocent but good young man who, at the age of twenty-six, thinks he should follow the Hindu scriptures and get married. He soon falls in love with his beautiful neighbour, Bindu (Saira Banu), who wears splendid modern western outfits and make-up but changes quickly to saris when she falls in love. Meanwhile, Bhola's uncle, Kunwarji (Om Prakash), who is old enough to be her father, and her music teacher, Masterji (Mehmood), also fall for her. Bhola realises that the way to win her is through music but, as he sings like a donkey, he gets his own guru, Vidyapati (Kishore Kumar), who runs a theatre group, to sing while he mimes to impress his neighbour. This creates situations for such classic songs as 'Mere saamnewali khirki' and the achingly funny *jugalbandi* (musical duel) between Masterji (playback Manna Dey) and Bhola's teacher (Kishore sings for himself but Sunil Dutt mimes), 'Ek chatura naar'.

Kishore had shown what a good comedian he was in films such as *Chalti ka naam gaadi*, and here he dresses up as a *paan*-chewing, floppy-haired musician. This was one of his last films, as he subsequently carved out a hugely successful career as a playback singer.

Saira Banu was one of the most popular female stars of the 1960s, her hits including *Junglee* and *Purab aur pachhim*. She was the second generation of women in her family to be in films; her mother, Naseem Bano, was a star in the 1940s, in films such as Sohrab Modi's *Pukar* (1939). Saira Banu married Dilip Kumar in 1966 but continued to act.

The real star of this film is Mehmood. Hindi cinema has always featured specialised comedians (Johnny Walker, Johnny Lever, and so on), who are usually set apart socially from the hero and heroine and who perform in a different style, often more closely allied to the popular, lower-class theatre. Here Mehmood, as the south Indian music teacher, is a caricature, both in appearance (his hair, clothes and gesture) and in his habits and outrageous accent. Masterji even has his own soundtrack of south Indian music that plays whenever he appears. A figure of fun for most of the film, as the servant who wants to marry his mistress, he is ineffectual (this trait attributed to his diet of south Indian rice-based *idlis* rather than northern wheat-based *parathas*) and slightly effeminate, but also becomes a sympathetic figure as he is manipulated by Bindu. (I am sure I was not alone in wishing he had found his own bride at the end.)

Dir.: Jyoti Swaroop; **Story**: Arun Choudhury's 'Pasher Bari'; **Scr./Dial./Lyrics**: Rajinder Krishen; **DOP**: K. H. Kapadia, Music: R. D. Burman; **Selected Cast**: Sunil Dutt, Saira Banu, Kishore Kumar, Mehmood, Om Prakash, Mukri; **Prod. Co.**: Mehmood Productions; Colour.

Pakeezah
India, 1971 – 175 mins
Kamal Amrohi

While courtesans feature in many films, mostly in minor roles, the two great films in which they are the main heroines are set in the nineteenth-century Avadhi court of Lucknow (*Umrao Jaan*), and in Delhi and the Punjabi princely state of Patiala in the early years of the twentieth century (*Pakeezah*), as these were two of the great centres of courtly Muslim culture of their time.

Shahabuddin (Ashok Kumar) is in love with a courtesan, Nargis (Meena Kumari), but his family will not let him marry her. Nargis dies in a graveyard where she has given birth to a daughter, who is brought up by her sister, also a courtesan. Sahibjaan (Meena Kumari) becomes a courtesan too and she also falls in love with a forestry officer, Salim (Raaj Kumar), whom she does not know is her father's nephew. They have some romantic moments together and want to get married but his family insists that he marries someone else. Sahibjaan is invited to dance at their wedding . . .

Pakeezah has very stylised aesthetics, with its beautiful actress, music and dance, the elaboration of scenery and in particular of clothing, tied to a certain nostalgia arising from the decline and disappearance of courtesan culture. The courtesan is a quintessentially romantic figure: a beautiful but tragic woman, who pours out her grief for the love she is denied in tears, poetry and dance. Yet although denied marriage and respectability, she is also a source of power. She ignores constraints on women's chastity and economic rights, succeeding through a combination of talent and education. Meena Kumari had a strong star persona, as a tragedian who was exploited by her parents and her lovers, despite her beauty and her talent as an actress and a poet. She had an alcohol problem, which killed her less than two months after *Pakeezah*'s release, when she was only forty. During the fourteen years it had taken to make this film, she and the film's director, producer and writer, Amrohi, were divorced.

Meena Kumari in *Pakeezah*

All this makes *Pakeezah* something of a camp classic. It has strong elements of foot fetishism: the lover leaves a note tucked into Pakeezah's toes on the train/('Aap ke paon bahut haseen hain. Inhen zameen par mat utariyega, maile ho jaayenge!/Your feet are very beautiful. Do not let them touch the ground, they will get dirty!') and dancing at her lover's wedding, she lacerates her feet on broken glass to leave symbolically resonant bloody marks on the white sheet of her performance. Although her sexual allure is constantly on display in the film, she calls her body a *zinda lash* ('living corpse') and writes romantic *ghazals* about love, maintaining the hope that she might marry, although her career would make this impossible.

The extended filming schedule meant that several of the crew and cast were rather old by the time it was finished. It was shot by Josef Wirsching, who had been a cameraman at Bombay Talkies in the 1930s. The songs from the film were beautiful, tragic compositions by Ghulam Mohammed, who wrote them in the late 1950s and died before the film's release, and they are often played even today, as well as commonly sampled in modern mixes such as 'Chalte chalte', 'Inhi logon ne', 'Thaade rahiyo', 'Chalo dildaar chalo', 'Mausam hai aashiqaana', and many more. Naushad stepped in to compose the background music for the film.

Dir./Story/Scr./Dial./Co-lyrics: Kamal Amrohi; **DOP**: Josef Wirsching; **Music**: Ghulam Mohammed, Naushad; **Lyrics**: Kaif Bhopali, Majrooh Sultanpuri, Kaifi Azmi; **Selected Cast**: Meena Kumari, Ashok Kumar, Raj Kumar, Pratima Devi; **Prod. Co.**: Mahal Pictures; Colour.

Parinda
India, 1989 – 154 mins
Vidhu Vinod Chopra

Vidhu Vinod Chopra is one of several graduates in the Hindi film industry from the Film and Television Institute of India in Pune. He began his career with small films, but gradually moved into bigger, more commercial movies in the 1980s, going on to make larger-budget movies such as *1942: A Love Story* (1994) and *Mission Kashmir* (2000). He also produces films, including the comedy hit *Munnabhai MBBS*. *Parinda* is usually regarded as his finest film and held in high esteem by most people in the Hindi film industry.

In order to survive and support his younger brother Karan (Anil Kapoor), Kishen (Jackie Shroff) has had to join a gang run by Anna (Nana Patekar). Anna is mad and kills without thinking but terrified of fire, although he burnt his own wife and child to death. Karan does not know that his brother is a gangster and although he does not join the police himself, in the tradition of two brothers in Hindi films (see *Gunga Jumna* and *Deewaar*), his best friend, Prakash (Anupam Kher), is a policeman and Karan falls in love with his sister, Paro (Madhuri Dixit). When Anna's gang kills Prakash in front of Karan, he finds out that Kishen is one of the gang. Karan joins the gang in order to destroy it from within. Anna finds out Karan's game and has Karan and Paro killed on their wedding night; Kishen avenges his brother by burning Anna to death.

Parinda is undoubtedly one of Hindi cinema's best gangster films, despite lacking plot twists or even a really good story. However, it does boast great cinematic and technical qualities, such as its images of Bombay, which really bring out the grittiness of the city, and its deployment of the motifs of pigeons (*parinda*/'birds') and fire. Vinod Chopra shows his mastery in key sequences, such as the assassination of Prakash and the fight in Anna's *godown* (warehouse). The film was edited by Renu Saluja, who was usually reckoned to be one of Bombay's best editors, and she keeps the film moving at a relentless pace with none of the usual diversions of the Hindi film into comedy and other tracks. The romantic element perhaps suffers from this lack of focus, or maybe it is the music, which is not particularly memorable (except when lifted directly from western songs such as 'When I Need You') and the unremarkable song picturisation. This is surprising considering that Vinod Chopra and R. D. Burman produced such remarkable music and memorable song picturisations in *1942: A Love Story*, although maybe this was because Sanjay Leela Bhansali worked on the latter film.

Nana Patekar is one of the most powerful and charismatic actors in villainous roles. Here he is dangerous and mad, but Anna was much loved by the audience. I think sometimes he overacts, but this view was not shared by the audience or by the critics, who gave him several awards for his performance. The much underrated Jackie Shroff really shines in the film, and this was the first time that he was taken seriously by the critics. Anil Kapoor and Madhuri Dixit, who made such a good pair in the several films they did together (including *Tezaab*), were outshone by these two, as their love story is one of the least successful parts of the film.

Parinda was regarded as the best gangster film in Bombay until Ram Gopal Varma made *Satya* and *Company* (2003). However, the debate continues, and many still regard *Parinda* as the best example of this type of film.

Dir./Story: Vidhu Vinod Chopra; **Scr.**: Shivkumar; **Dial.**: Imtiaz Hussain; **DOP**: Binod Pradhan; **Music**: R. D. Burman; **Lyrics**: Khursheed Hallauri; **Selected Cast**: Anil Kapoor, Jackie Shroff, Madhuri Dixit, Nana Patekar, Anupam Kher; **Prod. Co.**: Vidhu Vinod Chopra Films; Colour.

Phool
India, 1944 – 122 mins
K. Asif

Phool is not yet available on DVD or VCD but it is the first of the very
few movies made by one of India's great directors, K. Asif, whose
Mughal-e Azam is rightly regarded as one of the best Indian films ever
made. *Phool* is fascinating, as it mixes several 'Islamicate' genres, being
partly a Muslim social, that is a film set in the contemporary (or
seemingly contemporary) world, partly an Arabian Nights fantasy, with
veiled Arab princesses dancing on fabulous stage sets, and also one of
the few films to show 'Islamic' miracles.

   Safdar (Yakub) has promised to finish building a mosque but he loses
his money through his in-laws' scheming. When his daughter Shama
(Suraiya) is about to marry Salim (Prithviraj Kapoor), the latter suddenly
realises his duty as a Muslim and rushes off to fight for his *qaum*
('community') of Muslims in Turkey in the Balkan wars, leaving her a
flower (*phool*) and a model of the Taj Mahal. He falls under the spell of a
dancer, Princess Leila (Sitara Devi), who comes back to India with him,
touring Delhi, Agra, Cawnpore, Allahabad and Lucknow with an
amazing stage show.

   Leila's magic potion has made him forget Shama and his mother,
and believe he is Farid, not Salim. Even the sight of the flower he has
given Shama does not quite jog his memory. Rekha (Veena), their Hindu
friend, prays to Krishna and the image comes to life as Shama joins her
song. Salim's mother (Durga Khote) is injured in a struggle with her son
and Leila, only for her blood to restore his memory and he picks a
flower, which he takes to Shama. In the final resolution of the plot, the
in-laws' wicked son, who is trying to marry Shama, is struck down by
lightning outside the mosque, the couple are reunited and the film ends
with the cry, 'Allah ho akbar!' ('God is great!').

   Although singing star Suraiya shines as the heroine in the film, and
Veena has a smaller role as her best friend, the best female role goes to

Sitara Devi, 'the tigress from Nepal', as the famous Urdu writer Manto calls her in his *Stars from Another Sky* (New Delhi: Penguin, 1998). She plays an oriental(ist) temptress in the film, complete with a ring containing magic powder, veils that do not cover her body and her use of the occasional Arabic word (she calls Salim 'Habibi' and 'Hindi'). She performs the 'item number' of the film, an extraordinary song where the stage is made of piano keys, she dances on drums and women form the harp that she plays. Prithviraj Kapoor, the founder of the Kapoor dynasty that has dominated Hindi films for over seventy years and who was later to play the old Akbar in *Mughal-e Azam*, takes the role of the dashing hero.

The very stylised Urdu dialogues for the Muslims and more Hindi versions for the Hindus were written by Kamal Amrohi, who worked with Asif again on *Mughal-e Azam* before going on to make his own *magnum opus*, *Pakeezah*. The music is by Ghulam Haider, who was one of the most popular music directors after the success of *Khazanchi*.

Although this film is set in the period of the Caliphate (Khilafat) movement (1920s), showing students in India wearing *sherwanis* (long coats such as those worn by Nehru) and fezzes, the resonances with contemporary politics are clear. (The Pakistan resolution was made in 1940, while 1942 was marked by the Quit India movement, so it was hardly surprising that reports on censorship indicate that the sequence showing students marching through the street with the Caliphate flag, which looks almost identical to the Pakistan flag in black and white, was cut, though it was on the version I saw in the archives in Pune). However, the film makes a show of close friendship between the Muslim family and their Hindu friend Rekha, with the first song of the film being a spectacular Diwali number with Busby Berkeley-style effects.

Dir.: K Asif; **Story/Scr./Dial./Lyrics**: Kamal Amrohi; **DOP**: Kumar Jaywant; **Music**: Ghulam Haider; **Selected Cast**: Sitara Devi, Prithviraj Kapoor, Suraiya, Durga Khote; **Prod. Co.**: Famous Films; Black and white.

Purab aur pachhim
India, 1970 – 159 mins
Manoj Kumar

Although other films had already raised the issue of Indians in the diaspora, this film remains one of the most memorable even today. Following the early Indian nationalists, India, while lacking economic advantages, is seen as 'spiritual', while the west is wealthy but 'materialistic'. Yet the film actually complicates this polarisation as Indians and westerners experiment with 'eastern' and 'western' values, with 'good' and 'bad' characters found in both communities.

The film opens with the colonial powers' oppression of the Indian freedom fighters in Allahabad (the episodes set before independence are shot in black and white). Ashok Kumar is the good village priest who is actively involved in the struggle. Set against this is the character played by Pran, who betrays his family for money, snatching his son and leaving his wife (Nirupa Roy) and unborn child, to pursue material wealth in the UK. He is corrupted by money rather than by the west, but in the west he can become rich on 'the dogs' (greyhound racing), and his son (Prem Chopra) grows up with an amoral outlook on life, rejecting Indian family values. Meanwhile, another friend (Madan Puri), who left India earlier, manages to retain his inherent moral values despite marriage to a westerner (Shammi), but loses his way by trying to become modern, an effort that he later repents. (This is shown by his playing of K. L. Saigal records.) Our hero, Bharat (the Sanskritic name for India), played by the director Manoj Kumar, comes to study at Oxford but, while he is in the UK, he shows true Indian values to the diasporic Indians (as well as to westerners) and he brings them back to India. He falls in love with Preeti (Saira Banu).

The film puts great emphasis on religion, showing India as the home of Hinduism, Buddhism, Islam and Christianity, and stresses the role it plays in everyday life with the recurring theme of the popular *bhajan* 'Jai Jagdish Hare' (Victory to Jagdish Hare). Westerners are seen to be attracted to ISKON, with their mantra of 'Hare Krishna' in a quest to fill the spiritual vacuum in their lives. These are the most memorable songs, although Kalyanji–Anandji produce some very funky numbers.

A striking feature is the hero's lack of anger. Like Gandhi, he believes that the values he upholds will prevail, not through argument but through *satyagraha* (approximately, 'showing the Truth'), largely by example. He is willing to tolerate his fiancée's miniskirts, smoking and drinking, in the belief that she will change when she realises the error of her ways.

The film's rich visual culture spans religious sites in India, tourist attractions in London and a fascinating display of chromolithographs in Indian houses, which are contrasted with 'secular' images in the homes of diasporic Indians. At the beginning of her visit, the westernised heroine is terrified by the chromolithographs of the gods in her in-laws' house, but comes to worship the gods by the end. The costumes are wonderful, and the image of Saira Banu in miniskirt, glass of alcohol in one hand, cigarette in the other, has become iconic. The decadent pleasures of western life were undoubtedly one of the major attractions of this film for contemporary audiences, while the 'eastern' scenes of family life provided the emotional melodrama.

Dir./Scr./Dial.: Manoj Kumar; **Story**: Shashi Goswami; **DOP**: V. N. Reddy, **Music**: Kalyanji–Anandji; **Lyrics**: Santosh Anand, Prem Dhawan, Indeewar; **Selected Cast**: Ashok Kumar, Saira Banu, Manoj Kumar, Pran, Bharti, Nirupa Roy; **Prod. Co.**: Vishal International Productions; Colour/black and white.

Pyaasa
India, 1957 – 153 mins
Guru Dutt

Pyaasa is a masterpiece of world cinema, managing to use all the conventions of the Hindi film to make a movie that can be appreciated cinematically and narratively by both an Indian and an international audience. In the spirit of true Romanticism and that of the Urdu lyric, the film is about a hero thirsting (*pyaasa*) mostly for love, but also for a world where poetry and creativity are valued over material success.

Vijay (Guru Dutt), a poet, becomes a martyr to his art in a material world. When his brothers sell his poetry as wastepaper, he leaves home. He meets a prostitute, Gulab (Waheeda Rehman), who reads poetry and is looking for love. His first love, Meena (Mala Sinha), leaves him to marry a wealthy publisher, Ghosh (Rehman). When Vijay gives his coat to a beggar who is killed, Vijay is assumed to be dead. Gulab gets his poetry published by Ghosh. The book is a bestseller and a memorial meeting to the 'dead' poet is planned. Vijay attends his own memorial and denounces the world. Ghosh and his friends pretend that he is a madman claiming to be Vijay, and have him committed to an asylum. Eventually he gets out, Gulab joins him, and they leave together for a hopeful future.

Although Guru Dutt's earlier films (*Baazi* [1951], *Aar paar* [1954], *Mr and Mrs 55* [1955]) were not seen as autobiographical, his two dark masterpieces (*Pyaasa* and *Kaagaz ke phool*) are taken to be premonitions of his suicide and his suffering as an artist. Be that as it may, the character of Vijay is drawn in part from that of the poet, Sahir Ludhianvi, who wrote the lyrics for this and many other films, and was closely associated with the work of Yash Chopra. Again, this may be the reading of the poet into the poetry, but there are also direct references, such as the title of Vijay's poetry collection, *Parchhaiyan*, which is the name of one of Sahir's poems and also of one of his collections.

(*Opposite page*) Guru Dutt and Waheeda Rehman in *Pyaasa*

The outstanding features of this film are the songs and the cinematography. Some of the songs were originally poems whose language Sahir simplified by taking out the Persian words common to Urdu poetry. Their musical setting by S. D. Burman transformed them into some of the most loved and best-known songs in Hindi cinema ('Jinhe naaz hai Hind par', 'Jaane woh kaise log the' and the duet 'Hum aapki aankhon mein'), and their situational use in the film by Guru Dutt augments their impact, as does V. K. Murthy's exceptional cinematography. The film leaves lasting images, such as the lighting of Waheeda Rehman's face in 'Jaane kya tune kahi' (sung by Geeta Dutt) and the appearance of Vijay as the crucified saviour in the theatre for 'Yeh mehlon, yeh takhton' (sung by Mohammed Rafi). One of the songs that is often cited as a perfect example of a Hindi film song is the *bhajan* (Hindu devotional song) 'Aaj sajan mohe ang laga lo', in which all elements of the song and the picturisation are essential and integral to the whole film. Another hugely popular song is sung by Rafi and picturised on Johnny Walker – the comedy song of the masseur, 'Sar jo tera chakraye'.

This is a good choice for Hindi film novices, as its story is easy to follow and its use of the conventions of the Hindi film do not seem too unfamiliar.

Dir.: Guru Dutt; **Dial.**: Abrar Alvi; **DOP**: V. K. Murthy; **Music**: S. D. Burman; **Lyrics**: Sahir Ludhianvi; **Selected Cast**: Guru Dutt, Waheeda Rehman, Mala Sinha, Johnny Walker; **Prod. Co.**: Guru Dutt Films; Black and white.

Qayamat se qayamat tak
India, 1988 – 162 mins
Mansoor Khan

It was only when the young Mansoor Khan, Nasir Husain's son, released his *Qayamat se qayamat tak* (*QSQT*), ('From apocalypse to apocalypse') in 1988 that we see the return of the musical family-oriented romance that was to dominate the Hindi cinema of the 1990s. The story was a college romance but the plot still hinged around feudal structures: Thakurs (rich peasants and landlords) engaged in a family feud, the young couple from opposing factions falling in love à la Romeo and Juliet.

Ratan refuses to marry his pregnant girlfriend, Madhumati. When she kills herself, her brother Dhanraj Singh (Dalip Tahil) kills Ratan on his wedding day. With Dhanraj jailed for fourteen years, another brother in Delhi brings up his two young sons, who grow up to be Raj (Aamir Khan) and Shyam (Zutshi). Raj returns to the village, where he falls in love with Rashmi (Juhi Chawla), daughter of Randhir Singh (Goga Kapoor), Madhumati's brother. The families both holiday in Mount Abu, in Rajasthan, where Raj and Rashmi get lost in the woods together. Randhir decides to get Rashmi married, so the couple runs away, pursued by the family . . .

The fresh-faced, good looks of Aamir Khan, the male lead (and Mansoor's cousin), appealed as a role model and a boyfriend, and the former Miss India, Juhi Chawla, was a huge success as an innocent and bubbly heroine. They acted in several more films together, forming a successful pairing and becoming major stars of the 1990s, Aamir Khan in his later *tapori* films (including *Rangeela)* and then the Oscar-nominated *Lagaan*. One of Juhi's major hits was Yash Chopra's *Darr* (1993) with Shah Rukh Khan, and they became another popular screen couple, later going into production together.

For the first time for years, film music became cool among the college crowd, with everyone singing the catchy 'Papa kehte hain', a sort of 1950s' rock and roll song. 'Ay mere humsafar' 'and Ghazab ka hai din' were also popular and the songs echoed the the success of music in Nasir Husain's hits (such as *Teesri manzil* and *Yaadon ki barat*). This set the trend for a whole spate of musical films that followed soon afterwards, notably *Dil* (1990), *Dil hai ke manta nahin* (1991), *Joh jeeta wohi Sikandar* (1992), *Andaz apna apna* (1994) (all with Aamir, the last with Juhi also), *Aashiqui* (1990) and *Saajan* (1991). All these films promoted a new generation of stars and all were popular because of their music. A new generation of singers also emerged, including Udit Narayan, who first sang for *QSQT*. This was the time of the cheap (and often pirated) music cassette and the songs reached enormous audiences. The diasporic population emerged as a significant audience for the films, the VHS tapes (again, often pirated) reaching overseas, where a younger generation of viewers, also encouraged by the advent of Indian cable channels, enjoyed these films with young stars and catchy songs. These films of the early 1990s created the audience that eagerly received *Hum aapke hain koun . . .!* and *Dilwale dulhaniya le jayenge*, to set up a new dynamic between the Indian producers and the diaspora, and marking a return to cinema-viewing in India and overseas.

Dir.: Mansoor Khan; **Story/Co-scr./Dial**.: Nasir Husain; **Co-scr**.: Mansoor Khan, Aamir Khan, Nusrat Khan; **DOP**: Kiran Deohans; **Music**: Anand–Milind; **Lyrics**: Majrooh Sultanpuri; **Selected Cast**: Aamir Khan, Juhi Chawla, Ravinder Kapoor, Goga Kapoor, Dalip Tahil; **Prod. Co**.: Nasir Husain Films; Colour.

Qurbani
India, 1980 – 157 mins
Feroz Khan

The theme of sacrifice (*qurbani*) for the male friendship (*dosti*) is a great trend in Hindi movies. *Qurbani* is a stylish film, very much modelled on spaghetti Western cool, in a male world where the woman's narrative function is to act as an item over which the men negotiate friendship. The macho men use props, including guns, fighting, fast cars and motorbikes.

The film begins with an underworld theme, as Rakka (Amrish Puri) has married and then left Jwala (Aruna Irani) after stealing her money and getting her brother Vikram (Shakti Kapoor) convicted for crimes. We then meet Rajesh (Feroz Khan), a motorcyle stuntman and safe-breaker, who smashes up Rakka's Mercedes in a car park before going to a nightclub, where his girlfriend Sheela (Zeenat Aman) is performing. When Rajesh is jailed, after being caught by policeman Amjad Khan (Amjad Khan), he asks Sheela to wait for him but not to visit. Khan then ambushes a stake-out of Rakka during which he kills one of his own men, leading Amar (Vinod Khanna) to leave the gang. Amar and his motherless daughter Tina (Natasha Chopra) meet Sheela in a café, where he beats up a gang of hoodlums. Sheela and Tina become very close, while Amar falls in love with Sheela. Vikram and Jwala want Rajesh to rob Rakka's safe but Sheela tries to persuade him to refuse. Meanwhile, Amar and Vikram fight in a road-rage episode during which Rajesh saves Amar's life. When Rajesh introduces Sheela to Amar as his girlfriend, Amar sacrifices his hopes of a new family life for his friend. After Amar is once again saved from Vikram's gang by Rajesh, they attend an Eid ceremony, in which they sing and dance about *qurbani*. Vikram and Jwala kill Rakka, and Rajesh robs his safe and then arranges to be caught on a lesser job that will incur just a short prison term. However, Khan, realising the set-up, convinces Rajesh that Amar killed Rakka to frame him for murder so he could flee with Sheela and the money. Rajesh follows them to London where, after a fight with Amar, they are reunited, only to be pursued by Vikram and Jwala; more sacrifices ensue, as Amar finally dies in Rajesh's arms.

Feroz Khan, with his love for motorbikes and shirts open to the waist to reveal a medallioned hairy chest, is even more macho than Vinod Khanna, whose softness is shown in his portrayal of the loving father and his willingness to sacrifice his hopes of a new wife and mother for his daughter – and even his life – for the sake of his friend. However, Vinod still has his fighting moments and we can only imagine how his career might have developed if he had not taken a break from acting.

Amjad Khan, whose place in Hindi film history was made as Gabbar Singh in *Sholay*, steals the show with his characterisation of the tough and bluff cop with a wicked sense of humour. He raises laughs with his expressions, dialogues and fighting, and in one memorable moment puts on a wig, a beard and a frilly shirt to mime to the drums for 'Leila o Leila', one of the film's item songs.

Zeenat Aman provides more than enough sex appeal for the film, in her figure-hugging lamé outfits for 'Aap jaisa koi', her bikini, her chiffon sari (for mowing the lawn), which is then drenched by a hose, or a remarkably skimpy full-length dress.

Of all Kalyanji–Anandji's songs, the biggest hit was Nazia Hassan's rendition of 'Aap jaisa koi', which sparked a widespread craze at the time of the film's release. The song is shot twice, once with Feroz Khan as the viewer, once with Vinod Khanna. Zeenat's dancing is poor but the camera, clothes and movements all emphasise her curvaceous body – as indeed does the whole film. The backing group has a black drummer, and some large girls in white outfits and silver boots who seem to have no idea how to mime playing their instruments and no sense of timing when dancing.

Dir.: Feroz Khan; **Story/Scr.**: K. K. Shukla; **Dial.**: Kadar Khan; **DOP**: Kamal Bose; **Music**: Kalyanji–Anandji; **Lyrics**: Indivar, Farooq Kaisar; **Selected Cast**: Amrish Puri, Feroz Khan, Vinod Khanna, Zeenat Aman, Aruna Irani, Amjad Khan, Shakti Kapoor; **Prod. Co.**: F. K. International; Colour.

Ram aur Shyam
India, 1967 – 171 mins
Tapi Chanakya

The story of this film is taken up by *Seeta aur Geeta*, but I have included both films in my final selection, not only because the doubles are different genders and showcase two major stars but also because both of them were great hits and huge fun in different ways. The theme of identical twins has been present in many cinemas (this being one of the most basic 'tricks' available to cinema that was not available to live performances such as plays). Common to melodramas, it is taken to extremes in Hindi cinema, with not just identical twins (*Afsana* [1951], *Anhonee* [1952], *Gol maal*, *Hum dono* [1961], and others, including 'fake' doubles in *Jewel Thief*) but unrelated doubles (*Don*, *Kaho na pyaar hai*), while there are many other examples of non-identical brothers separated at birth (*Amar, Akbar, Anthony*, *Johny mera naam* and many others) as well as brothers who are opposites (*Mother India*, *Gunga Jumna, Deewaar* and so on).

Ram aur Shyam is also interesting for being one of several south Indian films that were remade in Hindi in southern studios. Shot in Madras, it was a remake of a Telugu hit starring N. T. Rama Rao, *Ramudu Bheemudu* (1964), whose director, B. Nagi Reddi, produced this film for a new director, Chanakya.

The timid Ram (Dilip Kumar) is terrified of his brother-in-law Gajendra Babu (Pran), who has bullied him all his life but, to protect his sister (Nirupa Roy) and niece, he suffers in silence. Gajendra wants Ram to marry heiress Anjana (Waheeda Rehman) so he can take her money as well as Ram's. When Ram realises that Gajendra will stop at nothing, he runs away. Meanwhile, we have met the lively and fearless Shyam (Dilip Kumar) who lives in a village, where he gets up to mischief and loves playing jokes, especially on his friend Shanta (Mumtaz). He goes to the city, where he rescues Anjana, who thinks he is Ram. They fall in love but he cannot convince her that he is not Ram. Meanwhile, Shanta falls in love with Ram, who has ended up in Shyam's village. Gajendra also mistakes Shyam for Ram, so is in for a shock when Shyam asserts himself. However, he finds Ram and imprisons him, then accuses Shyam of his murder; only later does it emerge that Ram and Shyam are twins separated at birth.

Dilip Kumar was known as the king of tragedy, so his debut in comedy was anticipated with scepticism if not amusement. However, as soon as Shyam appears, all doubts were dispelled, as he gives a hilarious performance as a villager hired to be a hero in a film who actually beats up all the baddies and is told that he will never make it in the movies. He is then soundly beaten by his mother for even thinking about joining the film industry. It must have been quite a shock when the film came out to see Dilip Kumar dancing and singing at a children's party, pulling faces and putting on silly voices. The others play roles with which they were usually associated. Waheeda and Mumtaz were well cast as opposing types. While Waheeda was already established as a major star, this was the film that moved Mumtaz onto the A-list of actresses, a position she would hold until her marriage. Nirupa Roy is saintly and long-suffering, while Pran is cruel and villainous.

The music for this film is not Naushad's best score but songs such as 'Aaj ki raat' were quite popular.

Dir.: Tapi Chanakya; **Story/Scr.**: D. V. Narasaraju; **Dial.**: Kaushal Bharati; **DOP**: Marcus Bartley; **Music**: Naushad; **Lyrics**: Shakeel Badayuni; **Selected Cast**: Dilip Kumar, Waheeda Rehman, Mumtaz, Pran, Nirupa Roy; **Prod. Co.**: Vijaya Vauhini International; Colour.

Rangeela
India, 1995 – 144 mins
Ram Gopal Varma

Although films about the film industry are regarded as a box-office risk in Hindi cinema (see *Kaagaz ke phool*), this film was a big hit and was soon regarded as something of a classic. Although Mani Ratnam's *Roja*, dubbed into Hindi from the Tamil original, had shot A. R. Rehman to fame as a music director, this was the first Hindi film for which he composed the songs.

Munna (Aamir Khan), a *tapori* (approximately, a streetwise guy), has been great friends with Mili (Urmila Matondkar) since their childhood. She is a junior artiste (extra) who dreams of being a star, for which she finally gets a chance. Her hero, Rajkamal (Jackie Shroff), is an established star who falls in love with her. This makes Munna realise that he is in love with his childhood friend and the love triangle begins.

Urmila, who was the child star of *Masoom*, returned with her first big hit and established herself as Ram Gopal Varma's top heroine. Her glamorous look and much-imitated outfits were created by Manish Malhotra, who gave many of the top heroines 'makeovers', notably Karisma Kapoor, Aamir's co-star in *Raja Hindustani* (1996), and created a new style of feminine glamour throughout the late 1990s.

In this film, Aamir Khan moved away from the 'chocolate-box heroes' (romantic leads) into a new *tapori* type that he made very popular in his roles in *Raja Hindustani*, *Ghulam* (1998), *Sarfarosh* (1999) and others. To some extent, the *tapori* is a 1990s' version of Amitabh Bachchan's Angry Young Man, though one who comes from the street and lacks the allure of his predecessor. The biggest star of the 1990s, Shah Rukh Khan, took on these roles occasionally, but he has been much more successful as the international or diasporic romantic hero in the films of Yash Chopra and his like.

Jackie was seen to play 'himself', in as much as he played a top hero. His role was one that is often played by the hero's friend, who is noble and self-sacrificing.

The film has a comedy track that contains several memorable scenes, such as when Munna and Mili go to a five-star hotel or when a heroine's mother makes unreasonable demands on the producer. Gulshan Grover, usually cast as a villain, plays the deluded director who sees himself as Spielberg (and is said to be modelled on a well-known director whose films feature in this book!).

Rehman's music was catchy and represented something quite new in Hindi cinema. Songs like Aamir's 'Yaaron suno zara' and Urmila's 'Tanha tanha' and 'Rangeela re' (sung by Asha Bhosle) were given a boost by the choreography of Saroj Khan and the young Ahmed Khan (one of the child actors in *Mr India*).

Rangeela was the first big hit Ram Gopal Varma had in Hindi. A very hit-and-miss director (one of his other successes being *Satya*), his films are always interesting and he is keen to experiment with genres not always popular in Hindi films.

Dir./Story/Scr.: Ram Gopal Varma; **Dial.**: Neeraj Vora, Sanjay Chhel; **DOP**: W. B. Rao; **Music**: A. R. Rehman; **Lyrics**: Mehboob; **Selected Cast**: Urmila Matondkar, Aamir Khan, Jackie Shroff, Gulshan Grover, Avtar Gill; **Prod. Co.**: Varma Corporation; Colour.

Roja
India, 1992 – 137 mins
Mani Ratnam

Mani Ratnam was already an established film-maker in Tamil cinema whose film *Nayakan* (1989) (recently chosen by *Time* magazine as one of the hundred best films ever made) had been quite successful nationally, when the box-office and critical success of the Hindi-dubbed version of *Roja* marked him as a major figure in the whole of Indian cinema. Although made in Tamil, *Roja* has come to be seen as a 'Hindi' film, with the Hindi-dubbed version being screened at film festivals and broadcast on Indian national television on Independence Day. *Roja*, along with Mani Ratnam's later films, has had a significant influence on Hindi cinema, with most people in the industry citing him as India's best contemporary director.

The film opens with the Indian army capturing Wasim Khan, a Kashmiri separatist. The focus then turns to a village girl, Roja (Madhoo), who has simple aspirations. Her sister is about to marry Rishi Kumar (Arvind Swamy) but, when she tells him that she loves someone else, he asks for permission to marry Roja. Rishi, a south Indian (though in the Hindi version, north Indian) cryptographer, is sent to Kashmir. Roja accompanies him as if on a traditional honeymoon, but he is soon captured by Kashmiri separatists, who demand that he is exchanged for Wasim. Roja tries to get her husband back by pleading with the army (in the Tamil version she does not understand Hindi, nor they Tamil) and a transfer is negotiated, but meanwhile Rishi is released by his captor's sister.

Roja is part of Mani Ratnam's 'trilogy', the other two films being *Bombay* (1995) and *Dil se* (1998). Unlike *Dil se*, Ratnam's only Hindi film until *Yuva* (2004), these two earlier movies were both made in Tamil, although they became national successes in their Hindi-dubbed versions. Among the few films to engage with contemporary issues about the Indian nation-state, it is striking that they were made in the Tamil cinema, which had earlier concerned itself more with the local political issues of Dravidianism and anti-Brahminism. Critics have suggested that, as they were made after the assassination of Prime Minister Rajiv Gandhi in 1991, they may represent a venting of collective guilt by subsuming Tamil nationality into an Indian one. All three films feature high-caste, if not Brahminical, figures, who travel throughout India rehearsing a high-caste Hindu national identity.

Much of *Roja* is set in Kashmir, formerly the major romantic location in Hindi movies, drawing on its associations of an earthly paradise, but which rarely features now due to political unrest. In one of the most memorable scenes, the hero, Rishi, is taunted by his captors, Kashmiri separatists, who burn the Indian flag. Rishi throws himself on it and is consumed by the fire, to the words of a song by the nationalist Tamil poet Subramania Bharati: 'India is dearer to me than life'. The film cuts to his impassive Muslim captor at prayer, reinforcing the image feared by followers of Hindutva of the disciplined and self-controlled Muslim linked to millions of other Muslims praying in a regimented manner.

The first film for which A. R. Rehman composed the music, songs like 'Choti si aashaa', 'Yeh haseen vaadiyaan' and 'Roja Jaan-e man' were huge hits. He has subsequently become the most acclaimed music director in India, working in Hindi and in south Indian films, as well as on international productions such as Andrew Lloyd-Webber's *Bombay Dreams* (2004). The beautiful cinematography is by Santosh Sivan, regarded as one of India's foremost cameramen.

Dir./Scr.: Mani Ratnam; **Story**: Sujata; **Dial.**: Umesh Sharma (Tamil original: Sujata); **DOP**: Santosh Sivan; **Music**: A. R. Rehman; **Lyrics**: P. K. Mishra (Tamil original: Vairamuthu); **Selected Cast**: Arvind Swamy, Madhoo, Pankaj Kapoor, Janakaraj, Nasser; **Prod. Co.**: Kavithalaya Productions; Colour.

Roti kapada aur makaan
India, 1974 – 159 mins
Manoj Kumar

This is an important film that tries to make political interventions around issues of poverty caused by unemployment and exploitation, which it regards as the root of most of society's evil.

Bharat (Manoj Kumar) is unable to marry his girlfriend Sheetal (Zeenat Aman) as he cannot find work, despite the engineering degree that his father had had to borrow money to finance. His sister (Meena) cannot marry, as her future father-in-law is demanding a dowry. Eventually finding work on a construction site, Bharat meets Tulsi (Moushmi Chatterjee), who has a small child, the result of her rape by the grocer, tailor and the builder (this is depicted graphically, as they attack her in the flour store, ripping off her clothes). The construction work is stopped and they all lose their jobs. Bharat's father dies, as his sons cannot afford to buy him medicine. Bharat realises that he must enter a life of crime in order to support his family. Meanwhile, his brother Vijay (Amitabh Bachchan) has joined the army, driven to leave home by Bharat's reproaches when he is tempted to take bribes; the younger brother Deepak (Dheeraj Kumar) joins the police. Sheetal has become secretary to the super-rich Mr Mohan (Shashi Kapoor), who wants to marry her. Eventually Bharat realises the scale of the corruption and a conflict between the brothers, two of whom represent the state (Vijay loses an arm as part of his sacrifice), erupts into violence as Deepak has to arrest Bharat. A complex denouement and reconciliation follows as all realise that they must abide by the traditional values of the *Ramayana* and act first as citizens rather than individuals.

The film begins with a long dedication to Sanjay Gandhi, Indira Gandhi's younger son who was killed in a flying accident. The preachy tone is then focused on Manoj Kumar, who wears an anguished expression for much of the film, especially when whispering some very *filmi* (overblown) dialogue. A great hero, who comes to epitomise Bharat (the name also means the country, or India), Manoj Kumar was hugely popular, but many find his patriotism too sanctimonious. However, the star cast here gives the film a boost, with the two heroines (Zeenat and Moushmi), as well as the veteran Kamini Kaushal as the boys' mother, the several heroes and the lion-hearted Sikh, Harnam Singh, played by Prem. The great songs here include 'Hai hai yeh majboori' (with Zeenat in a classic 'wet sari' sequence), 'Panditji mere marne ke baad' and 'Aur nahin, bas aur nahin', as well as 'Main na bhoolunga', which is repeated several times.

Dir./Story/Scr./Dial.: Manoj Kumar; **DOP**: Nariman Irani; **Music**: Laxmikant–Pyarelal; **Lyrics**: Santosh Anand; **Selected Cast**: Manoj Kumar, Zeenat Aman, Moushmi Chatterjee, Amitabh Bachchan; **Prod. Co.**: Vishal International Productions; Colour.

Sahib bibi aur ghulam
India, 1961 – 152 mins
Abrar Alvi

The failure of *Kaagaz ke phool* meant that Abrar Alvi, who wrote the screenplay and dialogues, takes credit for direction, although many think Guru Dutt himself directed this film, based on Bimal Mitra's Bengali novel.

Bhootnath (Guru Dutt), a middle-class young man, comes to work in the *haveli* (palatial house) of the wealthy landowning (*zamindari*) Choudhury family in late nineteenth-century Calcutta. The decline of the family's fortunes is exemplified in the fate of the younger daughter-in-law, Choti Bahu (Meena Kumari), whose husband (Rehman) prefers to spend his time watching dancing girls (*tawaifs*) to being with her. She manages to get him to spend some time with her when she starts drinking, but he returns to his girls and she becomes an alcoholic. She and Bhootnath become friends against the family's 'moral code' and her brother-in-law has her killed after they go on an excursion in Calcutta. Years later, Bhootnath comes back to the now demolished *haveli*, where they find Choti Bahu's skeleton.

The film is set in the world of *zamindars,* a class created by the Mughals in decline by the beginning of the twentieth century. Satyajit Ray's *Jalsaghar* (1958), one of the finest films made in India, documents this class with great sensitivity, simultaneously showing their decadence and their aestheticism and patronage of the arts. Here, the class is seen through the eyes of the innocent Bhootnath. He also represents a new class, the professional bourgeoisie, which came to dominate India in subsequent years. Although an educated Brahmin, he is still a villager, who eventually becomes an architect and marries a beautiful but ordinary girl, Jabba (Waheeda Rehman), a member of the modernising sect of the Brahmo Samaj.

The film is dominated by the wonderful performance of Meena Kumari as Choti Bahu. One of the iconic moments of Hindi cinema occurs when Bhootnath approaches her, first looking only at the carpet, then just at her beautiful feet, and then moving up to her *bindi*, her eyes and finally the whole woman.

Meena Kumari's performance reveals her frustrated desire, loneliness and alcoholism, which are said to parallel to her real life, a connection that certainly plays into the audience's reception of her role (see *Pakeezah*). Another great moment is her drunken rendition of 'Na jao saiyaan' in an emotionally saturated scene. Her friendship with Bhootnath is seen as a forbidden pleasure (it is said that a scene in which she puts her head in his lap during their excursion was cut), whereas her husband is able to take his pleasures elsewhere.

V. K. Murthy surpasses even his own usual high standards of cinematography in what is one of the most evocative picturisations of a *tawaif* song in Indian cinema: 'Saaqiya, aaj mujhe neend nahi aayegi'. The *tawaif* is neither pretty nor young but she dances in the light while

Rehman and Meena Kumari in *Sahib bibi aur ghulam*

her backing dancers are just figures, not people, moving in the shadows, their faces never seen. The film's beautiful costumes were designed by Bhanu Athaiya, one of the most skilled designers in the Hindi film.

With music by Hemant Kumar and lyrics by Shakeel Badayuni, the film boasts a great collection of songs. Three are sung by Geeta Dutt, herself a tragic figure: 'Na jao saiyaan', 'Koi door se awaaz', 'Piya aiso jiya mein'; while Asha Bhosle sings the *tawaif*'s song 'Saaqiya . . .' and 'Bhanwra bada naadaan'.

Dir./Scr./Dial.: Abrar Alvi; **Story**: Bimal Mitra's novel *Saheb Bibi Golam* (1952); **DOP**: V. K. Murthy; **Music**: Hemant Kumar; **Lyrics**: Shakeel Badayuni; **Selected Cast**: Meena Kumari, Guru Dutt, Waheeda Rehman, Nasir Hussain, Sapru; **Prod. Co**.: Guru Dutt Films; Black and white.

Sangam
India, 1964 – 238 mins
Raj Kapoor

Sangam is Raj Kapoor's first colour film and the first one that he shot abroad. Although other film-makers had gone abroad before, this movie created a trend that grew when colour cinema added to the spectacle, until by the 1990s it became almost mandatory to have scenes shot in Switzerland, however irrelevant to the story.

Sangam's story is a love triangle, in which two friends, Gopal (Rajendra Kumar) and Sunder (Raj Kapoor), are both in love with the same woman, Radha (Vyjayanthimala). She is really in love with Gopal and finds Sunder's desire for her unappealing but, when the latter returns as a war hero and declares that he only survived because of his love for her, she feels duty-bound to marry him. He is sure that she and Gopal are having an affair, despite Gopal's attempts to reassure him otherwise. Finally, Gopal commits suicide as the only way of convincing him of Radha's innocence.

This is one of many films (see *Qurbani*) where the primary relationship is between men rather than between men and women, where friendship (*dosti*) may be viewed as homosociality (male-bonding) or as homoeroticism. The distinction between the two is always blurred and this ambiguity may be one of the attractions of the theme to certain viewers and audiences.

Raj Kapoor once again plays an irritating, unattractive, immature type of man, as in he did in *Andaz*. It is unclear if this is to justify Radha's distaste for him here or whether this is considered to be an acceptable form of masculinity. Looking at some of the roles Shah Rukh Khan has taken in recent films, even though he wins over the audience with his charisma, the latter may be the case. However, here Sunder is ultimately shown to be sensitive, largely revealing this other side of himself through music. The film is also about how women can come to accept and even love their husbands, even if initially they think this is going to be difficult.

Publicity for *Sangam*

The film's songs have become classics of Hindi cinema. While they are good even outside their filmic context, it is their placement in the film that makes them great. The popular 'Bol Radha bol' is enjoyed no doubt for Vyjayanthimala's appearance in a swimsuit, although Raj Kapoor seems somewhat sleazy. Rajendra Kumar, the woman's choice, once again plays the sensitive man who has to suffer and die. This aspect of his character is expressed in his songs, such as the evergreen 'Prempatra', which is gentle and romantic. The song in which Radha teases Sunder for not giving her any fun (whatever that may imply) on their honeymoon, 'Budha mil gaya', is quite shocking, while 'Dost dost na raha' remains the song to quoted by Hindi-speaking Indians wishing to complain about the behaviour of friends. The way it is shot in the film, bringing out the characters' inner feelings, illustrates Raj Kapoor's total mastery of the medium of the Hindi film.

Dir.: Raj Kapoor; **Story/Scr./Dial.**: Inder Raj Anand, **DOP**: Radhu Karmakar; **Music**: Shanker Jaikishen; **Lyrics**: Shailendra, Hasrat Jaipuri; **Selected Cast**: Raj Kapoor, Vyjayanthimala, Rajendra Kumar, Lalita Pawar; **Prod. Co.**: R. K. Films; Colour.

Satya
India, 1998 – 170 mins
Ram Gopal Varma

A masterpiece and one of the best Hindi films of the last ten years, *Satya* deserved an international release as it could show how the Hindi-film way of telling a story can work even within such a well-defined genre.

The film charts the story of an outsider, Satya ('Truth'), about whom we never find out much. Satya (Chakravarty) comes to Bombay, drifting into the underworld and a life of crime. Unlike Amitabh Bachchan, he is neither cool nor fashionable and he has no righteous anger to unleash. After a bar-room brawl, Satya is sent to jail, where he befriends a gangster, who seems to be the real hero of the film, Bhikhu Mhatre (an outstanding performance by Manoj Bajpai). A touch mad, Bhikhu is in a loving though quarrelsome relationship with his feisty wife (Shefali Chhaya) and is as talkative as Satya is quiet. The other members of the gang, such as Kalu Mama (Saurabh Shukla), are more than just cut-outs, portrayed as individuals with their own stories. Falling in love with his neighbour, Vidya (Urmila Matondkar), who wants to be a singer, Bikhu begins to think about leaving the gang only to find himself too deeply involved.

The attractions of a Hindi film sit quite comfortably with the demands of the gangster genre. The film adds songs, including the hugely popular 'Goli maaro bheje mein', a dance at a wedding, 'Sapnon mein milti hai', and romantic numbers. The music is by Vishal, who later goes on to direct his own gangster movie, *Maqbool* (2003), while the lyrics are by Gulzar.

The romantic moments are not crucial to the film, except that they make Satya realise that he wants to leave the world of the gangsters. While Ram Gopal Varma's favourite, Urmila Matondkar, was the only big name in the film, Manoj Bajpai would emerge as a star. Some of his best scenes are with his screen wife, Shefali Chhaya, who has since gained a reputation as a good actress (in *Monsoon Wedding* [2001] and other

Publicity for *Satya*

films), though has perhaps not had the recognition she deserves.

Visually very strong, featuring graphic violence and shoot-outs, it is the film's depiction of the city of Bombay that is particularly striking. Its buildings, railways and streets host the action sequences (one of the best being the chase through a suburban railway station), while its beaches and nearby hill resorts provide the site for romance. With actual locations rather than sets, this use of the city may be traced back to *Ardh satya* and later *Black Friday* (2004). While Bombay's annual Ganpati festival, which forms the backdrop for the film's ending, has appeared in other films (such as *Agneepath* [1990]), it seems fresh and innovative here.

One of the film's strongest features, the script was written by Saurabh Shukla (who plays Kalu Mama) and Anurag Kashyap (whose two directorial ventures, *Paanch* [2003] and *Black Friday*, have been held up by the censors and court orders). The language in the film is extraordinary, the characters being defined and augmented by their style of talking, particularly that of Bhikhu Mhatre. The taut editing of Bhanodaya and Apurva Asrani keeps the pace moving throughout.

Ram Gopal Varma has subsequently made more gangster films, including the fascinating *Company* (2002), which is more glamorous and denser but lacks the sheer vitality and Bambaiyya atmosphere of *Satya*.

Dir.: Ram Gopal Varma; **Story/Scr./Dial.**: Saurabh Shukla and Anurag Kashyap; **DOP**: Gerard Hooper, Mazhar Kamran; **Music**: Vishal; **Lyrics**: Gulzar; **Selected Cast**: Chakravarty, Manoj Bajpai, Shefali Chhaya, Urmila Matondkar; **Prod. Co.**: Varma Corporation; Colour.

Seeta aur Geeta
India, 1972 – 162 mins
Ramesh Sippy

Hindi films have often used the popular theme of identical twins separated at birth (see *Ram aur Shyam*), but this film is outstanding for Hema Malini's performance and the excellent writing, which make it so much fun even after seeing the similar story in *Ram aur Shyam*.

Returning from a pilgrimage to Shirdi, a woman goes into labour. When she and her husband leave with the baby girl, the husband tells the childless couple who helped them that, had it been twins, they would have given them one of the babies. The childless woman then reveals to her husband that the visitor did indeed give birth to twins and that she has kept one for them. Seeta's (Hema Malini) parents die when she is young and she is brought up by her ineffectual uncle (Satyen Kappu), who is dominated by his wife Kaushalya (Manorama) and their spoilt daughter Sheela (Daisy Irani). They can access her fortune until she marries, so try to wreck every chance of this happening. Even the widowed grandmother (Pratima Devi) cannot prevent them from treating Seeta like a servant and it is only when the aunt's brother, Ranjit (Roopesh Kumar), makes sexual advances towards the girl that she runs away from home. The family inform the police, who mistake the stolen twin, Geeta (Hema Malini), for her sister. Geeta is the complete opposite of Seeta, a fearless and outspoken street performer with a total aversion to domestic chores and a taste for adventure. She joins in the pretence of being Seeta, especially when she falls for Dr Ravi (Sanjeev Kumar), who had been introduced to Seeta for a marriage proposal. She soon sets about putting the house in order, with the grandmother at the head of the family, the aunt back in the kitchen and the aunt's brother whipped into submission. Seeta, who had tried to commit suicide, was rescued by Rakka (Dharmendra) and takes Geeta's place, surprising everyone with her domesticity and religious devotion. The day the two girls are set to marry, Ranjit tries to persuade Seeta to marry him and the whole story emerges . . .

The script by Salim–Javed is well paced. Just as Seeta seems to have endured every torment, we are suddenly thrust into Geeta's world. Having seen the aunt tormenting Seeta, Geeta's revenge is all the more entertaining and amusing. R. D. Burman's songs are catchy, especially 'Hawa ke saath saath' (Kishore Kumar and Asha Bhosle), which Hema and Sanjeev perform on roller skates.

The undoubted star of the piece is the young Hema Malini, who gives a virtuoso performance in this double role, representing opposing aspects of a woman: a feisty spirit and a gentle caring type, playing up the strengths and weaknesses of both. While Sanjeev Kumar portrays the traditional doctor who falls in love with the sparky woman, Dharmendra is charming as the drunken ruffian looking for a stable family. Manorama is excellent as the aunt, her physique, gestures, clothing and language making her a far more interesting villain than Ranjit. With her sadistic behaviour backed up by a whole range of grotesque expressions, she would be well cast as a wicked stepmother in any pantomime.

Dir.: Ramesh Sippy; **Story**: Satish Bhatnagar; **Scr./Dial**.: Salim–Javed; **DOP**: P. Vaikunth; **Music**: R. D. Burman; **Lyrics**: Anand Bakshi; **Selected Cast**: Hema Malini, Dharmendra, Sanjeev Kumar, Satyen Kappu, Manorama, Daisy Irani; **Prod. Co**.: Sippy Films; Colour.

Shakti
India, 1982 – 177 mins
Ramesh Sippy

This film is always remembered as the one time that Dilip Kumar and Amitabh Bachchan played father and son. While both stars had played the role of the person who becomes a criminal but remains honest and decent, here the father is the police officer while the son is the outlaw with whom he comes into conflict. Although there have been debates about who is the better actor, I think such discussions are pointless. These are two of the greatest actors in Hindi cinema and should not be viewed as competitors.

Told in flashback, by the elderly Ashwini Kumar (Dilip Kumar) to his grandson (Anil Kapoor), in front of his daughter-in-law, Roma (Smita Patil), the film begins with the birth of a son, Vijay, to Sheetal (Raakhee Gulzar) and Ashwini, a police officer. Vijay is kidnapped as a small child but never forgets his father, choosing to stay within the law even at the risk of losing his son. The gangster who helps Vijay escape becomes more of a father to him, especially when he ends up on the wrong side of the law and comes into conflict with his father. Although Roma breaks most of society's conventional rules for women, she wants to unite her partner with his parents. However, his father must uphold the law and once again has to choose between that and his son's life . . .

Most of the songs are fairly forgettable, even though composed by R. D. Burman, the film being made chiefly by the powerful dialogues, which would stand alone as great speeches but are even more powerful delivered well and in character. The majority, of course, are between the father and son, who can both speak eloquently about love and justice but are incapable of saying that they love each other or talking about their feelings in order to discover that one is constantly misinterpreting the other.

Raakhee, who had played Amitabh's heroine in other films, becomes his mother here, while Anil Kapoor makes a guest appearance as the posthumous son. Amrish Puri plays J. K. the villain, with Kulbushan Kharbanda as the surrogate father figure. Smita Patil has a largely insignificant role in the film, although her transformation from the carefree girl who lives with a man she has only just met to a dutiful daughter-in-law gives her the desire for a family that leads to the final bonding of the fractured family.

Dir.: Ramesh Sippy; **Story/Scr./Dial**.: Salim–Javed; **DOP**: S. M. Anwar; **Music**: R. D. Burman; **Lyrics**: Anand Bakshi; **Selected Cast**: Dilip Kumar, Amitabh Bachchan, Smita Patil, Raakhee, Amrish Puri; **Prod**. **Co**.: M-R Productions; Colour.

Sholay
India, 1975 – 199 mins
Ramesh Sippy

Generally accepted to be the greatest Hindi film of all time, this film appeals to everyone and is always a good choice to show to people who have never seen a Hindi film before, as it needs no cultural explanations (even though they can add to the meaning).

Jai (Amitabh Bachchan) and Veeru (Dharmendra) are petty crooks, hired by Thakur Baldev Singh (Sanjeev Kumar), a former police officer. He has lost his whole family to the evil Gabbar Singh (Amjad Khan) in revenge for being sent to jail. Convinced that the law is inadequate, he is determined to take his own revenge, but Gabbar cuts off his arms. Veeru falls in love with the *tonga*-driver, Basanti (Hema Malini), while Jai is attracted to the Thakur's widowed daughter-in-law (Jaya Bhaduri). But they have to fight Gabbar and his gang . . .

The film's great foundation is its script and dialogue. Unforgettable scenes include the dismembering of Thakur, Jai's meeting with Basanti's aunt (Leela Mishra), and, of course, the episodes in Gabbar's camp. It is not unusual for people still to quote the dialogues today (especially Gabbar's 'Kitne aadmi the?' speech or his 'Tera kya hoga Kaaliya?'and 'Arre o Sambha', but also Basanti's 'Chal Basanti!' and her address to her horse, 'Chal Dhanno, aaj teri Basanti ki izzat ka sawaal hai', all of which were released on disk and now can be found on numerous websites).

The film also stands on the performances of the four major stars. Dharmendra as Veeru is the tough man with the soft heart, best remembered for his performance in the drunken scene. Jai is cool, quiet and composed but has a great sense of humour, as demonstrated in his meeting with Basanti's aunt. Hema Malini shines as the chatterbox of a *tonga*-driver who is forced to dance for Gabbar's sadistic enjoyment, while Jaya is silent apart from the flashback to the family's Holi party. This film shows why Sanjeev Kumar is considered to be one of Indian cinema's best actors. However, Amjad Khan as the evil Gabbar Singh has the best lines and is the baddie everyone loves to hate. The more evil he is, the more we are entertained.

The R. D. Burman songs include the hugely popular 'Yeh dosti', with its crazy sound effects and silly picturisation; the Holi song, 'Holi ke din', Basanti's tortured dance, 'Jab tak hai jaan', and the dance song performed by Helen, 'Mehbooba'.

Sholay has been called a 'curry Western' (rather than a spaghetti Western), no doubt in part because of its stylish baddies (Jai's resemblance to Clint Eastwood's characters has been noted), its bleak locations and the characteristics it shares with films like *The Magnificent Seven* (1960). While it has features that are unusual in a Hindi film, such as the absence of family ties (apart from those of the Thakur, which have been destroyed) and the presence of evil rather than just a villain, it is still very much a typical Hindi film, with songs, comedy and romance, as is clear from a comparison with its antecedents, in particular *Mera gaon mera desh*.

Dir.: Ramesh Sippy; **Story/Scr./Dial.**: Salim–Javed; **DOP**: Dwarka Divecha; **Music**: R. D. Burman; **Lyrics**: Anand Bakshi; **Selected Cast**: Amitabh Bachchan, Jaya Bhaduri, Dharmendra, Sanjeev Kumar, Hema Malini, Amjad Khan, Helen; **Prod. Co.**: Sippy Films; Colour.

Shree 420
India, 1955 – 177 mins
Raj Kapoor

Shree 420 was a worldwide hit on its release and even today it remains popular. Raj Kapoor reprises his Chaplinesque tramp of *Awaara* for this film. (The 420 of the title refers to the section of the Indian Penal Code that deals with fraud, so the film's title means 'Mr Fraudster'.)

Raju (Raj Kapoor) pretends to be knocked down by Seth Sonachand Dharmanand (a Rushdie-esque name to imply a rich hypocrite), whose car numberplate, 840, identifies him as a double cheat. Raju arrives in Bombay, where he meets a banana-seller (Lalita Pawar), who instantly becomes a mother figure. He then meets Vidya ('Knowledge'; Nargis) when he pawns his honesty-medal for Rs 40, which is stolen immediately. After several setbacks he encounters Vidya again, along with her disabled father, who together run a school for poor children. Raj finds work in the Jai Bharat ('Long-live India!') laundry and romances Vidya, but is picked up by Maya ('Illusion'; Nadira), who realises his skill at the card table. Seth Sonachand asks him to join his business and Raju takes one of Maya's saris from the laundry for Vidya to wear to a Diwali party at the nightclub, where he plays cards. Raju has to choose between Knowledge and Illusion. When Vidya runs away, Raju stays behind. Later he takes his winnings to her house, but she sends him away. Raju seems to have fallen into Maya's trap as he begins to work on various scams, including 'The Tibetan Gold Company', but when Seth Sonachand's housing scam proves too much for him, he is blackmailed into staying. Eventually, Vidya brings him back to the city in search of a better future.

The film, written by K. A. Abbas, the left-wing journalist, while drawing on Chaplin's tramp, is a story of the villager's journey to the city. Here, he quickly re-creates his networks, forming a family with the banana-seller and the pavement-dwellers, while seeking redemption in romantic love with the good woman, and eventually rejecting the temptations of the vamp and of money. The film shows how identities in

Raj Kapoor and Nargis in *Shree 420*

the city become fluid and uses the symbols of clothing and masks to illustrate how these can be put on and cast off, typified in the song, 'Mera joota hai japani'.

Along with the meaningful and well-constructed story, the film's strength lies in the luminous presence of Nargis. Said to be Raj Kapoor's lover, she worked with him on some of his greatest films before their relationship ended and she left him to return to her mentor, Mehboob, for her swansong, *Mother India*. Raj Kapoor, son of the great Prithviraj (star of India's first talkie, *Alam ara* [1931], and of many others, including *Phool* and *Sikander*, though best remembered now for his portrayal of Akbar in *Mughal-e Azam*), had now established himself as one of Indian cinema's leading directors, producers and actors, dominating Hindi film for four decades. He set up a team that was very similar to the old studio system where he began (in Bombay Talkies – see *Achhut kanya* and *Kismet*), with Nargis as his star and the Shankar–Jaikishen team as his music directors, along with a stable of personnel.

One of the glories of Raj Kapoor's films is the music, and every song in this film has a great tune and lyrics (by Shailendra and Hasrat Jaipuri), and is well picturised and integrated into the narratives. 'Mera joota hai japani' sets the theme for the whole film, while 'Ramaiya vastavaiya' highlights the good nature of the pavement-people and their capacity for joy. Then there is 'Mud mud ke na dekh', revealing to Raju the temptations of money, and Vidya's lament, where her image divides to stay behind and to run after him, 'Jaane wale mudke zara dekh ke jaana', as well as one of the all-time favourite love songs of the Hindi film, 'Pyaar hua, ikraar hua'.

Dir.: Raj Kapoor; **Story/Co-scr**.: K. A. Abbas; **Co-scr**.: V. P. Sathe; **DOP**: Radhu Karmakar; **Lyrics**: Shailendra, Hasrat Jaipuri; **Music**: Shankar–Jaikishen; **Selected Cast**: Raj Kapoor, Nargis, Lalita Pawar, Nadira; **Prod**. **Co**.: R. K. Films; Black and white.

Sikandar
India, 1941 – 146 mins
Sohrab Modi

The historical film is one of the oldest genres of Indian cinema, often closely linked with themes of nationalism and the freedom struggle. Favourite periods include the Mughal era (the most popular film being *Mughal-e Azam*) and, less often, classical India, often used to evoke the glory that was India or highlight how the Indian nation and its unity are rooted in the mists of time. The historical's popularity waned from the early 1960s but several have succeeded in the 2000s (including *Lagaan* and *Gadar*), experimenting with new periods (partition and even the 1960s).

Sohrab Modi, a Shakespearean actor, and his production company, Minerva Movietone, were always associated with this genre. His major historicals include *Pukar* (1939), which almost ousted *Sikandar* for its performances by Chandramohan and Naseem Bano, with able support from Sohrab Modi and others, its lavish sets and high drama; *Prithvivallabh* (1941), based on the novel by K. M. Munshi; *Jhansi ki Rani* (1953), documenting the fight by Queen Laxmibai against the East Indian Company; and the life of the great Urdu poet, *Mirza Ghalib* (1954), if only for Suraiya's songs. However, *Sikandar* is held to be his greatest film.

326 BCE. Sikandar (the Indian name for Alexander the Great) (Prithviraj Kapoor) has reached the Jhelum and is set to conquer India but has to defeat the Indian King Porus (Sohrab Modi). Sikandar's Persian lover Rukhsana (known in the west as Roxanna) (Vanamala), though shunned by Sikandar's tutor Aristotle (Shakir), pleads with Porus to spare Sikandar but Porus' only son (Zahur Raja) is killed in battle, and Porus is captured. However, the two heroes recognise kindred spirits and become friends. Sikandar releases Porus and begins his journey back home.

The film was epic in all senses. Its sets and battle scenes were lavish and no expense seemed to have been spared in creating the grandeur of ancient India. However, it must have been a great risk to make a film in 1941 (at the height of the freedom struggle) in which leaders debate nationalism and defeat. Nevertheless, apparently it managed to evade censor cuts, although it was not shown in cantonment towns (towns where the army was based).

The film is also remembered for the performances of these two imposing Shakespearean actors. Modi had worked in the Parsi theatre, specialising in Shakespeare, and Prithviraj Kapoor had also acted in Shakespearean touring companies. Both men began their careers in silent cinema. Prithviraj remained only an actor, starring in the first talkie, *Alam ara* (1931), and worked in New Theatres before returning to Bombay to appear in films such as *Phool*. From a generation who preferred theatre to cinema, he discovered that the latter paid the bills. His sons Raj (whose films include *Awaara*, *Shree 420* and *Bobby)* and Shammi (*Junglee*, *Teesri manzil*, among others) worked almost entirely in cinema, while a third, Shashi (*Waqt*, *Jab jab phool khile*, *Deewaar*, *Kabhi kabhie* and *Silsila*), despite a good film career, subsequently devoted his energies to the theatre.

Dir.: Sohrab Modi; **Story**: Sudarshan; **DOP**: Y. D. Sarpotdar; **Music**: Rafiq Ghaznavi, Mir Saheb; **Lyrics**: Sudarshan; **Selected Cast**: Prithviraj Kapoor, Sohrab Modi, Zahur Raja, Vanamala, Shakir; **Prod. Co.**: Minerva Movietone; Black and white.

Silsila
India, 1981 – 182 mins
Yash Chopra

Silsila was controversial from the start. Even before it was released there was gossip about the casting, due to persistent rumours that it depicted a real-life love triangle between Amitabh, his wife, Jaya, and his supposed mistress, Rekha.

Shekhar (Shashi Kapoor), an airforce pilot, and Shobha (Jaya Bachchan) are about to be married. He invites his younger brother Amit (Amitabh Bachchan) to meet her and they discuss the marriage with her mother. Amit falls in love with Chandni (Rekha) at a wedding. An aspiring playwright, he tells his brother that he intends to marry her but, when Shekhar is killed in the (1971?) war, leaving Shobha pregnant, Amit agrees to marry her to save everyone's honour. Amit is involved in a car accident in which Shobha loses the baby. Her physician, Dr Anand (Sanjeev Kumar), turns out to be Chandni's husband. Chandni visits Amit and, during a subsequent meeting, he explains why he had to leave her and their affair recommences. Meanwhile Shobha begins to fall in love with Amit. His friend, Vidyarthi, and Shobha become suspicious of his relationship with Chandni but nothing is said. Chandni knocks a boy down when she is out with Amit at night. They go to the police station and narrowly avoid meeting Dr Anand. However, the policeman turns out to be Shobha's cousin, and, recognising Amit, reproaches him. At Dr Anand's Holi party, Amit consumes too much *bhaang* (marijuana paste), and sings a traditional song about a cuckold. As he sings, his relationship with Chandni becomes clear to the other spouses, who later discuss this in parables. In a subsequent scene (dream sequence?), Shobha and Jaya agree to fight for Amit. Meanwhile, Amit and Chandni decide to set up a new life together. Chandni leaves while her husband is out of town, and Amit tells Shobha he is leaving her. Shobha declares her resolve to win him back. Amit and Chandni meet Amit's friend and go to his parents' golden wedding. The ceremony reminds them of the sanctity of marriage. Suddenly the phone rings: Shobha tells Amit that Dr

Poster for *Silsila*

Anand has been in a plane crash. Amit and Chandni return and, as Amit rushes to help Dr Anand, Shobha reveals that she is pregnant. Amit promises to come back to her. He saves Dr Anand, who leaves on a stretcher, accompanied by Chandni. Shobha and Amit are reunited.

Many Indian movies have dealt with extra-marital love, but this was the first one to show the consummation of adultery. While there is some justification for it, as the couple were lovers before Amit sacrificed their love, *Silsila* raises the question: can adultery be romantic? The film portrays the rapid decline of the relationship, which collapses when they realise that their loyalties lie with the partners they have hurt, and the innocent lovers become a sleazy couple.

In *Silsila*, Yash Chopra introduced the classical musicians Shiv (Shiv Kumar Sharma) and Hari (Hariprasad Chaurasia) as music directors. This was the first film he had made after the death of his friend, the poet and lyricist Sahir Ludhianvi, so he employed a team of lyricists, including Harivanshrai Bachchan, Amitabh's father, who wrote 'Rang barse'. The film contains the first lyrics written by Javed Akhtar, 'Dekha ek khwab to', 'Yeh kahaan aa gaye hum?' and 'Neela asmaan'. 'Dekha' and 'Yeh kahaan' were filmed partly in the Netherlands, the first of Yash Chopra's overseas shoots, which were to become his hallmark.

Despite widespread praise, the film did badly at the box office, partly because it went too far for many people but then drew back from taking a real risk. Karan Johar is now making a film, *Kabhi alvida na kehna* (2005), 'inspired' by *Silsila*, which is rumoured to be much bolder. Nevertheless, *Silsila* has now become something of a film classic, and is much loved for its music and performances, and, of course, because the so-called real-life triangle is still discussed more than twenty years later.

Dir./Co-scr.: Yash Chopra; **Story**: Preeti Bedi; **Co-scr.**: Sagar Sarhadi; **DOP**: Kay Gee; **Music**: Shiv–Hari; **Lyrics**: Javed Akhtar, Rajinder Krishen, Hasan Kamal, Nida Fazli, Harivanshrai Bachchan; **Selected Cast**: Amitabh Bachchan, Jaya Bachchan, Shashi Kapoor, Rekha, Sanjeev Kumar; **Prod. Co.**: Yash Raj Films; Colour.

Teesri kasam
India, 1966 – 159 mins
Basu Bhattacharya

This film script is adapted from Phanishwar Nath's short story, 'Mare Gaye Gulfam'. Produced by the great lyricist, Shailendra, it became famous as his nemesis, as the financial strains and stresses of making the film over four years, followed by its box-office failure, led to his early death. However, it won the national award, the President's Gold Medal for best feature film of 1966.

Hiraman (Raj Kapoor) is a bullock cart-driver who, after escaping from a police raid, makes his first vow in the film, which is that he will not carry stolen goods. After an accident, his second vow is that he will not carry bamboo. He takes a passenger to a *mela* (fair) who turns out to be a performer in *nautanki* (popular song and dance shows), Hirabai (Waheeda Rehman). On the way they talk and she is taken with his simplicity and his songs, in particular the tale of Mahua, a girl who is sold by her stepmother. Hiraman is in awe of Hirabai's beauty and is happy to spend a few days at the fair to see her performances. When another spectator calls her a prostitute, he gets into a brawl and Hirabai tells him he has no right to fight on her behalf, although she is moved by the fact that he regards her as a respectable woman. When she rejects the advances of the landowner (Iftikhar, unusually in a negative role), she decides that she has to leave the company. Hiraman returns to bid her farewell as her train leaves the village. He makes his third vow (*teesri kasam*), that he will not carry a *nautanki* performer again.

Although Raj Kapoor is somewhat old for his character, and both he and Waheeda look too upmarket for the roles, she excels in some wonderful dances and, as the relationship between them develops, in particular the last scenes when they part, we are no longer conscious of any discrepancy between the actors and the roles.

The film was shot by Subrata Mitra, who is most famous as the cameraman on *Pather Panchali* and many of Ray's films, as well as several early Merchant–Ivory productions. In the beautiful shots of the country, of the bullock carts, of villages and rivers, as well as of the train and the *nautanki* performances, the influence of Bimal Roy on Basu Bhattacharya is clear.

The songs by Shankar–Jaikishan and the apposite lyrics of Shailendra and Hasrat Jaipuri are memorable and well placed within the film. The songs Mukesh has for Raj Kapoor – 'Sajjan re jhoot mat bolo' and 'Duniya bananewaale' – set the scene and define his character, while those performed by Waheeda such as 'Paan khaaye saiyan hamaro', express her image of glamour and fragility.

Dir.: Basu Bhattachaya; **Scr**.: Nabendu Ghosh; **Story/Dial**.: Phanishwar Nath Renu's 'Mare Gaye Gulfam'; **DOP**: Subrata Mitra; **Music**: Shankar–Jaikishen; **Lyrics**: Shailendra, Hasrat Jaipuri; **Selected Cast**: Raj Kapoor, Waheeda Rehman, Dulari, Iftikhar, Asit Sen; **Prod**. **Co**.: Image Makers; Black and white.

Teesri manzil
India, 1966 – 172 mins
Vijay Anand

Sunita (Asha Parekh) goes to Mussoorie to investigate her sister Rupa's suicide. It seems she jumped from the third floor (*teesri manzil*) after being rejected by Rocky, the drummer in the hotel band. Rocky (Shammi Kapoor) falls in love with Sunita but does not let her know who he is. Sunita begins to suspect murder . . .

This film is a classic for its songs alone, and features some of the most enduringly popular hits of R. D. Burman, who was by now establishing himself as a music director of the first order, like his father, S. D. Burman. Asha Bhosle, who sang for the heroine and the vamp, was now the clear alternative to her sister, the legendary Lata Mangeshkar, for romantic numbers as well as for the dance style that she still dominates almost four decades later. Rafi showed his ability to sing in character as he becomes the voice of Shammi Kapoor. 'O mere Sona re', 'O haseena zulfonwali', 'Aajaa aaja main hoon pyaar tera' and 'Deewaana mujhsa nahin' are among some of the most popular film songs of all time.

Nasir Husain ensured his place in Hindi film history as the king of the teenage romantic musical. Having worked in Filmistan, he is best remembered now for his series of films with Shammi Kapoor, the 'Elvis of India'. His later classics, such as 'Yaadon ki baraat', brought style and panache to the movie, with his modern, fashionable young couples enjoying glamorous, consumerist lifestyles in Mussoorie locations, where they participated in hotel and nightclub culture. The bright and glossy images of youth, travel, consumerism and dance music that became core features of the Hindi movie romance in the 1990s owe much to Nasir Husain.

Teesri manzil drew heavily on his earlier *Dil deke dekho*, repeating the same cast and locations with an equally highly convoluted plot. The film's director, Vijay Anand (whose other films include *Guide*), was one of the masters of the brilliant modern look of the new colour in Hindi films of

Helen (in the iris) and Shammi Kapoor dance to 'O haseena zulfonwali' in *Teesri Manzil*

the 1960s, and was particularly suited to Nasir Husain's excellent song picturisations. The set for 'O haseena' is one of the most outrageous and stylish of all time and uses to great effect close-ups of hands and faces, with longer shots of chorus dancers and the 'live band' (whose drummer is Salim Khan, of scriptwriting Salim–Javed fame, as well as Salman Khan's father and Helen's husband). The shot begins with a close-up of the great dancer, Helen, then pulls back to reveal that she is in the 'iris' of a great eye with huge eyelashes. She gamely slips down slides, leaps around and pouts, while Shammi Kapoor hurls himself around in one of his most Elvis-like moments. The lyrics of the song draw on the traditional motif of the Urdu *ghazal*, the moth (the lover) who is fatally drawn to the flame (the beauty of the beloved). The costumes are no less elaborate, as Shashi wears a glittering tuxedo and Helen appears in a variety of outfits, including long gloves. While the other numbers 'jaa aa jaa' include wonderful picturisations, dances, and stylish outfits, this song remains one of the most effective picturisations of a Hindi film song to date.

Dir.: Vijay Anand; **Story/Scr./Dial.**: Nasir Husain; **DOP**: N. V. Srinivas; **Music**: R. D. Burman; **Lyrics**: Majrooh Sultanpuri; **Selected Cast**: Shammi Kapoor, Asha Parekh, Helen; **Prod. Co.**: United Producers and Nasir Husain Films; Colour.

Tezaab
India, 1988 – 173 mins
N. Chandra

N. Chandra's earlier films, *Ankush* (1986) and *Pratighaat* (1987), are often more highly rated than *Tezaab*, but this was his major hit. It is now chiefly remembered for its violence, its songs and its star performances, but in particular as the movie that really launched Madhuri Dixit as one of the greatest stars of Hindi cinema.

Mohini (Madhuri Dixit) has to work as a dancer to support her useless father (Anupam Kher). She wants to marry Munna (Anil Kapoor) but her father is determined to prevent this and gets a criminal, Lotiya Pathan (Kiran Kumar), to keep him away. When Pathan's brother tries to rape Munna's sister, Munna kills him and is sent to prison. After his release, Munna is exiled outside Bombay and becomes a criminal. Meanwhile, Mohini is kidnapped by Pathan, who has fallen out with her father. Munna saves her.

Anil Kapoor was already famous when he appeared in *Tezaab*. While never a handsome heart-throb, he brought an empathy to the many street roles (*tapori* characters) he played. Often overlooked, he is undoubtedly a good actor, with acclaimed performances in films like *Mashaal*, *Karma*, *Mr India*, *Parinda, Ram Lakhan* (1989) *Lamhe* (1991), *Virasat* (1997) and others. He appeared with the top female stars of the time, including Madhuri and Sridevi, in several films.

Although she had featured in Subhash Ghai's hit, *Ram Lakhan*, it was *Tezaab* that made Madhuri a superstar, a status she held for the next ten years. Her hits include *Dil* (1990*), Beta* (1992), *Khalnayak, Hum aapke hain koun . . .!*, and *Dil to pagal hai*. Although her acting was appreciated in this film, in particular during her scenes with her father, it is the 'Ek do teen' song that really made its mark. Saroj Khan's choreography for this song established her as the top choreographer of the female item song and she went on to win a string of awards for her big items (including for Madhuri, 'Choli ke peeche' in *Khalnayak* and

'Dhak dhak' in *Beta*). While the charge of vulgarity was levelled at the song's lyrics, music and performance, it was always Madhuri's trademark to achieve what so few of her rivals could, which was to look sexy without looking vulgar. She was one of the greatest female stars of Indian cinema, not just for her acting and dancing but for her sheer beauty and star power. Her item songs are perhaps what she is most remembered for, as she brought them to life and spawned a host of wannabes.

The song's writer, Javed Akhtar, was often ridiculed for the lyrics which count through the number of days she is separated from her lover. He would build on the dummy lyrics – in this case numbers – the music directors sang when they first presented him with a tune. However, as the audience becomes aware when he recites the lyrics at his public talks, it is actually a rather good poem.

Laxmikant–Pyarelal's music for this film was a hit. As well as 'Ek do teen', 'So gaya yeh jahaan' was particularly popular.

Shot at real locations, with many of the night scenes shot on the streets of Bombay, the film features plenty of violence, as the the title *Tezaab* ('acid') suggests. Chosen partly because Mohini's father threatens to throw acid at her, the title is also intended to highlight the general corrosion of values in society.

Dir./Story/Scr.: N. Chandra; **Dial.**: Kamlesh Pandey; **DOP**: Baba Azmi; **Music**: Laxmikant–Pyarelal; **Lyrics**: Javed Akhtar; **Selected Cast**: Anil Kapoor, Madhuri Dixit, Anupam Kher, Kiran Kumar, Chunky Pandey; **Prod. Co.**: N. Chandra Productions; Colour.

Trishul
India, 1978 – 167 mins
Yash Chopra

This multi-starrer is the story of Vijay (Amitabh Bachchan), the illegitimate son of Raj Gupta (Sanjeev Kumar) and Shanti (Waheeda Rehman), who seeks to avenge Raj's injustice to his mother, whom he abandoned even though she was pregnant in order to marry his boss's daughter. Raj, known as Mr R. K. Gupta, is head of a construction company in Delhi. He has two children, his heir Shekhar (Shashi Kapoor), in love with a businesswoman, Miss Varma (Hema Malini), and a daughter, Babli (Poonam), who romances Ravi. Vijay destroys his father's business and his family, eventually revealing his true identity and restoring his father's money, but the latter dies saving Vijay, and the brothers take over the business.

Trishul takes the common theme of the Salim–Javed outings for Amitabh a step further. In several of these films, Amitabh (or Vijay, as the character is often known), is devoted to his mother while his father is absent or dead. In *Deewaar*, his father had gone missing and Vijay has 'Mera baap chor hai/My father is a thief' tattooed on his arm. In *Trishul*, Vijay actually hates his father, because of his treatment of his beloved mother and he is determined to ruin him, an Oedipal drama given justification within the narrative. No film had gone this far before, and Yash Chopra cast two of Hindi cinema's most powerful actors, who were given a skilful blend of dialogue and silence.

The dialogues from this film are again among some of the most celebrated in Hindi cinema and are available on disk, including lines such as 'Jisne har roj apni maa ko thoda thoda marte dekha ho, usse maut se dar nahin lagta/One who has seen his mother die a little every day does not fear death'. Amitabh also enjoys some moments of stylised cool in the film, such as lighting the fuse for the explosives with his cigarette. These outshine the music by Khayyam, which nevertheless featured some hits, such as 'Gapoochi gapoochi gam' and 'Mohabbat bade kaam ki cheez hai'.

Dir.: Yash Chopra; **Story/Scr./Dial.**: Salim–Javed; **DOP**: Kay Gee; **Music**: Khayyam; **Lyrics**: Sahir Ludhianvi; **Selected Cast**: Amitabh Bachchan, Sanjeev Kumar, Raakhee, Shashi Kapoor, Prem Chopra, Hema Malini, Waheeda Rehman; **Prod. Co.**: Trimurti Films; Colour.

Umrao Jaan
India, 1981 – 145 mins
Muzaffar Ali

This film is based on the Urdu novel *Umrao Jaan Ada* by Mirza
Mohammad Hadi 'Ruswa', published in 1899, which presents the story
of Umrao Jaan, a courtesan of Lucknow and Kanpur, as supposedly true.
It is set at the last moment of Lucknow's glory: the 1857 uprisings occur
in the novel when Umrao Jaan is at the height of her power. The novel's
popularity has continued to the present, although the story of Umrao
Jaan is probably better known now from this film version, which has
been adapted considerably to fit the requirements of the Hindi film.
These include a focus on Umrao's romance and her transformation into a
beautiful woman, and the film creates nostalgia for a lost world, adding
the visual pleasures of cinema.

The child Ameeran (Umme Farwa) lives in Faizabad with her parents
(Muzaffar Ali plays her father) and her baby brother (Shaad Ali Sahgal,
Muzaffar Ali's son, who directed *Saathiya* [2002] and *Bunty aur Babli*
[2005]). Her father's enemy Dilawar Khan abducts her from her own
engagement ceremony and she, along with another girl, Ram Dei, is
sold in Lucknow. The *chaudhuriyan* (madam) (Shaukat Kaifi) of her
kotha (brothel) renames her Umrao and she is trained in dancing,
singing and poetry. She and her friend grow up (into Rekha and Prema
Narayan). Gauhar Mirza (Naseeruddin Shah), the son of one of the
tawaifs, pursues her but, once she begins to perform, a nawab, Sultan
Sahib (Farouque Shaikh), falls in love with her and she with him. When
the nawab and Umrao realise that they cannot marry, she runs away
with Faiz Ali (Raj Babbar), a bandit. When he is killed, she sets up her
own *kotha* in Kanpur where she meets Ram Dei, who has married a
nawab and laments her own fate. Mirza comes to take her back to
Lucknow, but she escapes during the 1857 uprisings. She finds herself in
Faizabad, where she continues with her career.

(Next page) Rekha as *Umrao Jaan*

The film showcases the talents of Rekha, one of the great divas of Hindi cinema. Although she was already an icon, this is her greatest performance and the film in which she looks the most beautiful. The film is obsessed with the exquisite aesthetics of a lost Islamicate culture. Muzaffar Ali, himself a member of one of the princely families of Lucknow, and latterly a clothes designer and music event organiser, has paid attention to every detail of these aspects to produce a visual gem. It is said that the extras are also members of princely families, who were asked to come dressed in their finest clothes and to lend items from their palaces. Since much of the film was shot on sets in Bombay, it seems more likely that the props were brought from markets such as Chor Bazaar.

The film has wonderful songs, especially Umrao's four *ghazals* (a popular genre of Urdu poetry), with music by Khayyam, lyrics by Shahryar and sung by Asha Bhosle. These are 'Justuju jiski thi', 'Yeh kya jagah hai doston',' In aankhon ki masti' and the most popular of all, 'Dil cheez kya hai?'. Although not classical music, they produce a similar effect and, as such, they are much loved even today.

The film is currently being remade, presumably only as a commercial venture, as any attempt to improve on it would be very risky indeed.

Dir./Co-Scr.: Muzaffar Ali; **Story**: Mirza Mohammad Hadi 'Ruswa''s novel *Umrao Jaan Ada* (1899); **Co-scr./Dial.**: Shama Zaidi, Javed Siddiqui; **DOP**: Pravin Bhatt; **Music**: Khayyam; **Lyrics**: Shahryar; **Selected Cast**: Rekha, Farouque Shaikh, Naseeruddin Shah, Raj Babbar; **Prod. Co.**: Integrated Films; Colour.

Upkar
India, 1967 – 172 mins
Manoj Kumar

Upkar, one of the most successful Hindi films of all time, winner of
Filmfare Awards and many National Awards, established its director and
star as a major figure of Indian cinema and creator of a subgenre of
Indian patriotic films of which it still remains the measure. This was the
first film that Manoj Kumar (Harikishen Goswami) directed, although he
had already made his mark as an actor. Manoj Kumar embodies India
(the Sanskrit and Hindi word, Bharat), in the character of Bharat, instead
of the more usual female representation of the nation, usually as the
female nationalist goddess 'Mother India' (see *Mother India*), although
there are many references to Mother Earth (Dharti Maa).

Bharat is a farmer who becomes a soldier after losing his land
through village machinations, thus also embodying the slogan of 'Jai
jawaan, jai kisaan/'Victory to the soldier and the farmer') promoted by
Prime Minister Lal Bahadur Shastri. Shastri encouraged Manoj Kumar to
make this film after seeing his *Shaheed* (1965), on the life of the
nationalist hero, Bhagat Singh. This earlier film refers directly to the 1965
Indo-Pak war and shows live footage of Shastri, identifying him as one of
the great Indian leaders, alongside the others mentioned in the song –
Nanak, Tagore, Gandhi, Bose and Nehru.

Upkar contrasts debauched westernised lifestyles with the noble life
of the farmer, on whose back the wealth of India lies, and with the
heroism of the soldier, willing to sacrifice his life for his country. The film
constantly refers to anxieties about farmers leaving the land and their
importance to the whole country. The heroine, a doctor who comes to
serve the villagers, reminds the farmer that her education and social
status are not more important to India than his labour and that there
should be no social division between them.

After *Upkar*, Manoj Kumar was so firmly established as Bharat, the
embodiment of India, that he found he could no longer portray a regular

hero, and he continued to play this character right up to the 1980s, in films such as *Roti, kapada aur makaan* (1974) and *Kranti* (1980). While Prem Chopra assumed his usual villainous role, Asha Parekh, the great dancing heroine of the 1960s, had a subdued role as a doctor, while Pran, well known as a film villain, took the role of Malang Chacha, a crippled family friend who ultimately sacrifices his life for them. Although there was controversy about picturising the song 'Kaasme vaade' on him, his success as this character led to new roles for him as the hero's friend, and he was often given a key song, such as 'Yaari hai imaan, mera yaar meri zindagi' in *Zanjeer.*

The film includes some classic songs composed by Kalyanji–Anandji, notably the great patriotic anthem of India, 'Mere desh ki dharti/The Land of My Home', sung by Mahendra Kapoor and picturised on Manoj Kumar as a *desh-bhakta* (great patriot), with striking images of peasant life blending a documentary style with that of the Hindi film.

Dir./Story/Scr./Dial.: Manoj Kumar; **DOP**: V. N. Reddy; **Music**: Kalyanji–Anandji; **Lyrics**: Prem Dhawan, Indivar, Gulshan Bawra, Qamar Jalalabadi; **Selected Cast**: Asha Parekh, Manoj Kumar, Pran, Kamini Kaushal, Prem Chopra; **Prod. Co.**: Vishal Pictures; Colour.

Waqt
India, 1965 – 206 mins
Yash Chopra

Waqt was a landmark in many ways: it is a multi-starrer with four main heroes and two major heroines; it set a trend for showing the lifestyles of the super-rich; it is a 'lost and found' film, a storyline that became a favourite in the 1970s; and it has memorable songs.

A prosperous merchant, Lala Kedarnath (Balraj Sahni), believes nothing can disrupt his happy family life until an earthquake tears his world apart and he loses everything including his loved ones. He is on

Raaj Kumar and Sadhana in *Waqt*

the verge of finding his eldest son but, hearing he has just escaped from an orphanage where he was beaten, Kedarnath kills the warden and goes to jail for twenty years. The eldest boy, Raja (Raaj Kumar), is raised by a criminal and becomes a professional thief, while the second son, Ravi (Sunil Dutt), is adopted by a rich couple and trains as a lawyer. They both live in Bombay, while the youngest, Vijay (Shashi Kapoor), looks after their mother in Delhi, where he falls in love with Renu (Sharmila Tagore), a rich college girl.

Raja and Ravi both love Meena (Sadhana) but Raja, finding a childhood picture of Ravi, realises that he is his long lost brother and sacrifices his relationship with Meena. Vijay has moved to Bombay, where he is hired as a chauffeur by Renu. Ravi reproaches Renu for having an affair with his driver, then Meena's parents object to Ravi marrying their daughter when they do not know who his parents are.

Raja throws a party to announce the identity of Ravi's parents. Although other members of the family bump into one another – such as Vijay and Kedarnath – no connections are made.

When Raja is framed in a murder, he hires Ravi as his lawyer. A courtroom drama ensues, in which Vijay appears as a witness; then his mother comes into court. Kedarnath recognises her and is reunited with Vijay, after which Raja reveals that he and Ravi are his other two children. The family returns to open a shop, with the two future daughter-in-laws settled into the family.

The film is an example of an early 'lost and found'. Although *Waqt* shows the family separated by an earthquake, probably referring to the Quetta earthquake of 1935, it requires only a little imagination to see this as a partition story, where the earthquake is a metaphor for a far greater human upheaval. The line of migration from Punjab to Bombay is the one followed by many in the Hindi film industry.

Waqt is justly famous for its whole new glamorous 'look' in clothing and lifestyle. While the outdoor locations were in Kashmir, Simla, Nainital, Bombay and Delhi, the film spares the viewer no detail of the lifestyle of the super-rich, who have motor boats, American cars, throw lavish parties and live in houses adorned with fountains, circular beds, sunken seating and grand pianos. This set the style for a whole 'look' for Hindi films, away from the drama of feudal riches to newly upwardly mobile social groups. The women are glamorous in every respect, displaying highly stylish outfits, diamond jewellery and elegant grooming. The men wear the tight suits that were fashionable at the time, while only the older generation appears in 'traditional' clothes.

Waqt has enduringly popular songs, composed by Ravi with lyrics by Sahir, including 'Ai meri zohrajabeen' (Manna Dey) (which Yash Chopra's son Aditya includes in his debut film, *Dilwale dulhaniya le jayenge*, as a love song for the older generation) and 'Aage bhi jaane na tu' (Asha Bhosle).

Waqt was the first colour film made by B. R. Films and established Yash Chopra as a major film-maker, a position he still holds nearly forty years later after directing films such as *Dhool ka phool* (1959), *Daag* (1970), *Deewaar, Kabhi kabhie, Trishul, Silsila, Chandni, Lamhe, Dil to pagal hai* and *Veer-Zaara* (2004), and producing other films, such as *Dilwale dulhaniya le jayenge*.

Dir.: Yash Chopra; **Story**: F. A. Mirza; **Scr.**: B. R. Films' Story Department; **Dial.**: Akhtar Ul-Iman; **DOP**: Dharam Chopra; **Music**: Ravi; **Lyrics**: Sahir Ludhianvi; **Selected Cast**: Sunil Dutt, Raaj Kumar, Shashi Kapoor, Sadhana, Sharmila Tagore, Balraj Sahni, Shashikala, Rehman, Achla Sachdev; **Prod. Co.**: B. R. Films; Colour.

Yaadon ki baaraat
India, 1973 – 164 mins
Nasir Hussain

This is one of many films in the 1970s that deals with a family broken apart, then brought back together through chance meetings and fate, usually called 'lost and found' films. The story of this film is not exceptional but the music was enormously popular and some of the songs are well known even today.

A happy family with three young boys (one played by the young Aamir Khan, later of *Lagaan* fame) is destroyed when the evil Shaakaal

Zeenat Aman in the song 'Chura liya hai' in *Yaadon ki baraat*

(Ajit) kills their father because he has seen him at the scene of a murder. The oldest boy, Shankar, witnesses his father's murder and as they run away they are separated. Shankar falls in with criminals and when grown up (Dharmendra), determines to take revenge on the man who destroyed their family. The middle boy, Vijay (Vijay Arora), is adopted by a widower, while the youngest, Ratan (Tariq Shah), brought up by the family's maid, becomes a hotel singer called Monto. Vijay romances Sunita (Zeenat Aman) and Monto courts Neetu Singh. The only thing that can bring them together is the song the family always sang on their birthdays: 'Yaadon ki baraat'. . .

Nasir Hussain is remembered for the music of his films and *Yaadon ki baraat* contains many memorable songs, with music by R. D. Burman and lyrics by Majrooh. 'Chura liya hai' (sung by Asha Bhosle) is one of the most popular Hindi film songs of all time, and its picturisation with the young Zeenat Aman in a white dress holding a guitar is an iconic moment of youth and glamour in Hindi cinema. Apart from the title song, the other best remembered numbers are 'Lekar hum deewana dil', again partly for the picturisation on the pin-up girl, Neetu Singh, and Asha and Kishore Kumar's duet, 'O meri soni'.

Although Dharmendra was the only major star in the film, the smaller roles are memorable. Jalal Agha played one of the few roles in which a Muslim is not depicted as a stereotype but as a normal person who happens to be a Muslim, and Ajit shows once again that he is one of Bollywood's best ever villains in his blond wig and dapper outfits.

Dir./Dial.: Nasir Hussain; **Story/Scr**.: Salim–Javed; **DOP**: Munir Khan; **Music**: R. D. Burman; **Lyrics**: Majrooh Sultanpuri; **Selected Cast**: Dharmendra, Zeenat Aman, Vijay Arora, Tariq, Neetu Singh, Ajit; **Prod. Co**.: Nasir Hussain Films; Colour.

(*Next page*) Amitabh Bachchan and Jaya Bhaduri in *Zanjeer*

Zanjeer
India, 1973 – 145 mins
Prakash Mehra

Although this film's primary reason for inclusion is that it was the first Salim–Javed film for Amitabh Bachchan and the one that set him on the road to superstardom, it also deserves inclusion in this book as a good film in its own right.

As a small child, Vijay witnesses his parents being murdered by a man whom he can only identify from his chain (*zanjeer*), from which hangs a white horse charm. He is adopted by a policeman but grows up having nightmares about a white horse. Vijay joins the police intent on cleansing the city of crime. He becomes friends with Sher Khan (Pran) and falls in love with a knife-sharpener, Mala (Jaya Bhaduri). Framed for taking a bribe, he leaves the force but continues his pursuit of the evil Teja (Ajit), realising only when he sees the horse charm that he was his parents' killer.

This was the first in a whole series of Salim–Javed films starring Amitabh Bachchan, many of which are included in this book. In *Zanjeer*, Vijay (the usual name Amitabh takes in these films) is already the Angry Young Man, seeking revenge for the wrongs done to his family, although he does not yet have the mother figure to whom he is devoted. Although Vijay falls in love with Mala, the romantic angle in the film is very much subordinated to the desire for revenge, with Mala finally telling Vijay that he should get this anger out of his system to free himself for romance before it burns him up from the inside. Vijay's enmity for Teja, which develops during his time in the police force becomes more righteous when he finally realises that the criminal is his parents' killer.

Although the music is by Kalyanji–Anandji, there are few songs, and Amitabh does not have a song and dance number, the songs being picturised on Jaya, Pran and Bindu. Mala's song 'Chakku churi' shows the young Jaya Bhaduri's vivacious charm, but the great song of the film is 'Yaari hai imaan mera', picturised on Pran. Pran, who had been one of Hindi cinema's most convincing villains (along with Ajit), first took on a good role with *Upkar*. Here he is a rogue, but with true Pathan values and a good heart. Many feel the song takes homosociality into homosexuality, emphasised by the view that Pathans prefer men to women, but it has been enjoyed by many as simply a celebration of *dosti* (male friendship). Many of the Salim–Javed films for Amitabh played up Vijay's relationship with his mother and with another male (often played by Shashi Kapoor) rather than with women.

Zanjeer raises some of the social issues surrounding unemployment and reveals how the honest can be framed. It also shows true villainy coming from the upper classes, who are ruining society by adulterating medicines and poisoning the ill. The depiction of the lower middle classes is quite realistic, in their housing, clothing and so on. Although Jaya wears rather glamorous ethnic outfits as a street girl, when she begins to enter into middle-class respectability, she switches to some rather ordinary saris.

The main murders in the film take place at Diwali when the festival is in full swing, crackers are exploding and people are celebrating. This is a favourite device in many kinds of cinema, from the depiction of Ganpati immersions in Hindi films (such as *Satya*) and in western films such as *Godfather: Part II* (1974).

Dir./Co-lyrics: Prakash Mehra; **Story/Scr./Dial.**: Salim–Javed; **DOP**: N. Satyen; **Music**: Kalyanji–Anandji; **Co-lyrics**: Gulshan Bawra; **Selected Cast**: Amitabh Bachchan, Jaya Bhaduri, Ajit, Bindu, Pran, Om Prakash; **Prod. Co.**: Prakash Mehra Productions; Colour.

Index

Page numbers in *italics* denote illustrations; those in **bold** indicate detailed analysis

List of Illustrations

Whilst considerable effort has been made to correctly identify the copyright holders, this has not been possible in all cases. We apologise for any apparent negligence and any omissions or corrections brought to our attention will be remedied in any future editions.

Achhut kanya, Bombay Talkies Workers Industrial Co-Operative Society. Courtesy of National Film Archive of India, Pune; *Andaz*, Mehboob Productions; *Anmol ghadi*, Mehboob Productions; *Aradhana*, Shakti Films; *Awaara*, R. K. Films; *Bandit Queen*, Kaleidoscope Productions/Channel Four; *Bhumika*, Blaze Film Enterprises; *Bobby*, R. K. Films; *Chalti ka naam gaadi*, K. S. Films. Courtesy of NFAI; *Chandni*, Yash Raj Films; *Deewaar*, Trimurti Films; *Dil to pagal hai*, Yash Raj Films International; *Dilwale dulhaniya le jayenge*, Yash Raj Films International; *Do aankhen baarah haath*, Sri Nirmala Devi Combines. Courtesy of NFAI; *Do bigha zamin*, Bimal Roy Productions/Kamat Foto Flash; *Garam hawa*, Unit 3 MM/Film Finance Corporation. Courtesy of NFAI; *Hare Ram Hare Krishna*, Navketan/Kamat Foto Flash; *Hum aapke hain koun....!,* Rajshri Pictures; *Jai Santoshi Maa*, Satram Rohra. Courtesy of NFAI; *Junglee*, Subodh Mukherjee Productions/Kamat Foto Flash; *Kaagaz ke phool*, Guru Dutt Films/Kamat Foto Flash; *Karz*, Mukta Arts; *Khalnayak*, Mukta Arts; *Kismet*, Bombay Talkies. Courtesy of NFAI; *Maine pyar kiya*, Rajshri Pictures; *Mother India*, Mehboob Productions; *Mughal-e Azam*, Sterling Investment Corporation Private Ltd/Kamat Foto Flash; *Munnabhai MBBS*, Vinod Chopra Productions; *Pakeezah*, Mahal Pictures/Kamat Foto Flash; *Pyaasa*, Guru Dutt Films/Kamat Foto Flash; *Sahib bibi aur ghulam*, Guru Dutt Films/Modern Studios/Kamat Foto Flash; *Sangam*, R. K. Films; *Satya*, Varma Corporation Ltd; *Shree 420*, R. K. Films; *Silsila*, Yash Raj Films; *Teesri Manzil*, Nasir Hussain Films/United Producers/Kamat Foto Flash; *Umrao Jaan*, Integrated Films. Courtesy of NFAI; *Waqt*, B. R. Films; *Yaadon ki baraat*, Nasir Hussain Films/Kamat Foto Flash; *Zanjeer*, Prakash Mehra Productions/Kamat Foto Flash.

The reproduction of all other images is courtesy of the producers. I am grateful to them for permission to use the images.